8.⁓

SEASONAL GUIDE TO THE NATURAL YEAR

EX LIBRIS

Gus K. Bell

Something from my past to
enrich your future - Cornelia

SEASONAL GUIDE TO THE NATURAL YEAR

A Month by Month Guide to Natural Events

North Carolina, South Carolina and Tennessee

John Rucker

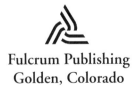

Fulcrum Publishing
Golden, Colorado

Cover photograph of Great Smoky Mountains National Park copyright © 1996 Tom Till
Interior photographs by John Rucker
Book design by Deborah Rich

Maps included in this book are for general reference only. For more detailed maps and additional information, contact the agencies or specific sites listed in the appendix.

We gratefully acknowledge the following contributors for the use of their materials:
Excerpt on page xxiii from *The Diversity of Life* by Edward O. Wilson
Copyright © 1992 by Edward O. Wilson
Reprinted by permission by Harvard University Press

Interior photograph on page 109 featuring Mary Lawrence Jellicorse in the Joyce Kilmer Forest, used with permission by Mary Lawrence Jellicorse.

"Poem of Preservation and Praise" reprinted on page 171 with permission by Stephen Lewandowski, copyright © 1986 by Stephen Lewandowski.

Interior photograph on page 280 featuring Sally Rollins and Tennessee coneflower, *Echinecea tennesseensis,* used with permission by Sally Rollins.

Library of Congress Cataloging-in-Publication Data
Rucker, John.
      Seasonal guide to the natural year : a month by month guide to
    natural events. North Carolina, South Carolina, Tennessee / John
    Rucker.
          p.   cm.
      Includes bibliographical references and index.
      ISBN 1-55591-270-2 (pbk.)
      1. Natural history—North Carolina—Guidebooks. 2. Natural
    history—South Carolina—Guidebooks. 3. Natural history—Tennessee—
    Guidebooks. 4. Seasons—North Carolina—Guidebooks. 5. Seasons—
    South Carolina—Guidebooks. 6. Seasons—Tennessee—Guidebooks.
    7. North Carolina—Guidebooks. 8. South Carolina—Guidebooks.
    9. Tennessee—Guidebooks.   I. Title.
    QH104.5.S59R83   1996
    508.756—dc20   96-28335
                                                                    CIP

Printed in the United States of America

0 9 8 7 6 5 4 3 2 1

Fulcrum Publishing
350 Indiana Street, Suite 350
Golden, Colorado 80401-5093
(800) 992-2908 • (303) 277-1623

The Seasonal Guide to the Natural Year Series

Pennsylvania, New Jersey, Maryland, Delaware, Virginia, West Virginia and Washington, D.C., Scott Weidensaul
New England and New York, Scott Weidensaul
Illinois, Missouri and Arkansas, Barbara Perry Lawton
Colorado, New Mexico, Arizona and Utah, Ben Guterson
Northern California, Bill McMillon
Oregon, Washington and British Columbia, James Luther Davis
Texas, Steve Price
North Carolina, South Carolina and Tennessee, John Rucker
Florida with Georgia and Alabama Coasts, M. Timothy O'Keefe

Forthcoming Titles

Minnesota, Michigan and Wisconsin, John Bates
Southern California, Judy Wade

In loving memory of my mother—whose encouragement and support enabled me to take the path less traveled.

North Carolina Hotspots

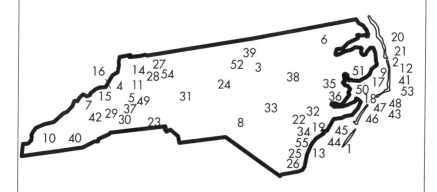

Seasonal Guide to the Natural Year

Site Locator Map

N

LIST OF SITES
North Carolina

1. Cape Lookout National Seashore
2. Cape Hatteras National Seashore
3. Eno River State Park
4. Grandfather Mountain
5. Chimney Rock Park
6. Merchants Mill Pond State Park
7. Joyce Kilmer Memorial Forest
8. Weymouth Woods Sandhills Nature Preserve
9. Pea Island
10. Nantahala National Forest
11. Mt. Mitchell State Park
12. Oregon Inlet
13. Shackleford Banks
14. New River State Park
15. Great Smoky Mountains National Park
16. Big Creek
17. Ocracoke Island
18. Portsmouth Island
19. Bald Head Island
20. Nag's Head Woods
21. Jockey's Ridge State Park
22. White Lake
23. FENCE
24. Piedmont Environmental Center
25. Cape Fear River Mouth
26. Battery Island
27. Blue Ridge Parkway
28. Doughton Park
29. Graveyard Fields
30. Lake Lure
31. Morrow Mountain State Park
32. Black River
33. Fort Bragg–Camp MacKall
34. Green Swamp Preserve
35. Millis Swamp Road Flatwoods
36. Millis Swamp Savanna
37. Craggy Gardens
38. Hemlock Bluffs City Park
39. Occoneechee Mountain
40. Transylvania County Waterfalls
41. Cape Hatteras
42. Richland Balsam
43. Gulf Stream
44. Rachel Carson Estuarine Preserve
45. Bear Island
46. White Oak River
47. Old Coast Guard Station
48. Fort Fisher
49. Hickory Nut Gorge
50. Pamlico Sound
51. Lake Mattamuskeet
52. Reidsville's City Lake
53. Buxton Woods
54. Bull Creek Valley Overlook
55. Sugarloaf Dune

SOUTH CAROLINA HOTSPOTS

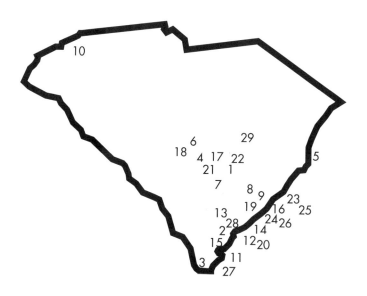

Seasonal Guide to
the Natural Year

N

SITE LOCATOR MAP

List of Sites
South Carolina

TENNESSEE HOTSPOTS

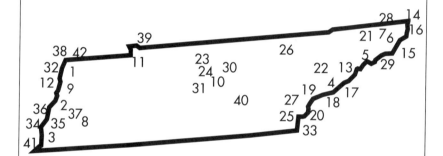

28 14
39
21 7 6
38 42 26 5 15
32 1 11 23 22 13 29
12 30
24
9 31 10 4
2 19 17
36 37 40 27 18
34 35 8 25 20
3 33
41

Seasonal Guide to
the Natural Year

SITE LOCATOR MAP

N

LIST OF SITES
Tennessee

1. Reelfoot Lake, Reelfoot Lake State Park
2. Fort Pillow State Park
3. Meeman–Shelby Forest State Park
4. Great Smoky Mountains National Park
5. Roan Mountain State Park
6. Watauga Lake
7. South Holston River
8. Hatchie National Wildlife Refuge
9. Chickasaw National Wildlife Refuge
10. Cedars of Lebanon State Park
11. Land Between the Lakes
12. Nebraska Point
13. Little Pigeon River
14. Virginia Creeper Trail
15. Roan Mountain
16. Holston Lake and Dam
17. Grotto Falls Grove
18. Ramsay Cascade Trail
19. Gregory's Bald Trail
20. Albright Grove
21. South Holston River
22. Sharp's Ridge
23. Warner Parks
24. Radnor Lake Park
25. Hiwassee River
26. Clinch River–Norris Dam
27. Roaring Fork Motor Nature Trail
28. Beaverdam Creek
29. Holston Mountain
30. Long Hunter State Park
31. Vesta Glade Coneflowers
32. Island 13
33. Cade's Cove
34. Mississippi River
35 Chickasaw Bluffs
36. Coal Creek Chute
37. Wardlow's Pocket
38. Phillippi Pits
39. "The Trace" Parkway
40. Savage Gulf
41. Overton Park
42. New Madrid Fault

Contents

Acknowledgments

To complete the writing of a seasonal guide for such a biologically complex region as the Carolinas and Tennessee within the allocated time frame would have been quite impossible if not for the generosity of others. How many times did a stranger agree to help me? In fact, I do not think I was ever turned down.

A Tennessee Natural Heritage botanist, a state park field biologist, an alligator biologist, some turtle network volunteers, a longleaf pine–wire grass savanna botanist, a western Tennessee birder and a couple who spends every weekend in search of tree frogs and other amphibians, all agreed to teach me the basics of their particular field of expertise. This book was not only an exploration of natural biospheres, but also of the generosity of the human spirit.

Walt Rhodes, a U.S. Fish and Wildlife biologist specializing in alligators, let me accompany him on a nighttime gator count. That experience taught me the "ethos" of the South Carolina lowcountry as nothing else could have. Milo Pyne of the Tennessee Natural Heritage Program took me out into the cedar glades in 95 degree heat and gave me the "key" to appreciating many of the subtle complexities of that little known ecosystem. Steve Roff, the biologist of Huntington Beach State Park in South Carolina, took me into a salt marsh and, while observing fiddler crabs, taught me to savor the semitropical fecundity of nitrogenous-smelling mud. Birders such as Fred Alsop III and FENCE's (Foothills Equestrian Center) Simon Thompson taught me the level of musical discernment that the ear of a lifetime birder can attain. Tim Landis took me to a tiny mountain creek to see spawning brook trout, which he "hunted" with a fly rod. Mike Ielmini of Chickasaw National Wildlife Refuge showed me oxbows of the Mississippi River from a canoe despite the whine of ten thousand mosquitoes.

Bill Mace, the ranger of Santee Coastal Preserve, who also was not deterred by the whine of thousands of mosquitoes nor the bites of truly fierce yellow flies, showed me how he floods old rice fields with rice "trunks" that he builds and installs himself. Bob and Pandy English took me out at night near Reelfoot Lake to "herpe" by ear, to listen to bird-voiced tree frogs, cricket frogs and others. Glen Criswell showed me his favorite location for seeing Mississippi kites: Island 13 of the Mississippi River. I would have never known of, nor found, Island 13 on my own.

Turtle network volunteers of Long Beach, North Carolina, let me help relocate doomed loggerhead sea turtle nests to locations where the eggs would not be submerged at high tide. Dick Thomas of Piedmont Environmental Center in High Point, North Carolina, drove me to the Carolina sandhills to show me his passion: the longleaf pine fire ecosystem. George Pyne of Eno River State Park showed me hillsides of yellow lady's slippers. Harvey Bradshaw flew me over Topsail Island, North Carolina, in a single-engine airplane, looking for leatherbacked and loggerhead sea turtles. Over the phone, Marty Hundley walked me through many word processor crises. Ruth Matthews Thomas provided invaluable research assistance. The field research for this book required being on the road nearly constantly, living out of my aging Dodge van. Darrell Newman correctly diagnosed various mechanical problems and talked me through their repairs over the phone. In a measure of true friendship, he drove to South Carolina to tow me home on one particularly frustrating trip.

One thing led to another. On a birding weekend Robin Carter told me of the spectacle of the great flying dung storm in the Mississippi River bottomlands, 500 miles west. A man cleaning catfish at Harry's Heart of the Lakes fish camp on Lake Marion told me of Bird Island and its fabulous rookery. These are just a few of the good people who have given you, the reader, a set of keys opening new doors to nature's mysteries, wonders and riddles.

Introduction

In September 1492, Christopher Columbus and his near-mutinous crew found themselves lost in the middle of the Sargasso Sea, north of the Bahama Islands. On September 20, Columbus wrote in his journal of seeing tiny songbirds—"singing birds" he called them—in the middle of the Atlantic. Taking this as a sign that land was nearby, Columbus continued his historic voyage with rekindled optimism.

For centuries ship captains continued to report seeing diminutive songbirds far out in the Atlantic, including the Gulf Stream waters off Cape Hatteras. Such a bizarre incongruity as a tiny chipping sparrow or a warbler a thousand miles out at sea was explained in the only plausible manner. These birds must have been blown off course during migration and were doomed in this endless landscape of heaving gray seamounts.

Yet in 1977, research was initiated by the Woods Hole Oceanographic Institute. Radar was placed on a ship located southwest of Bermuda in the middle of the Atlantic, 1,000 miles due east of Cape Hatteras. Other radar sets on Antigua also scanned the night skies in an attempt to solve the centuries-old riddle of the over-ocean songbirds. Nearly five centuries after Columbus's observation, the unthinkable was proven to be fact. In addition to the Atlantic Flyway and the Mississippi Flyway, another, heavily used over-ocean flyway existed for small songbirds as well as other avian species of the eastern United States headed for the wintering grounds in South America.

It is now known that many millions of birds undertake this do-or-die journey each autumn. It is estimated that from the Cape Cod, Massachusetts, area alone, on a single night of favorable weather conditions, as many as 12 million songbirds, woodpeckers, doves, swifts, kingfishers, plovers, birds of prey, ducks and other species may depart for the over-ocean route to South America. It is not known why birds choose to run this "survival of the fittest" gauntlet. They depart from a broad band of the eastern seaboard states. Some birds fly as high as 1.5 miles above the ocean. Moving at 30 miles per hour, small passerines such as wrens, kinglets, brown creepers, nuthatches and swallows must be able to fly nonstop for as long as three days and nights. There is apparently no thought of turning back. With normal fat stores, even the smallest birds are capable of flying more than 2,000 miles nonstop. Yet strong headwinds may increase the rate of calories per mile. The margin of error for birds with long flights is small.

When birds are tracked on radar from ships or from the mid-ocean island of Bermuda, it is noted that they overfly all the Caribbean islands. Apparently it would burn more energy to land there and find food, then regain altitude and momentum, than would be gained. It is estimated that as many as 100 million birds depart from the East Coast of the United States each fall, with departures peaking in October. Mortality may be high; this part of the equation is not known. For years the captains of fishing boats working the Gulf Stream off North Carolina's Cape Hatteras have reported sighting exhausted birds landing to rest on their boats, some barely able to fly.

There are safer migration routes to northern South America, such as following the North American coastline southward. Perhaps there is only enough food for a limited number of migrants to take the safer routes. No doubt the dynamics of these routes have been worked out over millions of generations of birds. For reasons known only to the collective consciousness of birds, this compelling commitment is made each year. The first night after a cold front has moved through, birds weighing as little as three-quarters of an ounce take to the invisible interstate highway in the night sky and move offshore as far as 1,000 miles. It is a highway with no rest stops.

Although perhaps the most compelling one, this is only one story that transpires yearly within the natural sphere of the three-state region of North Carolina, South Carolina and Tennessee and their offshore waters. All the rich biodiversity here teaches the same lesson that the constellation-navigating songbirds teach. The astonishing level of the genius and boldness of nature, as well as the simple, unpostured honesty and courage of its creatures like the tiny, open-ocean migrants, is the compelling lesson, retold in many ways.

The wildlife that inhabits the salt marsh, the barrier islands, the maritime forest, the longleaf pine forest, the cove hardwood forest of the southern Appalachians and the environs of the Mississippi River in western Tennessee teaches us to enjoy the simple pleasures offered by the sun, the rain and the moment. In terms of numbers of species among plants and animals, this three-state region ranks high among geographical regions of North America. On the level of natural community types and landscape-level biodiversity richness, it may be the equal of any area of comparable size in North America. Study in all the natural classrooms of North Carolina, South Carolina and Tennessee. Each one tells a tale all its own.

> The ethical imperative should therefore be, first of all, prudence. We should judge every scrap of biodiversity as priceless while we learn to use it and come to understand what it means to humanity. We should not knowingly allow any species or race to go extinct. And let us go beyond mere salvage to begin the restoration of natural environments, in order to enlarge wild populations and stanch the hemorrhaging of biological wealth. There can be no purpose more inspiriting than to begin the age of restoration, reweaving the wondrous diversity of life that still surrounds us.
>
> —E. O. Wilson, *The Diversity of Life*

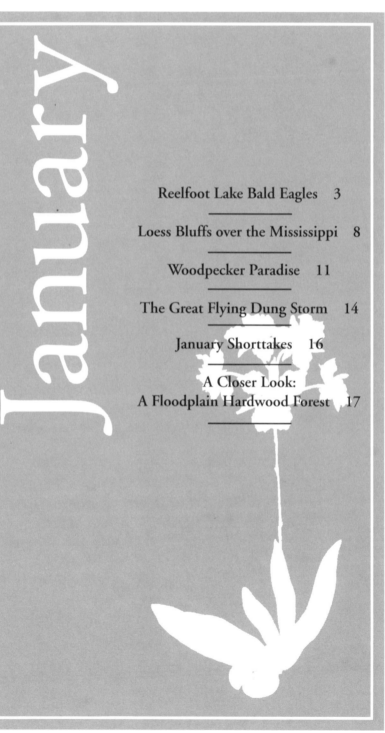

January

Notes

1

Reelfoot Lake Bald Eagles

Because Reelfoot Lake in Tennessee is so fertile, every season of the year sees large numbers of migratory birds arrive to take advantage of the lake's fabulous food chain. More than a half million ducks and geese overwinter here, venturing out into the adjacent tabletop flat agricultural lands in search of crops left behind during the fall harvest. White pelicans are often present in flocks numbering in the hundreds during this season. Shorebirds arrive in April and trade back and forth between the wetlands that border Reelfoot and the adjacent fields. April also witnesses the arrival of 20 species of brightly colored warblers from the tropics. The month of October may find as many as 20,000 cormorants converging on Reelfoot. They are impressive in flight, and form large gyres that revolve slowly, thousands of feet in the air, in the manner of sandhill cranes. The appetites of the snaky-looking cormorants, the diminutive warblers and all in between are satisfied by Reelfoot's generosity. It is balanced, at the other end of our three-state region, by the equally fertile Lakes Marion and Moultrie. Nothing exists between these two sister freshwater bodies that approaches them in terms of fertility. Reelfoot Lake and Lake Marion are strikingly similar in appearance.

Yet of all the avian migrants that place Reelfoot at the top of their itineraries, one species arouses more interest than all the rest combined. Each winter approximately 200 bald eagles reside here. This eagle population is a success story with origins in 1972, the year DDT was banned. Prior to that time, through widespread use this insecticide had invaded the food chain of America's wildlife from coast to coast. Avian species at the top of the food chain, such as falcons, ospreys and both golden and bald eagles, were in serious decline. Once ingested, DDT had the effect of thinning eggshells, causing them to break during incubation. Now that the chemical has been allowed to break down in the environment and no more has been added, numbers of all these species have made a healthy comeback. Most of Reelfoot's eagle population is an overwintering one, although a few pairs remain to nest during the breeding season. Most of the population returns to the Great Lakes and Canada to breed. There is a trend in the eagle numbers each year at Reelfoot. For instance, the bald eagle population of Reelfoot stood at 141 in early December 1994. January 1995 saw an increase to 188. By February the number had fallen to 68. Typically, by March most of the eagles have dispersed to the north.

These numbers represent a normal year's fluctuation on Reelfoot Lake. During a hard freeze, Reelfoot may freeze over, and many of the eagles will move to the nearby Mississippi River. Still others will migrate farther south. Before making a long drive to Reelfoot during cold weather, you may wish to call ahead to check conditions. However, even during a hard freeze, a handful of eagles will remain on the lake and offer an interesting birdwatching spectacle. These opportunistic feeders target the highly concentrated ducks and geese that remain on the small areas of open water during prolonged below-freezing weather.

The bald eagle, considering its imposing appearance, is rather plebeian in behavior. Dead fish are its principal diet, for it is only occasionally able to catch live ones. The osprey, or "fish eagle," is a far superior fisherman. The bald eagle often hazes the osprey in flight, forcing it to drop its honestly earned fish, which the eagle then seizes and eats. Bald eagles occasionally join crows and ravens as they feed on carrion. The bald eagle does catch many rabbits, ducks, squirrels, mice and snakes, and in this way is like its cousin, the golden eagle, which never eats carrion. Bald eagles mate for life and appear to form strong pair bonds.

If the number of eagles is high, as it tends to be in December and January, the birds will be scattered along the shoreline of Reelfoot. They can be seen in flight as well as perched in the cypress trees along the shoreline. The Air Park Inn area is an excellent location for observing eagles perched in cypress trees during the early months of the overwintering period. The Air Park Inn is the point of origin for eagle tours conducted by bus from

December 1 until mid-March. The boardwalk out into Reelfoot Lake at the Air Park Inn can be remarkable for the numbers of northern cardinals and other songbirds that feed in the partly submerged vegetation growing on both sides of the boardwalk during the winter.

The other area of concentration for Reelfoot eagles is the south end of the lake, near the visitor's center. Here eagles tend to gather as the winter season draws to a close. One reason may be that they are hand-fed at 11:00 A.M. each day by Bo Bentley at Bo's boat landing. At times as many as 30 eagles arrive at Bo's to eat fish scraps.

A soaring adult bald eagle, with white head and white tail, is one of the most impressive sights within the sphere of nature and never becomes commonplace. John Burroughs, consulting editor for T. Gilbert Pearson during the writing of *Birds of America*, spoke of the sentiments the eagle stirs in the heart of earthbound humans: "He draws great lines across the sky; he sees the forests like a carpet beneath him; he sees the hills and valleys as folds and wrinkles in a many colored tapestry; he sees the river as a silver belt connecting remote horizons. We climb mountain-peaks to get a glimpse of the spectacle that is hourly spread out beneath him. I would have my thoughts take as wide a sweep. I would be as far removed from the petty cares and turmoils of this noisy and blustering world." This quote is taken from *Far and Near* by John Burroughs.

Hot Spots

Reelfoot Lake, in the northwest corner of Tennessee, is reached by taking TN 78 north out of Dyersburg to Tiptonville. Air Park Inn is reached by driving 7.7 miles north of the little community of Tiptonville, Tennessee, on TN 78. To reach the Reelfoot Lake visitor's center take TN 22 east for 3 miles out of Tiptonville. As you drive these 3 miles, look in the large cypress trees around Bo's boat landing, Goch's boat landing and the American Legion Club. Immediately behind the Reelfoot Lake visitor's center is a large pen containing two bald eagles unable to fend for themselves in the wild. Inside the visitor's center are exhibits explaining in

Reelfoot Lake

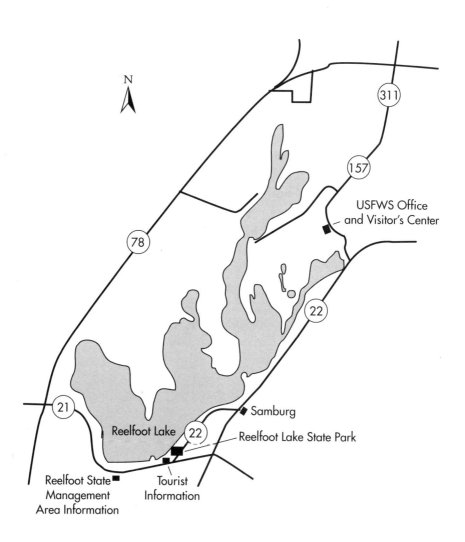

N

311

157

USFWS Office
and Visitor's Center

78

22

21

Reelfoot Lake 22

Samburg

Reelfoot Lake State Park

Reelfoot State
Management
Area Information

Tourist
Information

great detail how this lake was formed during the Great New Madrid Earthquake, which persisted from December 16, 1811, until March 8, 1812, and was the largest earthquake ever recorded in North America. Behind the visitor's center is a boardwalk out onto the lake, which enables you to walk among some of the old-growth baldcypress trees that grow in Reelfoot Lake. The Reelfoot Lake State Park public campground, located near the visitor's center, is closed during the winter months, when the eagles are present. However, the Air Park Inn campground is open year-round. Boyette's of Tiptonville, Tennessee, rents comfortable cabins by the night. Many naturalists visiting Reelfoot Lake stay here.

2

Loess Bluffs over the Mississippi

Tennessee, perhaps more blessed with geological wonders than any other state in the Southeast, possesses a gem in its crown of natural wonders that few people know about: the loess bluffs overlooking the Mississippi River. These bluffs provide a unique window through which to contemplate the incomprehensibly great powers that nature can activate. They bring this important lesson down to the simplest level—a handful of very unusual dirt.

The region presently occupied by the Mississippi River has seen great change. In the river's current floodplain, a mountain range over 4,000 feet in elevation, stood long before the Cretaceous Period. Millions of years later, what is now Memphis was in open ocean, in the center of a vast extension of the present-day Gulf of Mexico. Yet as recently as 12,000 years ago, the region was dominated by glaciers that stopped at the present-day course of the Ohio River, only a few hundred miles to the north of Tennessee's border with Kentucky. The ice sheets, roughly 2 miles thick and covering northern North America, Europe and Asia, retreated in a surprisingly short time because of unexplained and momentous climatic changes.

What the glaciers left behind challenges the imagination. Because of their great weight, the ice sheets ground millions of rocks and boulders as large as cars and houses into powder nearly as fine as flour. Billions of square yards of the rock powder that had been bulldozed along by the glaciers lay spread over the landscape for thousands of square miles to the north. Literally, the winds of change blew, creating dust storms that must have turned noon to dusk. The Chickasaw Bluffs, also called the Jackson Formation, which forms much of the western edge of Tennessee's coastal plain of the Mississippi River, towered nearly 100 yards over the mighty river at locations such as Meeman Shelby State Park and Fort

Pillow. These bluffs were smothered with the windborne rock powder, or loess, to a depth of 80 feet. The reconstituted boulders were blown southward and deposited as far away as Vicksburg, Mississippi, and as far north as Iowa and Minnesota. Finally the cogs of the great gears that somehow drive the engine of global cataclysmic change, slowed and the wind stopped. The Mississippi River ecosystem went to work, breathing life into a mantle of inert stone dust.

As you walk the bluffs of Fort Pillow, where Nathan Bedford Forrest's Confederates stormed the Union fort, you should go softly and thoughtfully, perhaps kneeling to sift the rich organic soil through your fingers and pondering the inscrutibility of life.

Fort Pillow State Park, overlooking North America's mightiest river, is a textbook example of a bluff ecosystem. The park's scenic overlook of Coal Creek Chute and the river has, arguably, the best view of the Mississippi in Tennessee. The bluffs are so rambling, steep and extensive that they give the impression of the Carolina foothills. The path from the old earthworks of Fort Pillow down the face of the bluffs to Coal Creek Chute is as steep as any you will encounter in the heart of the southern Appalachians.

By camping during the winter season, you benefit by having most of the campground to yourself. The other advantage only becomes apparent at night, as you sit by a campfire. During the winter, when the trees are bare, from the north loop of the campground you can listen to the calls of barred owls and watch the lights of barge traffic on Mark Twain's Mississippi. Powerful diesel tugs push barges nearly a quarter of a mile long, up the river as well as down. Each tug has its own searchlight mounted high above the cabin. These powerful lights probe the river in search of floating trees and snags. It is an eerie sight indeed.

The other textbook example of a Mississippi River loess bluff ecosystem is located in Meeman Shelby State Park, 8 miles north of Memphis. Some of the bluffs here have elevations of up to 300 feet above the river and 45 degrees of slope. Here some of the woodland creeks have cut erosion gullies where they follow the steep gradients, giving you opportunity to see the ancient, windblown depositions from the time of the glaciers. The park also offers a close-up view of the Mississippi River at Sasser boat ramp.

Hot Spots

To reach **Fort Pillow State Park**, on Tennessee's western border, follow TN 51 south from Ripley, Tennessee, for several miles. Look for TN 87 heading west. Follow TN 87 approximately 15 miles west to the entrance to the park. For information call (901) 738-5581. To reach **Meeman Shelby State Park**, take TN 51 south from Ripley. About 15 miles north of the city limits of Memphis, at the town of Millington, turn right at the second light onto Shelby Road. Go 10 miles, following signs for the state park. For information on Meeman Shelby State Park call (901) 876-5215.

3

Woodpecker Paradise

The Mississippi River floodplain hardwood forest may support more woodpeckers per square mile than any other place in North America. The vast stands of hardwoods, which in places still extend from horizon to horizon along the river, contain many dead and dying trees per acre. This moist, annually flooded, bacteria-rich, riverine ecosystem promotes decay at all levels, which in turn supports all manner of insects attractive to woodpeckers. The Mississippi River alluvial floodplain hardwood forest supports numbers of red-headed woodpeckers per acre that almost certainly exceed those of any other area in the three-state region. This woodpecker, with its bright red head and black and white body, resembles a large, colorful moth in flight and is an arresting sight. The robust population of red-headed woodpeckers found here is particularly noteworthy because the overall continental population of this species seems to be declining.

Although the red-headed woodpecker appears to dominate in this ecosystem, all other species of woodpeckers found across the region are well represented also. A drive to the Fort Pillow State Park interpretive center will reveal all the woodpecker species present, in every aspect of behavior. Yellow-shafted flickers flush from the ground near the road. Hairys, downys and red-bellied woodpeckers can be seen at dusk, flying up and out of the riverbottom forest to the trees on the bluffs overlooking the river, while you stand at the Mississippi River overlook at Fort Pillow. Bear in mind that unsettled weather conditions may halt the feeding activities of all bird species. The yelp of the lordly, crow-sized pileated woodpecker can frequently be heard.

Hot Spots

The riverbottom forest of **Chickasaw National Wildlife Refuge** (NWR), approximately 60 miles south of Reelfoot Lake, supports a healthy complement of woodpeckers year-round. In addition, Chickasaw's Ed Jones boat ramp may offer one of the best easily accessible locations for standing next to the Mississippi River in an isolated, uncluttered setting and taking one's measure of this great river. The yellow gravel roads of the refuge offer birding; you may park the vehicle and walk the gravel roadway, or walk the trail into the floodplain forest. Directions to Chickasaw NWR and Ed Jones boat ramp are lengthy. To reach the refuge headquarters for Chickasaw NWR, turn right (west) at the Exxon station/convenience store on TN 51 in Ripley, Tennessee. Proceed west on Edith-Central Road, which turns into Edith-Nankipoo Road, passing Moore's Store on the right, and then passing through the little community of Edith. In approximately 7 miles, you will come to the floodplain of the Mississippi River. To reach the refuge headquarters, turn left on the sandy road (Sand Bluff Road), which exits 100 feet before reaching the turn onto Dee Webb Road. Go one-half mile to the refuge headquarters.

To reach Ed Jones boat ramp and Nebraska Point on the Mississippi River, go back out to the blacktop and take Dee Webb Road across the floodplain of the Mississippi River. Several miles after turning onto Dee Webb Road, cross the Old Bed of the Forked Deer River and continue west. At 6.6 miles after turning onto Dee Webb Road, go past the turnoff to the large cement factory visible on the right side of the road. Here, bear left and proceed one-half mile to Ed Jones boat ramp. To reach Nebraska Point, continue past the turnoff to Ed Jones boat ramp and follow the sandy road through floodplain hardwood forest and cleared agricultural land for 4.8 miles. Upon reaching a large lake, turn right and wind through several miles of cleared agricultural land. When you come to a small power relay station (it has a small antenna), continue straight through the intersection and stay on the same road. After 1 mile, pass the New Mitchell Grove Baptist

Church and go 100 yards. Pass several homes and begin to look for a U.S. Fish and Wildlife Service sign that says "No vehicles beyond this point." Park and proceed on foot in a westerly direction for one-half mile across grass savanna. Follow a faint jeep trail until reaching the grassy point of the Mississippi River known as Nebraska Point. (See map on page 19.)

Fort Pillow State Park, 50 miles south of Chickasaw, is probably the premier location along Tennessee's section of the Mississippi for seeing the red-headed woodpecker and other woodpecker species. The forest here is old regrowth and the trees of Fort Pillow's bluffs and lowlands are truly impressive. The venerable hardwoods fairly ring with the staccato rapping and tapping of all manner of woodpeckers when the birds are actively feeding. Be sure to take the half-mile hike down to the earthworks of old Fort Pillow, the site of a controversial Civil War battle. The 25 miles of hiking trails in Fort Pillow allow you to savor the splendid hardwood forest during the winter, when it is most open, as well as the avian species most specifically adapted to it, the woodpeckers.

Meeman Shelby State Park (chapter 2) has a large number of standing dead trees, from the top of the bluffs down to the edge of the Mississippi River. The woodpecker population is diverse and robust here. Meeman Shelby's beech forest may be the most beautiful in America. There is no better time to see the stately beech trees of this park than during the winter, when the woods are free of foliage.

4

The Great Flying Dung Storm

The Mississippi River corridor of western Tennessee is a mixing grounds for eastern, western and southern species of birds, as well as an important migratory route. Yet of all the avian species that use both the Mississippi River Flyway and its fertile floodplain fields and forests, nothing is more symbolic of the scale of both the river and its bottomlands than the sight of a flock of five million blackbirds moving across a sunset.

These blackbirds are the lean "barbarians" that have replaced the sky, darkening flocks of naive passenger pigeons that, with their sheer weight, broke branches from the trees where they roosted. The mixed flocks of grackles, brown-headed cowbirds, starlings, rusty blackbirds, red-winged blackbirds and even robins are too smart for such archaic behavior. Monoculture agriculture has created huge monoculture flocking. The blackbird flocks are a wintertime phenomenon, for after March the flocks begin to break up as pairing for breeding season begins.

Apparently the combination of vast agricultural fields, rich in waste grain during the winter, and riverbottom forest has spawned this gargantuan entity. There is nothing more arresting than the sight of such a flock lifting out of the swampy lowlands of the vast Mississippi River where the blackbirds have been feeding in the leaf litter on the forest floor. The cacophony of their metallic "clanks," "checks" and other noises, as well as the roar of their wings, can sound as full as the ocean surf.

Often, when the blackbird flock has ceased its foraging under the leaves of the forest floor, it pauses in the trees on top of the bluffs overlooking the Mississippi River. As the last stragglers out of the riverbottom swarm into the trees, the blackbird flock may pause to express its huge collective approval of a fine, cold January morning. Then, with a soft boom that echoes like a mile-long wave collapsing on a beach, the flock takes wing, headed for the fields to look for waste grain. Their dung rattles on the dead leaves of the forest floor like rain. The great flying dung storm always seems to know exactly where it is going, the supreme example of collective consciousness. It is a most curious model to contemplate and may have implications regarding the behavior of humans.

The Mississippi River corridor of western Tennessee is truly a blackbird paradise. In addition to the vast mixed flocks that appear like smoke on the horizon, there is single-species flocking of blackbirds. Quite early in the new year, red-winged blackbirds are wearing the red shoulder epaulets they will use in courtship, and flocks of several hundred may be seen in cultivated fields. Similarly, brown-headed cowbirds flocks are seen, and like the red-winged blackbirds, are quite beautiful against the tilled soil. The brown-headed cowbird has a terrible reputation because it parasites warbler and other songbird nests. In some areas, where only small blocks of forest are left, cowbirds destroy the eggs of warblers, and substitute their own, in all the nests present. Yet the root problem is not cowbirds as much as the lack of large blocks of old-growth forest, which cowbirds are unable to penetrate.

Hot Spots Large blackbird flocks can be seen serendipitously around **Reelfoot Lake** (chapter 1) where they roost in the sawgrass marshes. Blackbird flocks can be seen in the areas of **Fort Pillow State Park** (chapter 2) and **Chickasaw NWR** (chapter 3) and as far as 100 miles east of the Mississippi River. West Tennesseans call Milan, Tennessee, north of Jackson, the blackbird capital of the world.

5

January Shorttakes

Overton Park's Remarkable Forest

Memphis's Overton Park is considered remarkable by those who study the eastern hardwood forest. This classic Mississippi River bluff forest is comprised of original old-growth trees and is one of the few places in the East where an old-growth forest survives outside the southern Appalachian ecosystem. In downtown Memphis miles of walking trails meander through more than 100 acres of red oak, white oak, cottonwood and beech trees. Also in this forest is the national champion shumard oak, which stands 190 feet tall, is 240 inches in circumference and has a crown spread of 88 feet. While a few of the trees may have been cut down when the area was a farm, most of the original trees are approximately 200 years old, which dates them well ahead of most of the rampant logging years. The park was acquired at the end of the 19th century, and the city of Memphis developed around it.

To reach Overton Park, enter Memphis from the east on I-40. Go west on Sam Cooper Boulevard, which becomes Broad Avenue and runs into Overton Park.

6

A Closer Look:
A Floodplain Hardwood Forest

The lower half of Tennessee's section of the Mississippi River takes in the largest blocks of remaining floodplain hardwood forest in the lower end of the river's winding 2,340-mile course. Chickasaw and Lower Hatchie Refuges, Fort Pillow State Park, Meeman Shelby State Park and Anderson Tulley form the anchors for an ambitious plan to connect these large forested blocks. Already the buying-up of blocks of cleared agricultural floodplain land between Chickasaw NWR and Lower Hatchie NWR is well under way. These cleared fields will be replanted with native riverbottom hardwoods. When completed, a vast, intact riverine-forest corridor will be created. Within the actual Mississippi River floodplain, much of the forested bottomlands of Arkansas, Missouri, Mississippi and Louisiana have been cleared for agriculture. As with the 100,000 acres of virgin hardwood forest in Great Smoky Mountains National Park, shared by Tennessee and North Carolina, once again Tennessee has the lion's share.

Within Tennessee's section of the river is the core of what remains of the lower Mississippi River floodplain hardwood forest. Although Tennessee has only approximately 10 percent of its original Mississippi River floodplain forest, it is still more than its neighboring states along the river. Environmentally, it is difficult to overstate the importance of Tennessee's blocks of old-growth riverbottom forest. The Mississippi Flyway is one of the major flyways for South American neotropical migrants headed for the oak-hickory forest of the Upper Midwest, Michigan's Upper Peninsula and the Canadian boreal forest. These migrants depend on the abundant food of Tennessee's Mississippi River floodplain forest as they migrate through the area. The flyway is critical for waterfowl using the prairie potholes region of Minnesota, North Dakota, Saskatchewan and Manitoba for breeding. Cerulean warblers, prothonotary warblers and other warbler species actively nest in the Mississippi River floodplain forest. Seventy-five percent of the high-density breeding range for these species along the lower Mississippi River falls between Tennessee's Reelfoot Lake and St. Catherine's Creek, near Natchez, Mississippi. Yet even within this region, Tennessee's large blocks of riverine hardwood forest along the Mississippi are the core area for prime warbler nesting habitat on the lower end of the river. The U.S. Fish and Wildlife Service considers protecting what remains of the lower Mississippi River floodplain hardwood forest its top priority in the southeastern United States, placing it ahead of even Florida's daunting environmental problems.

In a race against time, the most important warbler study in the country is being conducted within the Mississippi River floodplain hardwood forest. The principal study site is in Tennessee's Chickasaw NWR. Here, Paul Hamel of the Southern Hardwoods Research Laboratory of Stoneville, Mississippi, is studying the dynamics of cerulean warbler populations. This important indicator species has declined by 50 percent worldwide. Hamel coordinates his research in the Mississippi River floodplain forest with his ongoing research on the South American wintering grounds of neotropical migrants such as thrushes, vireos and warblers. The results of Hamel's cerulean warbler study in Chickasaw NWR, Meeman Shelby State Park and Delta Desha in Rohwer, Arkansas, will determine all alluvial bottomland forest management plans for neotropical migrants in the southeastern United States. The future existence of many warbler species, as well as other passerines, hinges upon the long-range success of this plan. Steps are being taken to increase the size of Tennessee's riverine hardwood forest. The Trust for Public Lands, located in Atlanta, considers Tennessee's Mississippi riverbottom lands its top priority. Other groups such as The Nature Conservancy and the U.S. Fish and Wildlife Service, as well as numerous individuals, are hoping for another environmental success story like the A.C.E. Basin in South

Chicksaw National Wildlife Refuge

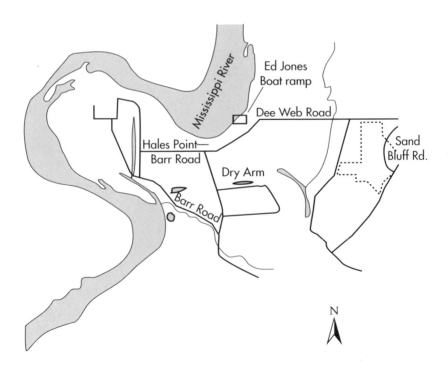

Carolina's lowcountry (see chapter 66). An even more ambitious preservation plan has been proposed by Gary Meyers, the present director of the Tennessee Wildlife Resources Agency in Nashville. Meyers is spearheading a plan to consolidate the Mississippi riverine ecosystem from Dyersburg to Memphis, restoring as much cleared agricultural land as possible to riverbottom hardwood forest, creating the largest restored and protected riverine ecosystem in the nation. The timing couldn't be better, for three hundred years' floods in less than a decade have made many owners of

Mississippi River corridor agricultural land amenable to the idea of selling.

Tennessee's Mississippi River floodplain forest offers the ecotourist an opportunity to see arboreal species diversity on a remarkable level. Along the bluffs overlooking the river in locations such as Fort Pillow and Meeman Shelby State Parks, one finds many of the same tree species of the cove hardwood forest of the southern Appalachian ecosystem. Yet as one moves down the bluffs into the riverine ecosystem, remarkably, three more forest community types emerge. The Southern Riverine forest ecosystem has indicator species such as the green ash, Carolina ash, white ash, eastern cottonwood, swamp cottonwood, black gum and various willows. The Southern Mixed Hardwood Swamp forest has, as indicator species, black tupelo, water tupelo, sweet gum, red maple, swamp hickory, water hickory, swamp chestnut oak, water oak, pawpaw and others. Finally, in the sloughs and oxbows and along the shoreline of the Mississippi River is the Baldcypress Swamp forest. Important indicator species of this natural community type are baldcypress, pond cypress, redbay, black willow and eastern sycamore. This forest community was once the home of the almost certainly extinct ivory-billed woodpecker.

Both the Mississippi River bluffs ecosystem and Roan Mountain, Tennessee, in the southern Appalachians, are alike in that numerous distinct forest types are found within their altitude bands. What is most astonishing about the Mississippi River bluffs ecosystem is that mere inches of change in elevation can be as significant as hundreds of feet in the southern Appalachians in terms of tree species variation.

For the ecotourist, the Mississippi River and its associated natural community types represent a very complex landscape-level biosphere. Yet it is almost completely unappreciated and unvisited by naturalists. Within the riverbanks, another vast web of life supports paddlefish, alligator gar, various catfish, as well as the alligator snapping turtle, the *Tyrannosaurus rex* of turtles worldwide. This fierce predator may reach a weight of more than 200 pounds.

The Mississippi River, one of the world's great rivers, is the site of migratory flights of waterfowl, neotropical migrants, eagles and pelicans. Each sunset during the spring, summer and early fall sees flocks of cattle egrets, herons and other wading birds flying over the river on their way to roost. As western Tennessee birders are fond of saying, "This river is one hell of a highway!" It is that, and so much more.

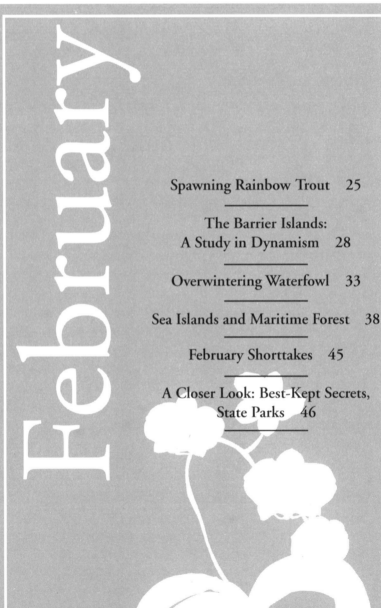

February

Notes

7

Spawning Rainbow Trout

One of the earliest natural events of the three-state region is the movement of wild rainbow trout to spawning beds in the small streams and rivers of the southern Appalachians. This spawning behavior takes place in the dead of winter because of the genetic memory left by the original McCloud River, California, rainbow trout eggs that were placed in the southern Appalachian streams. The spawning instinct of these trout is timed not to accommodate the southern Appalachian ecosystem but rather that of their ancestral river on the West Coast, many generations ago. Yet the rainbows are successful enough—too successful in the hearts of many who wish the native brook trout had not been forced out of most of its original range in the southern Appalachians by a non-native species.

The eastern brook trout is the only trout native to the southern Appalachian Mountains. Actually the brookie is not a true trout, but rather an arctic char that was able to migrate southward during the three-million-year Pleistocene ice age. But the native brook trout was naive, and was caught out of most accessible streams and creeks once fishing became a popular recreational activity. West Coast rainbow trout eggs were placed in watersheds on both sides of the continental divide in the southern Appalachians. The more aggressive and wily rainbows displaced "the poet's trout," the brookie. Brook trout still exist in the southern Appalachians, in very remote watersheds, above waterfalls and above fish barriers put in place to keep out brown trout and rainbow trout. It is possible to see spawning native brook trout on beds in October, for they are fall spawners, but it is far easier to observe the late-winter spawning efforts of the rainbows, which dominate most of the watersheds in the southern Appalachians.

To observe spawning rainbow trout you should seek out sediment-free streams and brooks, preferably within or adjacent to Great Smoky Mountains National Park, in order to ensure excellent water quality. Look in moderately swift water that is between 6 and 24 inches in depth. The gravel on the stream bottom should range in size from fist-sized stones to pea-sized gravel. Spawning pairs of rainbow trout will often select the tail of a pool or a side riffle out of the main current. Any spawning bed, or "redd," will be scoured clean and free of algae, in contrast to the surrounding riverbottom, by the active pair of fish. Pairs of spawning rainbows are easily spooked. Creep up slowly behind a tree or other cover when approaching any likely-looking water, and look for a nervously swimming pair of fish, which usually range from 5 to 10 inches long. Look for spawning colors, a bright pink mark down the side and white-tipped fins. Look for surface disturbance as the male chases away any potential intruders. The best time is from mid-February until mid-March, depending upon the severity of the winter.

If you are successful in finding spawning rainbows, the following autumn you may wish to try observing the brilliantly colored spawning brookies. You will need to begin locating a brookie population well in advance of the spawning season, for as already mentioned, the brookies are not easy to find anymore.

Hot Spots

Great Smoky Mountains National Park has more than 800 miles of streams and brooks; most of those that are at least 6 feet wide support populations of rainbow or brook trout. One of the easiest locations to reach is **Big Creek,** on the Tennessee–North Carolina state line, on the eastern end of the park. To get to Big Creek, take I-40 west of Asheville, heading for Knoxville. Cross into Tennessee and immediately begin looking for the Waterville exit. Take this exit, go under the interstate and turn right. Cross the bridge over the Pigeon River and head back toward North Carolina. At the Carolina Power and Light station, bear to the right and begin driving along Big Creek. Rainbow trout are present in all the pools from this point going upstream. Park in the vicinity of the power station and begin your search on foot.

Another good location, which has many miles of excellent rainbow trout habitat, is the **Little Pigeon River** on the north end of the park. To reach this handsome river, take the Greenbriar entrance off US 321, approximately 5 miles east of Gatlinburg, Tennessee. Follow the signs for the Ramsay Cascades Trail. Stop anywhere there is a parking pullout along the river and look carefully for spawners. This section of the Little Pigeon supports several pairs of river otters, released here to feed on the overabundant and stunted rainbow trout population. If you are fortunate, you may see these large, playful predators, perhaps in pursuit of their principal prey species, the descendants of the McCloud River, California rainbow trout.

8

The Barrier Islands:
A Study in Dynamism

North Carolina's protected Cape Hatteras and Cape Lookout National Seashores stretch over 160 miles from just north of Oregon Inlet to Cape Lookout. There are no barrier islands like these anywhere else in the world. A strong case could be made that these barrier islands are the most distinctive feature of one of the most unusual coastlines in the world. Alexander and Lazell, in *Ribbon of Sand*, bring attention to what they call "America's bony elbows"—the capes of Cod, Hatteras, Lookout, Fear, Romaine and Canaveral. Four out of six of these capes fall within the three-state region. No other coastline in the world is blessed with so many sandy protrusions into the world of oceania.

Like Cape Horn at the tip of South America, Cape Hatteras is truly an intrusion into the marine environment. The Outer Banks of North Carolina extend farther out into the ocean than any others in the world, and the ocean off this cape is a very unusual one. Here, "Hatteras Style Lows" are spawned. These potent weather systems are caused by the collision, off Hatteras, of the Gulf Stream, riding up from the tropics, and the frigid Labrador Current. Only the east coast of Australia has a similar interplay of two powerful, incompatible, global currents that produce weather as violent as that off Cape Hatteras. Powerful thunderstorms, waterspouts (over-ocean tornadoes) and hurricane-force northeasters are all part of living 20 miles out at sea in a particularly dynamic part of the Atlantic Ocean. With the exception of Florida's coastline, no part of the southeastern United States is as vulnerable to hurricanes as North Carolina's Outer Banks.

North Carolina's inlet-rich Outer Banks form a permeable dam that backs up the greatest collection of brackish water sounds

The tip of Cape Hatteras as seen from the Cape Hatteras Lighthouse.

in the world: Currituck, Core, Albemarle Bogue and Pamlico. These brackish water sounds and the vast freshwater systems draining into them give North Carolina the second largest estuary on the East Coast; only Virginia's Chesapeake Bay is larger.

"Outer banks" protect the Gulf states of the south-central United States and Mexico's eastern coastline as far south as Tamaulipas. Even Brazil has a series of barrier islands. No other continent has anything else of significance in the way of sandy capes and barrier islands. Yet, as Alexander and Lazell claim in *Ribbon of Sand*, regarding all other outer banks across the world, "They are outer—not Outer."

Until the early 1960s, it was thought that the Outer Banks of North Carolina were anchored to a series of unmoving Pleistocene coral reefs. A young graduate student from Louisiana State University named Robert Dolan arrived in Manteo, North Carolina in 1959, armed with a portable drilling rig. Dolan, working on his doctorate in coastal geology, discovered something heretofore undreamed of: The Outer Banks of North Carolina are nothing but a 30-foot-thick lens of sand, nearly as fluid as the sea, which migrated inland and southward during periods of warm weather or back out to sea during ice ages, when sea levels dropped. Dolan's views were strengthened by the writings of a young botanist from the University of Massachusetts, Paul Godfrey, who wrote a paper in 1970 stating that occasional overwash by storms and hurricanes did not harm salt-adapted, native plant communities. He went on to claim that overwash fans on the west side of barrier islands created new, beneficial marshlands, and that high, artificially sustained dunes blocked this process. The Dolan/Godfrey theory was gradually modified to accommodate another major factor: the opening of new inlets through the barrier islands. It is now understood that new inlets pull sand, migrating down the coastline, into the brackish water sounds behind the barrier islands, thus helping to move the western shoreline and sand base of the "ribbon of sand" in a southwesterly or inland direction. Through the seminal work of Dolan, Godfrey and others, it gradually became apparent that the philosophy of stabilizing barrier islands was inherently flawed and completely impossible. The war mentality of holding back the sea, which had evolved since the early 1930s in the U.S. Army Corps of Engineers and the National Park Service, was gradually questioned and is now being discarded. The legacy of this strategy is thousands and thousands of homes built upon a carpet that is slowly being pulled out from beneath them.

This story illustrates dramatically just how complex natural systems can be. It also demonstrates the importance of understanding natural systems and building and living to coexist within them, before a crisis situation is reached. Perhaps nowhere in America are more dynamics, including economic ones, at work than on North Carolina's Outer Banks. The Outer Banks seem to strengthen the credibility of the increasingly popular axiom,

"Nature is not only more complex than Man thinks, but is more complex than Man *can* think."

North Carolina's Outer Banks, which invite "overwash" by storms and hurricanes, are utterly different from barrier islands (or "sea islands," as they are commonly called in South Carolina and Georgia), which support maritime forests. These islands are relatively stationary and may support the same forests that have existed there since the last ice age, as Bald Head Island is theorized to have done. Because of the extraordinary dynamism of the Atlantic Ocean at Cape Hatteras, the barrier islands there do not resist the sea by growing forests to anchor sand, but rather move with it.

The naturalist who wishes to visit these superlative barrier islands may do so on three levels of potential aloneness. To walk the "ribbon of sand" without the clutter that now exists from Bodie Island and Nag's Head northward, you need only drive to any section of North Carolina's Outer Banks south of Oregon Inlet. The beaches opposite Pea Island visitor's center are a good choice for a long, satisfying walk. You can walk the unaltered beach here all the way to the town of Rodanthe. To get away from the surfers, bathers and shell gatherers who come during the summer months, take the ferry from Hatteras to Ocracoke Island. Finally, in order to have miles of barrier island beach strand entirely to yourself, have a waterman on Ocracoke deliver you to **Portsmouth Island.**

One other way to reach a barrier island that has no highway connections like Portsmouth Island and Cape Lookout National Seashore, is to take the Shackleford Ferry to **Shackleford Banks.** From late April through late October, the ferry takes foot passengers departing at 9:00 A.M., 1:30 P.M. and 4:30 P.M. Look for the sign that reads "Shackleford Ferry" along the Morehead City waterfront. Operated by Mystery Tours, the ferry also offers a naturalist-led crossing to the banks at 10:00 A.M. For more information call (919) 240-2177 or (919) 728-7827. Bring your own food and drink with you if you intend to spend the whole day there.

North Carolina's Outer Banks

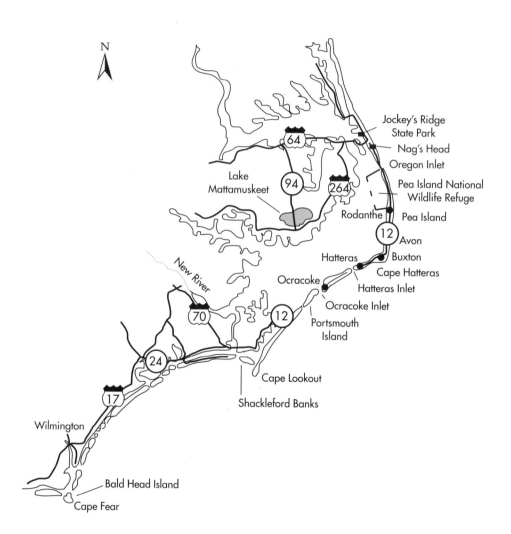

9

Overwintering Waterfowl

Perhaps the best way to beat the February blahs is to travel to the Charleston, South Carolina, area and the elegant Lowcountry that surrounds it. Summer never feels far away here in this semitropical environment. There is no more gracious city in the three-state region, or anywhere for that matter, than Charleston. It is surrounded by wildlife. Forty-five miles to the south is the 350,000-acre A.C.E. Basin, the most pristine salt marsh–estuarine–swamp forest region on the East Coast. Less than an hour's drive north of Charleston are Cape Romaine NWR, Santee Coastal Preserve, Tom Yawkey Wildlife Center and Hobcaw Barony, which form another huge block of undeveloped maritime forest, salt marsh and estuary so unspoiled that it is studied as a model for future restoration of all East Coast intertidal zones. Even within the Charleston city limits there are areas rich in wildlife. Crab Bank Island, off Shem Creek in Mt. Pleasant, is a highly productive colonial nesting site for pelicans and other species of waterbirds. During the summer, night heron rookeries are found both in Washington Park and in the live oaks of The Battery in the heart of the city. Spend a Valentine's Day weekend in Charleston, exploring nearby salt marshes and maritime forests and observing waterfowl overwintering in the old flooded rice plantations, and combine elements of history, nature and romance. What could be more balanced?

Hot Spots In the first weeks of February, overwintering waterfowl are still widely scattered throughout the lowcountry, even though spring dispersal is only a few weeks away. One of the most interesting locations for observing puddle ducks and other waterbirds is **Magnolia Plantation**, 10 miles north of Charleston. Although there is an admission charge, this destination offers the naturalist an excellent opportunity to see wildlife on the 125-acre flooded impoundment, which is managed for waterfowl. A raised levee forms the perimeter of the former rice field. A footpath and an observation tower allow you to observe ducks, gallinules and even alligators on warm, sunny days in February. On most Saturday mornings year-round, bird walks led by naturalist Perry Nugent convene at the snack shop. Call (803) 571-1266 for more information. Magnolia Gardens has an active rookery located in Ravenswood Pond, adjacent to Audubon Swamp. To reach the Magnolia Plantation, take SC 61 north out of Charleston for approximately 10 miles. Look for signs to the plantation.

The **Pitt Street Causeway** is an interesting destination for the naturalist within the city limits of Charleston. This pedestrian causeway enables you to walk through the salt marsh environment. At dusk, even in February, this ecosystem can be quite active as clapper rails, marsh wrens, various sparrow species and wading birds move about. To reach the Old Pitt Street Bridge, enter Mt. Pleasant from US 17. Travel as if you were going to Sullivan's Island or Isle of Palms. At the Scotchman's convenience store, bear right on Whilden Street. Go to McCann Street and turn right. Finally, turn left on Pitt, go to the end, park and proceed on foot.

At the south end of Folly Beach County Park, just south of Charleston, is a splendid example of an ocean inlet. Here the Atlantic Ocean rushes in like a river on incoming tide. There is always a chance to see bottlenosed dolphins in the inlet as well as in the Folly River behind Folly Island. Ocean inlets possess great dynamism because here the ocean and the highly productive salt marsh meet, concentrating predator and prey species. Another such inlet, Jeremy Inlet, is located at the north end of Edisto Beach State Park, 40 miles down the coast as the crow flies. If you happen to be a military aircraft buff, you're in luck, for all manner of dark, sinister-looking warplanes are constantly in the sky over the Charleston area.

Less than an hour's drive south of Charleston on US 17, you can observe overwintering waterfowl in the heart of the

350,000-acre region known as A.C.E. Basin, in **Bear Island WMA** (Wildlife Management Area). A.C.E. Basin is regarded as a model ecosystem. In the upper reaches of the large basin formed by the Ashepoo, Combahee and Edisto Rivers are undisturbed upland forests. After heavy rains, all three rivers overflow and flood the bottomland forests. Here pollutants settle out and are absorbed, maintaining the pristine qualities this region is known for. At the lower end of the basin, 91,000 acres of tidal marsh interact with the freshwater ecosystem of a vast "jigsaw puzzle" of lowland, upland, marsh and estuary. The 26,000 acres of old rice fields are kept flooded to provide habitat for waterfowl.

Bear Island WMA offers probably the best opportunity to experience the otherwise difficult-to-access A.C.E. Basin. From January 21 to October 31, the entire Bear Island WMA is open, except on Sunday. During the rest of the year, you may observe waterfowl only from the blacktop road. During the winter months, marsh hawks, mallards, pintails, widgeons and other puddle ducks, as well as abundant wading birds, are present. To reach Bear Island WMA take US 17 approximately 10 miles south of Jacksonboro, then look for SC 26 (Bennett's Point Road). Take SC 26 south for 2 miles. Look for the entrance to Bear Island WMA. To get a sense of how vast this basin is, stay on the refuge road, heading south. At a sign that reads "Aquatic Construction Co.," bear to the right. Drive less than 1 mile on a dirt road. Park at B and B Seafood, and look across a splendid salt marsh.

Less than 50 miles up the coast from Charleston is another regionally important location for overwintering waterfowl. At **Santee Coastal WMA** there is a brief window of opportunity for the naturalist to enjoy this biodiversity hotspot. The preserve is open from February 1 through October 31, but the mosquitos and yellow flies own it for most of the year. They seem to be attracted to insect repellent, and are generally unbearable, even for the most determined stoic, after May 1. The beauty of Santee Coastal WMA in February is that the wintering waterfowl are still there, but the insects are a few

Santee Coastal Wildlife Management Area

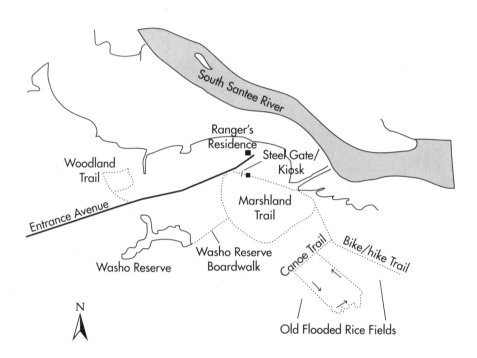

months away. This 24,000-acre preserve is one of the great overwintering locations for waterfowl on the East Coast. In February higher water levels in the old rice fields are maintained by an ingenious floating trapdoor device called a "rice trunk," whose design has not been improved upon in 300 years. The rice trunks allow the freshwater from the Santee River into and out of the rice fields, according to the desired levels. South Carolina has more than 500,000 acres of coastal marsh, far more than any other east coast state, and Santee Coastal WMA is one of the most biologically productive management areas in this vast region. More than 50,000 mallards, pintails, widgeons, Canada and snow geese and other species overwinter here. If you want more information on the antebellum rice culture that shaped much of the South Carolina Lowcountry ethos, stop in nearby Georgetown and visit the Rice Culture Museum.

To reach Santee Coastal WMA, head south out of Georgetown on US 17. One mile after crossing the bridge over the South Santee River, turn left on SC 875 and proceed for 1.5 miles. At a small church and a brick schoolhouse, look for the sign to Santee Coastal. Turn left here and drive down a sandy lane to the preserve. You will pass through fire-managed longleaf pine first, then past picturesque live oaks, before reaching the home of the refuge ranger. To reach the parking area for the levees and old rice fields, go straight after reaching the iron gate. Drive past the kiosk and continue straight, passing the maintenance shed. Continue ahead until reaching a small parking area sign. Walk down the sandy lane for a quarter mile to the old rice fields.

10

Sea Islands and Maritime Forest

In a broad sense, a sea island and a barrier island are one and the same, yet one might arbitrarily separate them according to certain characteristics. A barrier island, in the purist sense, is best represented by North Carolina's Outer Banks. These low-profiled islands "invite" the sea to overwash them on a regular basis. Before the human hand "stabilized" this strand of sand by planting millions of grass and sea oat seedlings and installing sand fences, it was fluid. Oregon Inlet, for example, once migrated southward at the rate of 82 feet per year. During the ice ages, the Outer Banks of North Carolina stood 50 miles east of their present location. Yet the Suffolk Scarp is clearly visible in photographs taken from space. Remnants of ancient barrier islands can be seen snaking across the landscape of North Carolina's coastal plain, running just west of Edenton and Plymouth, south to Morehead City.

A sea island tends to be more stationary and even invites forests to flourish in the upland regions of the larger islands. It is thought by some botanists that the live oak forest of Bald Head Island, near Wilmington, represents old-growth maritime forest never inundated by post–ice age seas. Maritime forests come in a number of configurations, yet without a doubt the loveliest maritime forest type is the live oak forest. These graceful evergreen trees with small, oblong leaves have a low profile. Their branches are extremely long and are often nearly horizontal to the ground. The live oak offers a low profile to hurricane-force winds, in contrast to a poplar or a pine. The live oak is the only hurricane-evolved tree species, and therefore tends to become the dominant tree on islands that offer protection from salt spray. The largest live oak island forest on the East Coast is on Georgia's Cumberland Island, just off the coast of the Georgia-Florida border. Yet live oak forests within the Carolinas, such as those at Bald Head or Edisto Island, are extensive and offer splendid examples of this ecosystem.

Hot Spots

Along the coastline of the Carolinas are several maritime forest community types. **Hunting Island State Park** has the best example of slash pine–palmetto forest in the Carolinas. The 4-mile beach and associated maritime forest are unique in South Carolina in that they are considered the most tropical beach in the Carolinas. The dead and dying trees at the ocean's edge are a sure sign of swiftly eroding shoreline. The best way to get an overview of this unusual maritime forest and the adjacent marsh systems is to walk to the top of the Hunting Island lighthouse. Do not miss the excellent visitor's center in this state park, where you can find photographs and explanations of barrier island dynamics. As you drive to the visitor's center, you will have a good view of the slash pine–palmetto ecosystem of the island's interior. To get a good look at a grass prairie (an extensive salt marsh dominated by spartina grass), turn south as you leave the visitor's center. Drive approximately 1 mile and park at the turnout for the plank boardwalk. These salt marsh flats extend as far as the eye can see. To reach Hunting Island State Park, take US 17 approximately 55 miles south of Charleston. Take SC 21 south through Beaufort to Huntington Island State Park.

Edisto Island is worth a visit for many reasons. The state park campground here allows you to camp close enough to hear the surf of one of the best shelling beaches in the Carolinas. Most of the shells are broken, but prize specimens of conchs, scotch bonnets, scallop shells, whelks and others can appear any morning. Edisto Island Tours takes shellers to more remote beaches. Call (803) 869-1937 for more information. **Jeremy's Inlet,** at the north end of the park, several miles up the beach from the primary campground, is an example of an ocean inlet and an excellent place to see wildlife as the tide rushes in and out. The overflow campground at Edisto Beach State Park allows you to camp within an old-growth live oak forest.

For a hike through a splendid live oak forest, Edisto Island is hard to beat. Drive a quarter of a mile north of the entrance to the main campground on SC 174. Turn left at the blue sign that reads "Nature Trail." Park at the trailhead for the Spanish Mount Trail and walk the 4-mile loop. Even during the winter, seed ticks can be terrible. Take the hike early in the day when temperatures are coolest and the ticks least active. Inspect your body carefully for these tiny fiends; their bites itch acutely. There have been no recorded cases of Lyme disease here. To get rid of ticks in your clothing, put the clothes in a plastic garbage bag, spray with an appropriate insecticide, tie the bag closed and leave it overnight.

At the end of the Spanish Mount Trail is the largest Native American shell midden on the coast of the Carolinas. This large pile is composed of oyster, clam, whelk, mussel, mud snail and cockle shells, as well as animal bones and pottery fragments. If you are blessed with good fortune, you will see a family group of bottlenosed dolphins pass by the midden mound in the tidal creek used by the Edistow Indians.

To reach Edisto Beach State Park, take US 17 south of Charleston, approximately 6 miles beyond the little town of Ravenel. Look for SC 174 south, which goes to the town of Edisto and Edisto Beach State Park. To reach another of South Carolina's superlative salt marshes, drive approximately 5 miles north of Edisto Beach State Park on SC 174, where a small brown sign on the right side of the highway reads "Steamboat Landing." Take this sandy lane, which passes beneath live oak branches that meet over the road, giving the illusion of a tunnel, to the end of the road and Steamboat Landing boat ramp.

You may wish to visit some of the plantations of the Edisto area. Their names are as beautiful as the Lowcountry itself: Dawhoo, Airy Hall, Ashepoo and Redcliffe. You will hear the musical Gullah language spoken here. One could make a strong case that the South Carolina Lowcountry is the most evocative and romantic part of the three-state area.

Bald Head Island is the most "bittersweet" sea island of the Carolinas. The "sweet" part is the simple fact that this grove of live oaks was not cut down during the age of sailing vessels. Considering the demand for the strong, resilient live oak timber used as ribs or knees in ship construction, and the

Bald Head Island live oak forest and salt marsh.

proximity of Wilmington, one of the busiest ports anywhere during the Age of Sail, it is a miracle that the Bald Head live oaks survived the ax and saw. The "bitter" part was the failure of the State of North Carolina to buy the island, which contains Cape Fear, the only sandy cape in America not protected from development (see chapter 18). Still, in fairness to the Bald Head Corporation, in the past at least, great pains have been taken to preserve the live oak forest and the ambiance of this unique island. The golf course was built with as little impact as possible on the live oak forest. The stunning news from the Bald Head Corporation is the newly unveiled plan to build condominiums on the very tip of Cape Fear! (See chapter 18.) You can walk the shaded lanes of this splendid live oak forest, bicycle it or even rent a golf cart from Bald Head Corporation, all without fear of meeting cars, for they are prohibited on the island. The general public is welcome on Bald Head Island, even though it is used primarily by property owners. There is a fee to use the ferry.

Underscoring the importance of Bald Head Island as an important climatic ecotone is the fact that extensive live oak forests do not occur north of this point on the East Coast. In contrast, the maritime forest of Hammock's Beach State Park 80 miles to the north, as well as Buxton Woods at Cape Hatteras, are composed of mixed loblolly pine, scattered small live oaks, red bay, dogwoods, red cedar and others. We simply do not see significant examples of salt spray climax forest north of Bald Head Island. To reach Bald Head Island, take US 17 south of Wilmington 20 miles to the little town of Supply, North Carolina. Here take NC 211 into Southport. Look for signs to Indigo Plantation–Bald Head Island Ferry. Park in the lot. The ferry is for foot traffic only.

Finally, there is **Nag's Head Woods,** a maritime forest extraordinaire. In fact, according to The Nature Conservancy, which oversees this preserve, a combination of maritime deciduous forest and maritime swamp forest is known to exist in only four places in the world. Nag's Head Woods has been designated a globally endangered forest ecosystem. Because of its location behind Jockey's Ridge, the largest sand dune in the eastern United States, this 1,100-acre publicly and privately owned preserve supports more than 300 plant species, as well as the most diverse reptile and amphibian fauna on North Carolina's Outer Banks. With Jockey's Ridge protecting this maritime forest from salt spray and other harsh maritime influences, it became like no other. Remarkably, the environment behind the great dune system is so stable that species such as oaks, hickories, pines and many other mainland species were able to flourish on a barrier island. Nearby is Jockey's Ridge State Park; try to visit this 120-foot-high dune system on a windy day, for the wind brings out the kite flyers. They can often be seen from the wildest, windiest, grittiest vantage

Jockey's Ridge State Park on North Carolina's Outer Banks near Nag's Head.

points flying, with consummate skill, their fighting kites, triple-decker kites—indeed, all manner of kites. The top of Jockey's Ridge offers a superb view of all three remarkable landscape-level ecosystems found here: the ocean, the brackish water sound and the barrier islands. The Nag's Head Woods preserve is open on specific days of the week, varying with the different seasons of the year, for those not belonging to The Nature Conservancy. For Nature Conservancy members the preserve is open at all times. For information, call The Nature Conservancy's Nag's Head Woods office at (919) 441-2525. Youth internships are available for college students and children's nature camps are held here each June. The preserve offers naturalist-led hikes as well as self-guided trails. To reach Nag's Head Woods, you must drive through considerable unnatural clutter. Get on NC 158 west, on the north end of Nag's Head. At mile 11.5 look for Pigman BBQ on the left; here, make a left turn. In 0.6 mile, pass the "Rustic Woods South" subdivision sign on the left. Continue 0.4 mile and turn into The Nature Conservancy Center.

11

February Shorttakes

The Angel Oak

Six miles south of Charleston, South Carolina just off of SC 700, stands the Angel Oak. Considered one of the oldest and largest live oak trees in America, this survivor of many hurricanes shades 17,500 square feet of earth, yet is only 65 feet tall. It is thought that the live oak tree may have evolved long limbs but short trunk height in order to present a profile less vulnerable to hurricanes. The longest limb of the angel oak is 89 feet, which is greater than its height. This massive tree has been regarded as a patriarch for over a century. While coring live oaks to determine age is problematic, because heart rot is present in all old trees, this oak is estimated to be approximately 1,400 years old.

12

A Closer Look:
Best-Kept Secrets, State Parks

Ideally a trip designed to bring one closer to nature should not cease to do so at sundown. The most satisfactory arrangement is to remain within the natural sphere, spending your quiet time before bedtime, cooking and even sleeping, without breaking connection to the sounds, smells, rhythms and peace of nature. The state parks of the three-state region offer the ecotourist clean, safe and economical havens overseen by rangers who often work as volunteers. Each park is designed to highlight the special ambiance that draws people to it. For example, at Cade's Cove Campground in Great Smoky Mountains National Park, you may hear red wolves howling at night or at dawn from your tent or camper. A doe and spotted fawn might feed confidently a stone's throw away as you cook breakfast or supper over a cookstove. An evening stroll before bedtime in Big South Fork National River and Recreation Area, northwest of Knoxville on the Tennessee–Kentucky state line, will give a view of night skies most of us have forgotten still exist, due to light pollution from our cities. From Cape Point Campground near Cape Hatteras, you can walk for 10 minutes down a sandy, cedar-lined lane to stand on the most geographically important cape on the East Coast, and feel the power of the ocean. From this location, you have the same view of the night sky as a sailor on the open ocean. At dawn or dusk, you might see approaching weather systems slowly rear their heads far offshore. At night, you can watch thunderstorms flashing over the Gulf Stream from a comfortable seat in the dunes on the beaches of Cape Hatteras. It is terribly important that the delicate connection to these natural wonders, most of which are quiet and retiring when compared to the human-made clutter that sprawls across the landscape, not be broken.

At Huntington Beach State Park, south of Myrtle Beach, South Carolina, you might be lucky enough to hear a bellowing alligator. A little farther down South Carolina's superb coastline, you can walk 100 feet from your camper or tent at Edisto Beach State Park through palmetto palms and onto a beach that is nearly deserted during the winter season. From the overflow campground at Edisto Beach State Park, you can camp in a virgin live oak forest. In Roan Mountain State Park in the mountains of eastern Tennessee, the fireflies resemble thousands of strings of tiny Christmas tree lights, flashing over the meadows at dusk. Later in the evening, when the female lightning bugs have moved into the trees, with just a little imagination you can pretend that the stars of the heavens now shine from the forest itself. Here hundreds of thousands of nighttime cicadas carry a rhythm until the mountains resound in a single vast, ratcheting, chanting voice. At Fort Pillow State Park during the winter months, when the woods are bare, a camper can sit at night by the campfire on the north loop of the campground and watch the red and green lights of barge traffic on the mightiest river in North America. The hoots of barred and great horned owls in the vast Mississippi River floodplain hardwood forest can be heard as they begin their courtship activities in midwinter. At Buck Hall State Campground, south of McClellanville, South Carolina, huge wood storks fly overhead as they return from the sea islands of Cape Romaine NWR. A family of bottlenosed dolphins hunting jumping mullet in the intercoastal waterway might swim by the Buck Hall campground. At Land Between the Lakes, on the Tennessee-Kentucky border, you can camp in an ocean of fall color at a site on Kentucky Lake. From the public campgrounds along North Carolina's Blue Ridge Parkway, you can look upon a mountain vista as unsullied by humans as when the Cherokee ruled it, either in glowing fall colors or new leaf.

All the biodiversity of the three-state region is accessible through its splendid state parks. The wonder of it is that so few people avail themselves of these parks. For some of the more popular campgrounds, such as those of Great Smoky Mountains National Park or Cape Hatteras National Seashore, you should make reservations, especially during the peak of vacation season. However, during the week sites are often available except during the busiest periods.

The people who do a great deal of camping in these state parks become extremely knowledgeable on the subject and often camp with simple gear, preferring a screened bug-proof tent that allows the ocean breeze to pass through it to an expensive, air-conditioned, gas-guzzling motor home.

The fee for camping at these campgrounds is quite reasonable. For instance, winter rates at Edisto Beach State Park in South Carolina are $12 a night while summer rates are $17 a night. Public campgrounds on North Carolina's Outer Banks are closed after Labor Day, but privately owned ones remain open. To determine which campgrounds of the various state parks are open after Labor Day and during the winter months, you will need to check them on an individual basis.

March

Notes

13

Purple Martins

Long before Europeans arrived in the New World, humans and martins had established a relationship. Choctaws, Chickasaws and other tribes began placing gourds on poles to attract the handsome purple swallows. This practice was observed by slaves, who erected their own martin houses. The idea was simply too good not to catch on, and by the early 1800s, martin houses were scattered throughout the land.

Perhaps the most easily understood reason for this bond becomes evident after a particularly harsh winter. Seeing the indigo-colored "scouts" arrive during the drab month of March is proof that spring is on the way. Martins bring new energy to the landscape when the human spirit needs it most. Although people in the 1700s and 1800s could not have known that the martins were coming from Brazil's Amazon Basin, they may have suspected that these large swallows were arriving from some warm, sunny place.

To further understand the appeal of martins, you need only spend an hour or two near a martin colony. Unlike the "lesser" swallows, swifts and nighthawks that arrive in the three-state region from the Amazon Basin at the same time, martins seem to genuinely seek out and enjoy the company of humans. Their vocalizations are a series of gurgling, melodic chips and chirps that are pleasing to the human ear and indicate a highly gregarious and nonviolent social order. Their wheeling, banking, graceful flight is beautiful to watch. There is much in their joyful behavior, flight and personality that humans share and recognize. The martin's penchant for chasing away hawks attracted by farmyard poultry, and its assumed dietary predilection for mosquitos, have certainly earned it additional points. There is even an element of resignation in the martin's personality that further endears and cements its place in our hearts. Martins sometimes tolerate particularly

Purple martins in baldcypress tree on Reelfoot Lake.

brazen and resolute English sparrows as next-door neighbors in their martin apartment houses, as if in recognition of the fact that the world is an imperfect place.

There is hot debate over the martin's diet. It is firmly documented that one of the largest components is dragonflies, which eat mosquitos, but it has never been proven by studies in the field that martins eat mosquitos. They actually eat the ultimate mosquito predator, the dragonfly—but no matter. Whatever the martins eat, all is forgiven, and they are welcome, for as the poet Keats stated in *Endymion,* "A thing of beauty is a joy forever."

Martins occupy the entire three-state region. In order to give some sense of this species' time of arrival, it should be noted that Greensboro, North Carolina's **Lake Townsend Marina** and **Lake Higgins** anticipate the arrival of the male martin "scouts" by the third week of March, depending on the severity of the winter. By the second week of April, the males have claimed their domiciles and are advertising for females who wish to set up housekeeping. In the coastal plains of the Carolinas, the timetable is even earlier. Along the shoreline of **White Lake,** 45 miles southeast of Fayetteville, North Carolina, on NC 87, martin houses are a prominent feature of the landscape. A little farther to the south, many of the fishing docks along the shores of **Lakes Marion and Moultrie** (chapter 33) have martin apartment houses. **Reelfoot Lake** (chapter 40) has a fabulous martin population. While the American water lotus plants are blossoming in July, many hundreds of martins in family groups can sometimes be seen perching in the tops of the baldcypress trees that grow at Reelfoot Lake.

But it is within the intertidal zone of the South Carolina Lowcountry where people believe most steadfastly that martins would never commit such an unchivalrous act as to not eat mosquitos. Here, the human residents extend the hand of hospitality not only to the martin, but also to the bottlenosed dolphin. This is reflected in the architecture of the martin houses and in the dolphin weathervanes. South Carolina Lowcountry communities such as **McClellanville** or **Georgetown** welcome these genteel birds. At 405 Pinkney Street in McClellanville, across from the municipal offices, is a handsome "antebellum" martin house. A dolphin silhouette weathervane is nearby. These are two sure signs of a community with strong ties to the natural world.

14

Spring Ephemerals

In early March within the rolling piedmont of the three-state region, and even earlier in lower elevations, one of nature's cleverest strategies is played out each year. This strategy is lilliputian in size but ranks high in audacity, for the risk of a late freeze is considerable. While the surface of the forest floor is quite brown with dead leaves in late winter, the ground underneath is rich in nutrients accumulated over the fall and winter, for the plant community has yet to make demands on them. Seizing this opportunity, the earliest spring wildflowers appear as tiny flecks of color against winter's drabness in their prevernal grab for sunlight and nutrients. Many of the wildflowers of the forests are timed in such a way to appear before the leaf canopy of the forest blocks out the sun. Yet the early wildflowers in evidence by mid-March are cued to arrive not only before the leaf canopy, but also before other wildflower species arrive in April, May and June. Some of the earliest March wildflowers are bluets, violets and the toad trillium, with its beautifully mottled light and dark green leaves. Another group of wildflowers, the ephemerals, appear so early in the year that some of them actually expend part of last year's stored energy to burn a hole through lingering ice or snow. Trout lilies, spring beauties, wood anemones, windflowers, bloodroot, golden corydalis, Dutchman's breeches, cutleaf toothwort and rue anemones are some of the better-known ephemerals. The wildflowers known collectively as spring ephemerals have a strategy similar to the mayfly, a small, graceful, streamborn insect that emerges from the cold-water, gravel-bottomed rivers of the region. Both the spring ephemerals and the mayflies appear briefly, perfect in design, color and timing, and then are gone from the landscape, leaving no trace. Each demonstrates perfectly the concept of "strategy" in nature.

The parameters for inclusion in the spring ephemeral group of wildflowers are very specific. Although other woodland herbs such as hepatica, woods phlox, trilliums, jack-in-the-pulpit and wild ginger appear at approximately the same time as the ephemerals, they retain leaves and ripen fruit long after the leaf canopy has closed. They are "patient" in their wait for the pollinator and for sunlight, in contrast to the ephemerals, which die back completely, leaving no flowers or leaves, by the time the leaf canopy has closed overhead. Within a few weeks they will have stored up enough energy reserves in their underground tubers, corms, bulbs or fleshy rhizomes to bow out of the ongoing aboveground dialectic altogether—a most interesting strategy. Learn to appreciate nature's ingenious strategies, interdependencies, ploys, deceptions, misrepresentations and mimicries. Remember that all is grist for nature's mill. Though big can be beautiful and audacity can be effective, there is room for the small as well. Let the spring ephemerals "downsize" your level of perception and awareness of nature's cleverness; worlds will be opened up to you.

Hot Spots

While the spring ephemerals, as a class of wildflowers, are common and widespread, one must know which particular woodland community types are ephemeral-friendly. The ephemerals do not do well in pine woods, unshaded fields or marshy areas. The oak-hickory forest is best. **Eno River State Park** contains excellent spring ephemeral habitat (see chapter 24). The Eno riverbottoms are so rich in ephemerals (and wildflowers in general) that Michael Godfrey was moved to make the following statement in his book *A Closer Look:* "The Eno River near my home in the Piedmont ... reflects off an ancient granite mass for a mile or two ... . Along the Eno's edge and up these slopes grows the greatest collection of spring ephemerals I have ever seen. Except for squirrel corn, a mountain plant, every eastern ephemeral mentioned grows here." Two more good locations for spring ephemerals are **Chimney Rock Park** and **Grandfather Mountain** (see chapter 26). Finally, both **Roan Mountain State Park** (chapters 26 and 31) and **Great Smoky Mountains National Park** (chapter 26) in Tennessee, being the wildflower treasure troves they are, are spring ephemeral hotspots.

15

Early Avian Events

During the bleakest winter months, one may find opportunities for birding if one knows where to look. Some of the most unremarkable environments, such as golf courses, open pastures, wintertime apple orchards and even large lawns, may harbor an avian event. Against the drab colors of the winter landscape, several hundred high-spirited, red-breasted robins, which have dropped in to claim a golf course, are a welcome sight. Open pastures provide perfect habitat for robins seeking earthworms. Before wild fruit, beetles and caterpillars are available, angleworms are a primary food item for robins. After a heavy rainstorm, walk pasturelands along creeks and lowlands; here the rising water table will flush worms to the surface of the ground. Locate a large robin flock working a pasture and determine the general direction in which the flock is feeding. Move well ahead of the robin flock. Seat yourself unobtrusively and try to blend in with the landscape. The robin flock will feed past you and ignore you if you do not threaten them, allowing you to watch these consummate worm predators at work. The flock may be composed of either the large, colorful eastern robin or the slightly smaller and paler subspecies, the southern robin. These same robin flocks may roost by the thousands in cedar thickets.

These proud thrushes, with their erect posture as they march, pause and seem to listen for worms, are one of the species that human manipulation of the environment has actually benefited. Late in the winter, one of the earliest signs of spring is the animated carolling of these birds, as the longer days turn their thoughts to courtship. Once the birds have started pairing off, the robin flocks disperse until next winter.

Another species you can count on through the entire winter, for it is nonmigratory, is the pileated woodpecker. This crow-sized woodpecker is remarkable in that it has proved to be so adaptable, in spite of the fact that its two giant relatives, the imperial woodpecker of Mexico and the ivory-billed woodpecker of the baldcypress swamp ecosystem, were far less adaptable. Since nature seems to be continuing the trend of "downsizing" since the last mass extinction, which took out the dinosaurs, large size has been a liability to many species. Not so with this magnificent woodpecker. From the sea islands of the Carolinas to the Mississippi River floodplain hardwood forest, the flickerlike yelp of this thriving avian dinosaur is part of the landscape.

The hope of seeing a pileated is a fine excuse for a winter woods walk down a mountain ridge, valley or wherever there are relatively old stands of mixed hardwoods. This bird was once widely hunted for table fare, which may explain, in part, the remarkable wariness of the species. Their numbers may now be the highest of any time during this century. The sight of this strong flier, with its bright red head and great size, is something one must never take for granted.

Another early avian event takes place in the three-state region, one that attracts almost no attention: the arrival of shorebirds at Santee Coastal WMA. (See chapter 9.) Yet the timing of this South Carolina Lowcountry birding event could not be better because for much of the year, biting insects make enjoyment of this location almost impossible. At the end of March, intensifying as April progresses, shorebirds such as black-bellied plovers, red knots, black-necked stilts, willets, yellowlegs and others arrive. For two to three weeks in April, the water level in the old rice fields is drawn down, in large part to accommodate the growing wood stork population. By lowering water levels, important food species for the wood stork, such as jumping mullet and shrimp, are concentrated, making feeding a simple matter. Recognizing an opportunity, shorebirds search the exposed mud flats at this time for small crustaceans, insects, mollusks, worms and vegetable material. To check on the arrival of the shorebirds and the spring drawdown at Santee, call (803) 546-8665.

Bobolinks took advantage of the rice fields during the eighteenth and nineteenth centuries, earning the nickname "ricebirds," and even timed their migration to coincide with the ripening rice crops each year. The bobolinks no longer stop here, but two different avian entities, the wood storks and the shorebirds, have filled the vacated niche, once again demonstrating nature's astonishing adaptability and resiliency. Taking the place of the ravenous flocks of bobolinks that were much hated by rice planters, shorebirds in bright courtship colors quietly begin to trickle in around the end of March on their way to the northern breeding grounds. With this avian event, timing is everything. Remember that as May draws near, the mosquitos and yellow flies become the undisputed masters of the Santee Coastal preserve.

Hot Spots

Robin flocks can be found anywhere there are large grassy areas. At times the drab **wintertime apple orchards between Hendersonville and Bat Cave,** North Carolina, can harbor large flocks of robins. To reach the apple orchards, take US 64 east from Hendersonville. Pass through the community of Edneyville, then turn left onto Mills Gap Road. Drive approximately 1 mile. Do not take the turnoff to the right for Old Bearwallow Road. Rather, turn right on Bearwallow Road, which is the next turn. Stay on this road. Remember that these orchards are privately owned and must be enjoyed from the road. You may wish to return in the spring of the year to see the apple blossoms.

Pileated woodpeckers are present in good numbers in most hardwood forest ecosystems. They can be found in relatively urban settings such as High Point, North Carolina's **Piedmont Environmental Center.** The national forests of western North Carolina and eastern Tennessee are at carrying capacity for this species.

16

Early Spring Amphibians

The first signs of spring are missed by many people. The male purple finch and the bright red male cardinal are two of the first birds to sing lustily. In February the mourning dove begins his courtship song, a sad, unbirdlike cooing. Listen carefully and you will notice that the vocalizations of the birds of the year are quite awkward and haphazard. The young male mourning doves will not perfect the phrasing and pitches until the "big boys" are moved to song, providing a perfected model. You can count on the young mourning doves to get it right, for the heart of a lady dove will not be won by a clumsy minstrel. In late February or early March, depending on the elevation, the maple trees take on a reddish tint as their tiny flowers begin to sprout. Yellowing weeping willows move with the freshening breezes of late February. Early in the morning, in weedy fields and on hillsides along the roadway, the first spiderwebs of the season are silver with dew. They are easily visible before the sun dries them. There may be thousands, each several inches in diameter, in a weed field of half an acre. Yet there is one tiny announcer of spring that nearly everyone notices, and it resides in the most ordinary of freshwater boggy spots, in a pasture, along a creek and perhaps most often of all, along the road. The courtship call of the male spring peeper is one of the defining sounds, even as winter still grips the landscape, of the most miraculous transformation of the year.

Even though most of us see the gray winter landscape as lifeless in February and early March, the amphibian does not. Depending on elevation, the first rainy nights of January, February or March, which provide temperatures between 45 and 50 degrees, will see them converging on the same boggy puddles and ponds where they themselves were initially deposited as eggs. Often these breeding locations are little more than depressions filled with rainwater during the early spring. The amphibians' choices of breeding sites may seem peculiar to us, but these temporary wet environments contain fewer predators, such as fish, which reside in permanent ponds and pools.

Amphibians choose vernal pools that traditionally remain moist at least until early June. By that time all eggs will have reached maturity and the young wood frogs, salamanders and toads will have left the breeding pools for some niche in the forest. For a species like the spotted salamander, this brief breeding period is the only time of year when they can be seen, for they spend the rest of the year underground.

Perhaps the amphibian aspect that makes them so interesting is their secretive nature. You will likely have your favorite amphibian breeding sites all to yourself. Amphibian watching is definitely not fashionable. Yet, as with virtually any link in the biodiversity chain, amphibians can be fascinating.

There is great order in the breeding pools. The wood frog, a northern species that terminates its southern range around the foothills of Statesville, North Carolina, is the first to arrive. By the time the spring peepers are evident, the wood frog egg clusters will be a full month toward maturation, and the adult frogs will have departed for the forest. Many weeks before the arrival of the strident peepers, those stalwart few who watch and wait for the wood frog may be rewarded by hearing the courtship call of the male of this species, a soft, low quack, somewhat like a duck's.

The large spotted salamanders arrive at about the same time as the wood frogs, and these two species are the principal depositers of visible egg clusters in the vernal pools of the three-state region. Spring peeper eggs are too small to see, and the smaller species of salamanders like the common dusky salamander leave their eggs in wet seeps where they are not readily seen by humans. The eggs of the American toad are deposited in long "necklaces" or chains, and are easily distinguished from those of the wood frog and the spotted salamander.

The wood frog egg clusters can be discerned from those of the spotted salamander by several characteristics. Wood frog egg clusters tend to float near the surface of the water, where they are attached to a twig. Each embryo resides in an individual egg sac, which is clearly visible within the large egg cluster. The fist-sized spotted salamander egg clusters tend to be well beneath the surface of the water. Never remove egg clusters from the pools; examine them without touching them. Within the spotted salamander egg clusters, the individual egg sacs cannot be seen as clearly as those of the wood frog; rather, the entire cluster forms a large blob.

After a week or so of warm weather (a cold snap will put development of the embryos on hold), you may wish to return to examine the vernal pools that contain egg clusters of the spotted salamanders and wood frogs. The wood frog tadpoles should be evident at this time, easily visible throughout the pool. To examine the young spotted salamanders, use an aquarium dip net to gently stir up leaves and other debris from the bottom of the pool, catch it in the dip net and deposit the material in a pail of clear water. The immature spotted salamanders should become evident in the pail, even though they are difficult to see in the pool itself, where they hide under the leaves on the bottom. After examining the young salamanders, place them back in the pool. Among the egg clusters of the wood frogs and the spotted salamanders, you may see some smoky-colored embryos that are obviously dead. They may have been killed by either acid rain or ultraviolet light pollution, or they were never fertilized by the male.

Weeks after the wood frogs and spotted salamanders have departed from the vernal pools, the music of the spring peepers announces to the world that they have arrived at the recently vacated pools. Standing in a bog amid hundreds of piping male spring peepers on a still night can be painful to the ears. Look closely for a tiny tan frog the size of a dime. The inflated air bags on their throats are clearly visible in the beam of a flashlight. Remember, a rainy night is the catalyst that brings them out in the greatest numbers. Hip boots are helpful, but the most ideal place is a marsh with a boardwalk, such as the one in the FENCE (Foothills Equestrian Nature Center) near Tryon, North Carolina. The American toads arrive at the same vernal pools concurrently with the peepers, although spring peepers tend to be a little earlier.

You will stumble on a spotted salamander breeding "orgy" only with the greatest luck. It is best to be on a "standby" list and have a knowledgeable observer checking a proven site each rainy night of the late winter season. You can do this through an environmental organization such as FENCE or High Point, North Carolina's Piedmont Environmental Center. Should you be fortunate enough to witness this event, you will see dozens of these handsome yellow-spotted beauties, some reaching 10 inches in length, in the act of procreating. Perhaps it is best that they are so difficult to catch on the breeding grounds, for at this time the spotted salamanders are extremely vulnerable to poachers. They fetch a shocking price as aquarium pets. For this reason many naturalists are reluctant to release their proven yellow salamander breeding pools to the public.

Timing is critical in this environmental loop. If you're a week late, all you will see are gelatinous masses full of developing eggs, some free-floating and others attached to twigs. Although the peepers are relatively easy to locate because they are so noisy, the other species mentioned in this chapter are more difficult. Still, the rewards are great. You may be one of the few to witness the dance of the spotted salamanders. You may be privileged to hear a chorus of American toads, their melodious calls sounding much like the one-pitch tremolo of the screech owl. At times the toads seem to be trying to harmonize. The best strategy for finding toads singing in a breeding pond is to visit each boggy place where peepers peep. Visit these places in mid-March when the dogwood trees are blossoming and listen carefully for a persistent, fluttering, reedy vocalization on one pitch, superimposed over the shrill piping of the peepers. For a taped recording of the American toad, purchase "Voices of the Night," compiled by the Cornell Laboratory of Ornithology. Bookstores specializing in birding books and related publications will order it for you.

You must listen carefully for the music of the humble toad. Yet it is surprisingly commonplace across the landscape once you learn to discern it. Toads may converge in shallow arms or coves of large lakes, as well as in small bogs. The males sit in the water, in groups of perhaps a dozen or so, advertising their availability to the females. There are many more males than females and the competition is fierce. At times the males swim boldly out into ponds in search of reddish-brown females without the much smaller yellowish males riding them like determined little jockeys. You may see some copulating pairs underwater, while other pairs sit with their heads above the waterline. Often the surplus male toads wrestle with each other, perhaps out of frustration. It is quite a spectacle and strongly suggests a bacchanalian orgy. Softer, more intimate vocalizations come from the copulating pairs, as the air sacs of the male toads work slowly in the flashlight beam. Toad "orgies" also occur during the daylight hours, particularly on a cloudy or rainy day.

Amphibians are both benefitting and suffering from changes in the environment. The reintroduction of beavers has created countless wetlands that are inhabited by amphibians. The "beaver meadows," which are gradually formed as beaver dams fill with silt, are ideal breeding environments. However, tens of thousands of salamanders are collected each year and sold to bait shops as "spring lizards" for fishing bait. Most ominous for all amphibians, on a worldwide scale, is depletion of the ozone layer. This potentially killing blow to all amphibians is greatly reducing the chances of eggs even reaching maturity. It has recently been discovered that amphibian egg clusters are hypersensitive to ultraviolet radiation pollution. Acid rain may be playing a role in the puzzle of the vanishing amphibians. Amphibian numbers are dwindling all over the world, even in places where their environment is unchanged. The golden toad of Costa Rica, plentiful as recently as 1987, is already extinct.

The amphibians are not the superstars of the threatened and endangered species, but they need all the friends they can get. You may want to begin your own amphibian awareness course by listening for peepers this spring. You might only find clusters of frog, toad and salamander eggs by the time the peepers alert you. You can turn back the clock and go higher in elevation. The following year you will know where to look, before the peeping chorus limbers up. You may become one of the strange breed of human that others see in their headlights, with collecting pails in hand, rescuing spotted salamanders and toads from the fate of becoming roadkills on the first warm, rainy nights of late winter. You may want to begin your early spring amphibian search anywhere there is a freshwater pond, a marsh, a seep, a cattail slough or even a roadside gravel pit full of water. The peepers will guide you in.

Hot Spots

An excellent place to become acquainted with amphibians is High Point, North Carolina's **Piedmont Environmental Center,** located off Penny Road. The staff naturalists here are very keen on amphibians, and the center has a large lake, complete with trails and a short boardwalk, where naturalist-led walks are conducted on a regular basis. For information call (910) 883-8531. **FENCE,** another nature study center, is located in the foothills of North Carolina in Tryon. Like the Piedmont Environmental Center, FENCE offers naturalist-led nature walks, including trips especially to see amphibians. FENCE's yearly salamander swamp tromp is usually planned for the third week of February. For information call (704) 859-9021.

An excellent location for amphibian breeding pools is the boggy lowlands around the **Virginia Creeper Trail,** which runs along the Tennessee-Virginia border in upper northeast Tennessee, near the town of Damascus, Virginia. Go to Mt. Rogers Outfitters in Damascus, and obtain a map of this superlative 34-mile mountain bike and foot trail. The trail follows the roadbed of the Virginia Creeper narrow-gauge railroad line, which hauled out most of the timber of the watershed of Whitetop Laurel Creek at the turn of the century. The valley of Whitetop Laurel Creek has now returned to a natural state and the evidence of human alteration of the environment is now hardly discernible.

One of the top experts in the field of amphibians in the region is Carlton Burke, of the Western North Carolina Nature Center of Asheville. For information call (704) 298-5600.

17

March Shorttakes

Itzhak Perlman of the Thickets

A pair of male and female brown thrashers is a model of cooperation and mutual admiration. The fierce yellow eye of this species is no sham. The thrasher will stand and fight a nest-raiding black rat snake. Across the Carolinas and Tennessee the male can be found on a prominent bough or snag during the cool hours of the morning or evening. His musical couplets are wondrously complex, precise and liquid. If he has won the heart of a lady thrasher, she often sits several branches beneath him, in unconcealed admiration for her mate. When she is quite sated with his musicianship, she may fly up to his perch as if to say, "That was wonderful. Now you're needed at home." The pair is seldom separated and exhibits a level of no-nonsense, shared responsibility and purpose. Their relationship is clearly on a different level from that of most other songbirds.

The more you observe this secretive species, the more you will come to admire the brown thrasher. Listen carefully during the first warm days of March for this unobtrusive yet passionate minstrel.

The Santee Fish Lift

The Lake Marion–Moultrie complex is one of the few freshwater impoundments on the East Coast with a direct link to the Atlantic Ocean. Runs of blueback herring, American shad and gizzard shad enter the fresh water of the Cooper and Santee Rivers and migrate to the spawning grounds in the Marion-Moultrie complex during March and April. The fish are assisted by being "locked" into the lakes in the same manner as salmon are "locked" around the dams on the Columbia River of the West Coast. At the Santee Canal Rediversion Project you can look through a glass window at schools of migrating herring, anadromous shad, as well as sea-run striped bass and huge, predatory catfish that stalk the hordes coming in from the sea. Recently a 100-pound Arkansas blue catfish was videotaped as it cruised by the window, before being locked in the lakes. Often hundreds of cormorants are here as well to feed on the migrating fish. Fish propagation ponds where striped bass are raised are also open to the public.

The fish lift is in operation 60 days of the year (typically from March 1 until April 30) in order to assist the sea-run fish in their migration to the spawning grounds. To reach the Santee Fish Lift follow directions to Angel's Landing (see chapter 47) but pass the turnoff to Angel's Landing. Continue for 14 miles until SC 45 meets SC 52 and turn right. Go south for 12 miles. You will then see a sign for the Santee Canal Rediversion Project and a second sign for the fish lift and visitor's center.

Lake Moultrie Passage

Late March is a good time to walk or bike the Lake Moultrie Passage section of South Carolina's Palmetto Trail. The bugs are not out yet, gators are beginning to sun themselves, anadromous fish are moving through the locks and the loop trail sections of the Lake Moultrie Passage are open. This 26-mile trail runs through large areas of the Marion-Moultrie complex. Primitive campsites with hand-operated water pumps are available for no fee. The trail offers access to sandy beaches, eagle nests and wooden footbridges across wetland within a truly fertile ecosystem. The loop goes through scenic areas that are closed from November 15 until March 1 in order to isolate nesting waterfowl. For information on this trail write to the Supervisor, Forestry and Undeveloped Lands, Santee Cooper Land Division, 1 Riverwood Drive, Monck's Corner, South Carolina 29461 or phone (803) 761-8000.

The trail begins just north of the steel bridge over the diversion canal on SC 45, which is just south of the entrance to Angel's Landing. The trail is new, so the entrance is not easy to find; it's best to check with Al Jones at Angel's Landing for detailed directions.

Turtles on the Brink

The great sea turtles of the earth face a dim future. All dwell primarily in the tropical waters of both hemispheres where they are relentlessly pursued. All species are vanishing and are among the most endangered animals in the world. They are hunted by the Orientals, who covet their eggs for aphrodisiacs, their flippers for expensive leather, tortoiseshell for ornamental objects and meat for sale in gourmet markets. On the open ocean turtles mistake plastic garbage bags for jellyfish and suffocate when they eat them. Hawksbills are still actively sought for their shells, from which tortoiseshell items are made, in spite of a moratorium on these products. Cataracts are showing up in relatively young turtles. Blindness and starvation ensue. Since sea turtles spend their entire lives in full exposure to ultraviolet rays on the ocean's surface, they are among the most vulnerable species to the effects of ozone depletion, which allows harmful radiation to penetrate the atmosphere.

The green turtle is called the most valuable reptile in the world. It is one of the species which is disappearing most rapidly. Its delicious flesh is eagerly sought for sale in the gourmet market. Turtles off our own coastline are regularly struck and killed by boats. Others are drowned in shrimp nets and trawl nets, although turtle excluder devices or "TEDS" have moderated this problem to some degree. Ultimately the turtle crisis is a global one and is deeply metaphorical for the fate of biological diversity on our planet. The Kemp's (Atlantic) Ridley turtle is nearly extinct. Since much of their nesting effort takes place on one beach near Tampico, Mexico, the United States and Mexico have enacted a protection treaty as a last ditch effort. In those parts of the world where a hunter-gatherer lifestyle is still prevalent, there may not be time for the sea turtles' dwindling gene pool to be stabilized. The harvesting of a single female is made even more tragic by the fact that between 20 and 30 years are required before sexual maturity is reached and a single clutch of eggs is laid. Only education can bring home the ramifications of harvesting such precious brood stock, and education is a long way off in many parts of the world. It is thought that there are fewer than 1,000 female leatherback turtles worldwide. With a gene pool this small, it is not certain whether this species will be able to continue to produce viable eggs. If the mysterious world travelers vanish, the oceans of the world will be a much lonelier place, for extinction is forever.

18

A Closer Look:
The Only Unprotected
Cape in America

North Carolina's Cape Fear River, where it meets the Atlantic Ocean at Southport, south of Wilmington, is one of the most important ecotones, or meeting places of distinctly different ecosystems, on the East Coast. The only ecotone comparable to it in the three-state region is Buxton Woods at Cape Hatteras.

Underscoring the unusual character of this location, the Cape Fear River mouth has a unique Florida-Caribbean connection that no location farther north can claim. The water manatee was once present here. A few show up even now in the estuary of the Cape Fear River. This species might someday be reintroduced, further enhancing an already extraordinarily rich flora and fauna.

The lower basins of the Cape Fear and its sister river, the Northeast Cape Fear, are considered regionally significant in terms of plant species diversity. Here The Nature Conservancy maintains two preserves, Green Swamp and Lanier Quarry. Within these longleaf pine–wire grass savanna ecosystems, you can actually find the greatest small-scale diversity of flowering plant species in the world, including the Amazon River Basin. On certain sites within the Green Swamp preserve, you may see as many as 50 species of flowering plants in a 1-square-meter plot. The Lanier Quarry Preserve may have more than 100 species per square meter. Green Swamp supports more species of insectivorous plants than any other place in the world, with the exception of New Zealand. Here, Venus's-flytraps, pitcher plants, bladderworts, butterworts and sundews can all exist within a 1-square-mile area.

On the north end of Green Swamp is Lake Waccamaw, a nearly perfect example of a Carolina Bay. These elliptical, shallow lakes are thought to be depressions in the landscape left behind as ancient seas retreated during ice ages. These unique geological features are found nowhere in the world but in the coastal plains of North Carolina and a few northern counties of South Carolina. The lower Cape Fear Basin possesses some of the best preserved examples of Carolina Bays. Other Carolina Bays are White Lake, Jones Lake and Singletary Lake.

Unknown to most residents of North Carolina, Lake Waccamaw belongs to a select group of lakes that includes Russia's Lake Baikal, Lake Tanganyika in Africa and certain volcanic lakes of the Philippines. These lakes are all noted for a phenomenon called "speciation," the subject of one of the hottest debates in the scientific community. Speciation is not yet completely understood, but is presently defined as a process of rapid evolution from parental stock into a new, genetically different species within a relatively short period of time. Studies of Darwin's finches on the Galapagos Islands have recently proven that genetic modification to improve chances of survival can occur after only one year of severe environmental modification. Because Lake Waccamaw is only several thousand years old, it is remarkable that four species have evolved here that are genetically distinguishable from their parental stocks in nearby lowland streams. The Waccamaw shiner, the Waccamaw darter, the Waccamaw killifish and the Waccamaw silverside occur nowhere else in the world. These four species, along with the Ocracoke or "intercapes" king snake of North Carolina's Outer Banks, place the state in a unique position in terms of rapid-evolution fauna.

Other Carolina Bays exist at the northern end of North Carolina's coastal plain, yet they sit in the middle of one of the grandest American environmental disasters perpetrated during the last quarter of a century. Lake Pungo and Lake Phelps, once two splendid examples of Carolina Bays, are located on the Albemarle-Pamlico Peninsula, which was cleared by Japanese and French investors along with a North Carolina trucking company to create huge corporate farms. After the swamp forest that once existed between Swanquarter and Plymouth was first clear-cut and then drained, there was no buffering ecosystem to absorb and

Bald Head/Cape Fear River—Wilmington

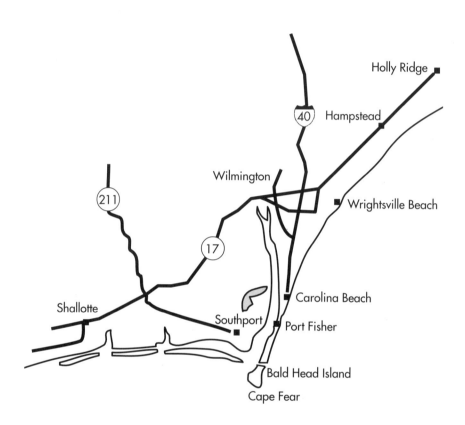

filter the pesticides and sediment released into the environment by large-scale, intensive agricultural operations. The upshot of the clearing of the peninsula is that the vast Albemarle–Pamlico Sound ecosystem has now been designated the nation's first "estuary of national concern." These unique brackish water sounds will not be productive and clean until the swamp forests that once protected them are returned. Lakes Phelps and Pungo offer an unfortunate contrast to the Carolina Bays in the lower Cape Fear Basin.

Battery Island, located in the mouth of the Cape Fear River a half mile offshore from the waterfront of Southport, is one of the most important waterbird rookeries and roosting islands on the East Coast. It has been stated that no area of equal size in North Carolina supports so great a volume of such diverse bird life as this small island. Terns, black skimmers, snowy egrets, Louisiana herons, glossy and white ibis and herons nest in high densities.

There is much that is remarkable about the region at the mouth of the Cape Fear River, the only major North Carolina river to flow directly into the ocean. The Cape Fear Museum in downtown Wilmington has many exhibits on this river and the surrounding region (see chapter 28). The town of Southport is remarkable in itself, for it is literally within a live oak forest. Yet the real jewel of the lower Cape Fear is Bald Head Island. The historical significance of this island, which is tipped with one of the six protruding sandy capes of the East Coast, is difficult to overstate. Giovanni da Verrazanno, an Italian navigator and explorer, mentions it in his log in 1524. The ship carrying John White, governor of what would become the Lost Colony on Roanoke Island, used it as a navigational checkpoint and nearly wrecked on its shoals while returning to England. These dangerous shoals were used by pirates during the eighteenth century and by blockade runners during the Civil War to elude pursuers.

In *Islands, Capes and Sounds*, Thomas Schoenbaum calls the live oak forest of Bald Head "the only extensive barrier island forest now remaining on the North Carolina coast." Although live oak forest once extended from Florida to Virginia on the East Coast, Bald Head's forest now marks the last significant occurrence of this climax stage of barrier island forest, as one moves up the Atlantic Coast. Here, live oaks 4 feet in diameter are common. Some botanists believe the live oak trees on Bald Head Island are descendants of a forest that, because of its elevation above sea level, was never inundated by the sea level rises of the post-Wisconsin ice age.

This 12,000-acre island, with 3,000 acres of upland forest, provides varied wildlife habitat. Very large alligators live on the island, and it is the most important loggerhead turtle nesting site on the North Carolina coastline. Yet the winds of change are blowing across this most beautiful of all North Carolina sea islands, and these winds may affect the character of the island more than did the melting of the glaciers or Hurricane Hazel in 1954.

Development of Bald Head Island has been under way since the mid-1980s. During phase one of the development program, a golf course was built, lots were sold and homes were built in the live oak forest as well as in the dunes. Yet in fairness to the new owners of the island, the Mitchell family of Texas, great pains were taken to preserve the island's character. Few large trees were cut as houses were built. The golf course was designed to fit inside the live oak forest, and especially large live oak trees were left standing on the edges of the fairway. The lagoons built along the course have actually become the favored habitat of large alligators and other wildlife. During dry weather these lagoons are actually the alligators' most dependable refuge from the heat and lack of moisture.

But the Bald Head Corporation has now announced that it may soon begin phase two of the development scheme in the summer of 1996. This would involve platting 50 acres into 35 more homesites, seven tennis courts, a swimming pool, a beach club, a convenience store, a bed and breakfast and a multi-family unit. All of this building would occur on the very tip of historic Cape Fear. The wild, windswept ambiance of Cape Fear and its infamous, historic Frying Pan Shoals would certainly be sacrificed (see chapter 17).

Cape Cod, Cape Hatteras, Cape Lookout and Cape Romaine on the East Coast are all protected, either as national seashores or as national wildlife refuges. Cape Canaveral is protected from development by its inclusion in the John F. Kennedy Space Center. Point Reyes, north of San Francisco, is a national seashore. Cape Blanco in southern Oregon is a state park. This covers every protruding, sandy cape in America except Cape Fear, the only one that is privately owned.

It is the fervent hope, not only of many property owners on the island but also of generations who enjoyed Bald Head before it was purchased by the present owners, that good stewardship be practiced here. Some of the old men of nearby Southport can still remember riding down to Bald Head's ocean beach on the backs of female loggerhead turtles as they returned to the sea after laying their eggs among the dunes. Residents of Southport in the early 1800s stood and watched flocks of passenger pigeons passing overhead with a sound "resembling a gust of wind" on their way to feed on the acorns and roost in the live oak forest of Bald Head Island. As contact with the natural world diminishes and human population swells, the concept of wildness may be relegated to myth. The value of places that serve as windows through which wildness can be viewed may become more valuable than anyone living today can grasp.

Here's an update on Cape Fear. On May 23, 1996, a letter was sent to property owners on Bald Head Island outlining a plan to preserve 93 acres, including the tip of historic Cape Fear, which was slated to be developed by the owner of the island. As a result, Smith Island Land Trust, a non-profit organization, is now being formed. In a race against time and the developer's agenda, the Land Trust is negotiating with the owner of the island to purchase the tip of the cape. Anyone interested in contributing should call (910) 457-6187 or write Smith Island Land Trust, P.O. Box 3203, Bald Head Island, North Carolina 28461.

April

Notes

19

Spring Colors Along the Blue Ridge Parkway

The fraternity of truly great scenic drives across the world is select; only a few qualify. Among them are the famed Fourteen-Mile Drive of Carmel, California; US Highway 1 from Monterey south to Big Sur, California; Italy's Amalfi drive and the Moynne Corniche outside the municipality of Monte Carlo. The Pan American Highway, which runs from the U.S.-Mexico border to Puerto Montt, Chile, is world-class where it crosses parts of Central America.

Along Mather Memorial Parkway, which follows the White River in Snoqualmie National Forest in Washington state, the traveler sees gargantuan Douglas fir trees along a "boulevard of giants." Across Puget Sound the Olympic Highway, Route 101, encircles the Olympic Peninsula and offers views of the Juan de Fuca Strait and the Cascade Range. Montana's Beartooth Highway winds between Red Lodge and Cooke City, Montana, where more than 25 peaks rise over 12,000 feet. Yet within this group, there is one scenic drive that towers above the others: the Blue Ridge Parkway. This 469-mile parkway is universally recognized as the world's premier scenic drive and is made up of Virginia's 105-mile Skyline Drive, the 33 miles of US 441 that passes through Great Smoky Mountains National Park and North Carolina's 331 miles of the Blue Ridge Parkway.

The Blue Ridge Parkway and two other, shorter scenic drives in New York state, the Taconic State Parkway and the Palisades Interstate Parkway, were all designed and constructed at roughly the same time. Yet the Blue Ridge Parkway emerged as the pièce de résistance of the scenic drive concept, an idea that took on a truly grand scale as architect Stanley Abbott and planner/coordinator

Edward Abbuehl took it across the ridges and through the valleys of North Carolina and Virginia. The North Carolina route was chosen over a Tennessee route because two national forests that provided a corridor for the parkway were already in place in North Carolina. But there was bitter contention between the two states over which one would be selected by the planning commission. By good fortune, the parkway was undertaken during the Depression, when the Civilian Conservation Corps provided unlimited cheap labor. It is highly unlikely that any scenic drive will ever be attempted on such a scale again.

Although hundreds of thousands of people make the pilgrimage to the parkway each autumn to see the fall colors, relatively few think to drive it during the other peak season for color. In about mid-April, depending on the elevation, five striking colors—lime green, red, orange, purple and white—begin to emerge from the otherwise drab mountains. These colors, especially when backlighted by the sun, strongly suggest the pointillism technique of some Impressionist painters. Against a wintry brown background, each tree of the earliest species to leaf out, the yellow poplar or tulip tree, forms a dab of bright green. On mountainsides where the poplar is the dominant tree, thousands of dabs of light green are interspersed with dabs of orange and red where red maple flowers and unfurling orange-tinted maple leaves form bursts of color. Puffs of white are interspersed where dogwood and serviceberry blossom. Finally, and most striking of all, is the lavender blossom of the redbud or Judas tree. This small tree favors forest edges and is often found along the highway right-of-way. There is probably nothing in these forests more colorful than acres of blossoming redbud, made even more vibrant by the backdrop of last winter's forest floor.

Take a walk in the early spring cove hardwood forest, for the openness of the winter woods is still present and the leaf color is fresh and light. One of the most delightful aspects of the emerging foliage is the way the dogwood and serviceberry blossoms seem to hang in the distance as you walk through the greening forest. Once the woods are fully leafed out, this "depth of field" will vanish.

Hot Spots

The area around **Doughton Park,** approximately 20 miles south of the Virginia state line on the Blue Ridge Parkway, is a favorite location for both fall and spring foliage color. Another is the **Graveyard Fields** area of the parkway, located just north of Brevard between NC 276 south and NC 215, which provides both unusually open vistas and good foliage color. The drive down NC 9 toward Bat Cave, southeast of Asheville, and then down NC 74, through the **Hickory Nut Gorge,** combines cascading waters and brilliant foliage. The area around nearby **Lake Lure** is another good choice for leaf color. The granite domes here, the site for the filming of *The Last of the Mohicans,* are superlative. The New River in and around **New River State Park,** northeast of Boone, North Carolina, is also an excellent destination for viewing both spring and fall leaf colors.

The drive on NC 321 between Boone and Hampton, Tennessee, is an excellent place to see the cove hardwood forest spring colors. From the Tennessee state line to the community of Hampton, near Roan Mountain, the soil apparently favors the redbud. If you can hit the peak of the redbud blossoming in this area, which occurs around April 12, you will see a profusion of color. At this time there are the added bonuses of blossoming dogwoods and serviceberry or "sarvis," not to mention one of the most beautiful lakes in the TVA chain, **Watauga Lake.**

Other spots for spring colors as the cove hardwood forest leafs out are nearby **Roan Mountain State Park** and **Great Smoky Mountains National Park.** In both parks the early spring colors continue to come in well into May at the higher elevations.

There is no better way to enjoy the first spring foliage color than from a canoe. **Watauga Lake** in eastern Tennessee is one of the most beautiful lakes in the entire TVA chain. The forested mountains tower over this impoundment, creating a bowl filled with Watauga Lake's brilliantly blue water. To reach it, take US 421 west out of Boone. Where 421 and 321 split, take US 321 and cross the state line into Tennessee.

Follow US 321 toward Hampton, along the shoreline of Watauga Lake. At the Rat Branch boat ramp, put in your canoe and paddle toward the concrete dam, which is visible straight ahead. Upon reaching the main body of the lake, bear right. Nearby **Holston Lake** is the equal of Watauga Lake in terms of beauty. Holston Mountain, with the Appalachian Trail running down its spine, towers dark and huge over this lake, filling the horizon. The best access to Holston Lake is off US 421, east of Bristol, Tennessee (see chapter 34). Another foliage hotspot for the canoeist is North Carolina's **Santeetlah Lake,** on NC 129 north of Robbinsville. This trip is easily combined with a walk through the virgin grove of nearby Joyce Kilmer Memorial Forest. Follow signs for Joyce Kilmer Forest on NC 129 out of Robbinsville. North Carolina's ancient **Uwharrie Mountains,** between Asheboro and Albemarle, have spring and fall color weeks after the mountain locations have peaked. **Badin Lake,** on the western edge of Uwharrie National Forest, offers both spring and fall colors as well as a large body of water for the canoeist. Begin this trip from **Morrow Mountain State Park.**

20

Gators!

Observing alligators in a wild setting, where they are not accustomed to humans, provides a unique window into the world that existed 180 million years ago, during the age of dinosaurs. Far from being clumsy, slow and dull-witted, there is no more efficient predator in the Carolina coastal environment than the alligator. The success of this species in avoiding extinction proves this beyond all question. No predator is quicker in bursts of speed, is more patient, expends less energy during periods of rest or uses food more efficiently. Nothing is wasted; even the shells of turtles and skeletons of captured prey are dissolved and digested. Their variable metabolic rate allows energy to be conserved during periods of inactivity, unlike most warm-blooded species.

The female alligator *Mississippiensis* is a remarkably tender and attentive mother, and is the only social reptile. Unlike sea turtles and other reptiles, the female alligator stays with her nest and guards it aggressively. When the little ones make peeping noises as they struggle underneath the mound of vegetation serving as their nest, the mother gator sometimes gently crushes the eggshells in her jaws to help them out. Mother alligators are known to carry their young in their mouths to more suitable locations. Fossilized remains of recently discovered dinosaur egg "nurseries" suggest that certain species of gregarious dinosaurs behaved much as alligators do today.

The alligator is the only player left from the age of dinosaurs that moved among them as an equal, which is to say, it ate dinosaurs and was eaten by them. The ancestral crocodilians reached lengths of 45 feet, had 6-inch teeth and were larger than many species of dinosaurs. Except for their smaller size, today's crocodilians are little changed from those of 180 million years ago. You will experience a certain awe while observing the American alligator, a prominent member of the crocodilian family, the oldest reptile group on earth. This ultimate survivor was there when the big meteor struck the Gulf of Mexico, near Merida, with the force of thousands of atomic bombs exploding at once. So much dust and debris were thrown into the atmosphere that the sun was blocked out and much of the global flora died back. Yet by totally using whatever food it was able to catch, by expending energy with astonishing penury and by downsizing a little, the gator did what no other large reptile from the Age of the Dinosaurs did: It made it through the mass extinction bottleneck. The gator now finds itself on the stage with a whole new cast of flighty, posturing, extravagant actors: the mammals!   After being nearly extirpated between the 1890s and 1966, when it came under the protection of the Endangered Species Protection Act, the American alligator has exercised an extraordinary ability to rebound. Prior to gaining protection, gators were hunted relentlessly for the hide trade, as well as for meat, and were captured live for zoos. By 1902 it is estimated that the gator populations of Florida and Louisiana had been reduced by 80 percent. In a little more than 30 years since becoming protected, however, alligators are at carrying capacity across much of their range in the southeastern United States.

The American alligator and the Chinese alligator are the only two alligator species in the world. The other 27 species of crocodilians are jacare, caimans and crocodiles, and are much more saltwater-adapted than the American alligator. That there could be only two species of alligators, separated by half the globe, underscores the southeastern U.S.–southern China floral-faunal connection discussed in chapter 21.

The gator's place in the food chain is clearly at the top. A large alligator may measure more than 14 feet in length. Now that gators are protected from humankind, no predator stands over it. Most of the diet of the Carolina gators consists of crabs, crawfish, rough fish such as jumping mullet, carp, gar and menhaden, as well as snakes, turtles, carrion and other small gators. Raccoons are taken whenever the opportunity presents itself. One of the most interesting interdependent relationships in the coastal intertidal zone exists among three species: nesting waterbirds, raccoons and gators.

Because the coon can both climb and swim, it is a highly successful predator. One of its most productive tactics is to climb into trees containing active nests of wading birds, such as ibis and herons, and eat both eggs and young. The raccoon population all across America has exploded because they are no longer shot or trapped in significant numbers. Entire waterbird rookeries have been forced to relocate because of raccoon predation. It is thought that the large waterbird rookery on Bird Island in Lake Marion (chapter 28) is composed largely of birds that relocated from a former rookery in Charleston Harbor, where they were more easily accessible to raccoons. Waterbirds now often locate their rookeries on sites that force raccoons to swim across open water in order to reach them. The waterbirds seem to know that alligators will get every coon that tries, for the raccoon is the gator's favorite food. Gators will also attack any dog with absolute abandon, perhaps because the dog's anatomical form and behavior are close to those of the raccoon. A light-colored, long-legged dog may not be at as great a risk as a darker, short-legged, more coonish-looking dog. Large alligators have been known to snatch a dog on a leash away from its horrified master. A swimming dog is in even greater danger. Never send your dog into the water to retrieve a ball if there is the remotest chance that a large gator is near. Fortunately, American alligators have no interest in attacking humans. However, their cousins, the saltwater crocodiles of Australia and the Nile crocodile, take humans whenever they have an opportunity.

Gator watching can be done from a canoe, on foot or from a vehicle. It is not recommended to take a dog in a canoe where it may been seen by a gator. Even in January and February, gators will emerge from their dens to sun themselves on particularly warm days. April and May are the best months to see them because they are hungry for the warmth of spring. Because the evenings are still cool in April or May, gators actively seek the sun's warmth from midmorning to midafternoon. Look for gators under 3 feet long sunning on logs or any sort of floating platform. The big ones will haul themselves out on favored locations on mud banks or sandbars, exposing their entire length to the early sun of the spring season. During the oppressive heat of summer, they avoid the sun and seldom lie out in the open. September and October also see the gators actively seeking the last warmth of the year, but never as aggressively as in the first weeks of warm spring weather.

One of the most interesting times to go gator watching is during courtship. In May, and into early June, the bull gators bellow to attract females. The sound may resemble that of a mooing cow, or, if the gator is a large one, the bowing of a string base in the distance. Cow gators bellow too, but in a higher range. The pitch of the bellow of a large bull gator is extraordinarily low. In fact part of the courtship song of a large bull alligator is below the auditory range of the human ear. Only when a bellowing "Pavarotti" moves into the high end of his vocal range can humans hear him. People who maintain large alligator farms in Florida have claimed that gators will bellow back to a sustained B-flat note played on a woodwind instrument. No other pitch moves them to song. If you are fortunate enough to hear a bellowing gator, you will instantly know what the dinosaurs knew: This is no lightweight!

The courtship song of the American alligator occurs only very sporadically and serendipitously. It is best to have the resident naturalist of a state park, or someone who lives near a gator hotspot, give you a phone call when the big boys start bowing their string bases in the springtime.

Even if you do not get to hear them, a sure time to see alligators is at night, in the beam of a flashlight, when their eyes show up as red embers or yellow-green jewels. Look for them actively swimming or floating with just their eyes and a few other knobs above the waterline. If you are fortunate enough to be invited to go with the South Carolina Department of Fish and Game on a nighttime gator count, accomplished from the back of a pickup truck moving slowly across the levees of the old rice fields, you will probably be amazed by the many hundreds of pairs of glowing eyes. The sweeping beam of a powerful flashlight illuminates a remarkable scene. While the jumping mullet skip across the surface of the water, the gators float placidly, their glowing eyes staring vacantly across the vastness of the old rice fields. The Santee Delta and other Lowcountry rice areas were once cleared of cypress forest and then leveed by hand with slave labor at a terrible price in terms of human suffering and death from malaria. They now once again belong to the jumping mullet and the alligator.

Hot Spots

Savannah NWR is one of the best places to see gators because of its abundance of freshwater habitat. To reach Savannah NWR from US 95, on the Georgia–South Carolina border, exit at Hardeeville (Exit 5) and head south on US 17. After traveling 6 miles, US 17 splits. Do not take alternate 17, but rather stay on US 17. Look for signs for the refuge. Impoundment 18 is excellent for alligators. The gates to the refuge are closed automatically by a timer; be careful not to get locked inside.

Lake Marion, South Carolina, provides the canoeist an ideal opportunity to see gators. One productive area is the shoreline and islands of **Santee NWR**, just east of where I-95 crosses the lake on the north side. Go to Santee State Park, located just east of where I-95 crosses the lake, to get a map of this area of the lake. To reach the visitor's center at Santee State Park, leave I-95 at Exit 98 (Santee) and go west on SC 6 for 1.2 miles. Here, turn right on Road 105 and go 2.4 miles to the park entrance. Do not paddle a canoe across open expanses of this lake, for it can become very rough and dangerous.

Huntington Beach State Park provides perhaps the most accessible gator population. Look in the freshwater lagoon on the right side of the road as you drive across the little causeway into the park. By sitting in the gazebo built at the edge of the freshwater lagoon, you will likely see gators cruise by at dusk. Look for sunning gators on the small island directly out from the gazebo. The entrance to this park is located opposite the entrance to Brookgreen Gardens, on US 17 between Litchfield Beach and Murrells Inlet. For the more adventuresome gator enthusiast, **Santee Coastal WMA** (chapter 8) offers miles of levees through the old flooded rice fields, where a gator population thrives. Remember that insects make this location all but impossible to enjoy after May 1.

21

Birding: The First Wave

With the appearance of the earliest green buds of April, the birder's thoughts turn naturally toward the semitropical South Carolina Lowcountry and coastal plain, with its evocative swamp and riverbottom forests. Here, the first of the neotropical migrants— the warblers, thrushes, vireos, flycatchers and kites—begin to drift into the Carolinas. They arrive in small groups that build quickly in size as the month progresses. These superanimated bits of jewel-like color gladden the spirit of the early birders, just as the first trillium, lady's-slipper or bloodroot thrills the wildflower fancier, and just as fly fishermen are excited by the first mayfly hatches that miraculously rise from the southern Appalachian rivers. Early birders who come to the swamp forest are seeking assurance that the miracle is poised to happen again. And if they do not walk the boardwalk trails through the flooded forest too early in April, the first trip is usually satisfying.

The warblers and other songbirds are eager to lay claim to the eastern seaboard forests of North America. Some species, like the prothonotary warbler, the Mississippi kite and the great crested flycatcher, will spend the entire breeding season here. Others will move quickly through on their way to the Appalachians. Still others, such as the hermit thrush, the Swainson's thrush and the Wilson's warbler, will have their homing systems set on locations as far north as Canada's boreal forest. But regardless of destination, a great many neotropical migrants pass through the region, peaking in late April and the first week of May. All are eager to be back, in song and in full courtship colors.

Hot
Spots
There are no two better places to see the first waves of neotropical migrants than **Congaree Swamp National Monument** and **Francis Beidler Forest.** Each of these locations offers the warblers and other species a rare commodity on the East Coast: large blocks of old-growth forest. The two locations are similar in some ways, for both appear swampy. Yet to the trained eye, they are quite different. Beidler Forest, 1 mile wide by 7 miles long, is a true swamp environment, and the core area remains submerged all year. For this reason the baldcypress tree is the dominant species here. The tupelo gum and the cypress outcompete the other water-tolerant tree species. Located in the famous Four Hole Swamp, Beidler Forest (see chapter 22) attracts warblers and other neotropical species because of both its abundant insect life and its plentiful nesting cavities in the ancient trees. Both the prothonotary warblers and the great crested flycatchers are cavity nesters. For some reason the great crested flycatcher nearly always incorporates a shed snakeskin into the construction of its nest.

Congaree Swamp National Monument, on the other hand, is a floodplain forest. On average, 10 times a year the Congaree River floods cover 80 percent of the park. When the floodwaters recede, nutrients are left behind, greatly enriching the soil and accounting for the great biodiversity found here. More than 320 plant, 41 mammal, 24 reptile, 52 fish and 200 bird species inhabit the park. In contrast to Beidler Forest, where the cypress clearly dominates the tree community, 90 different species of trees grow here, with no single species dominating. Eleven thousand acres of the monument are true old growth, and were never logged. The obvious king of Congaree Swamp National Monument is the loblolly pine. Across much of the Carolinas, this pine is considered unremarkable, but here the loblolly achieves its highest expression. The Congaree's loblollies grow more than 150 feet high and are the tallest trees east of the Mississippi River. Many are more than 10 feet in circumference. To reach Congaree Swamp National Monument from I-26, take Exit 116, which may be marked to SC 48. Here, pick up I-326, which may still be marked SC 48. Head east and cross the Congaree River. Look for the exit for SC 48 in 6 miles. Turn right (east) on SC 48, go approximately 8.5 miles and turn right onto SC 734 (Old Bluff Road). From this point follow signs to Congaree Swamp National Monument. In both Congaree and Beidler, stop at the visitor's centers and ask about trails and maps. To reach Beidler Forest, call (803) 462-2150. To reach Congaree National Monument, call (803) 776-4396.

Another attraction for the birder in this part of South Carolina is **Super Sod**, a grass turf farm located near Orangeburg. The hundreds of acres of manicured sod, faintly suggesting a vast football field or golf course, have countless depressions. After several days of rainy weather, they fill with water and create a large wetland habitat that shorebirds find irresistible. The Super Sod Corporation allows birders to drive their vehicles along the sandy lanes and set up spotting scopes. All visitors must stop at the office to check in before driving onto the grounds. Some of the more interesting species here are American pipits, lapland longspurs, buff-breasted sandpipers, American golden plovers, pectoral sandpipers, upland sandpipers, stilt sandpipers, dowitchers, turnstones and yellowlegs. Shorebirds migrate through this region along with the neotropical migrants and can be seen in late April and May. July 1 through mid-September is considered the peak time for Super Sod. During this period, a storm front will usually push shorebirds along ahead of it, and the Sod Farm is a favorite stopping-off point for them. At such times, entire birding clubs will descend on the Sod Farm and you may hear the refrain, "Anything's possible at the Sod Farm." Remember that this human-made shorebird attractor is open to the public only through the generosity of the Super Sod Corporation. Do not drive the lanes of the Sod Farm if they are too wet, for they will be deeply rutted by your tire tracks. During dry weather there will probably be no standing water in the depressions in the landscape of the Sod Farm, and thus no shorebirds. To reach Super Sod, take the Orangeburg-Santee Exit, southeast of Columbia, on I-26. Take SC 301 toward Orangeburg, go a quarter mile; the entrance is on the left.

22

The Second Oldest
Living Thing in America

In nature's endless thoroughness, no niche where life might gain even a tenuous foothold is ever overlooked. Sometimes the most interesting things happen in the most precarious of environments. In many coastal plains rivers, the primeval waters were nutrient-poor and stained with tannic acid. Yet nature put on its biodiversity hat and started experimenting. The result is the splendid tree with "knees" that is the very soul of most coastal plains lowland tree communities, from Merchant's Mill Pond and Great Dismal Swamp in northeastern North Carolina, to South Carolina's A.C.E. Basin, south of Charleston, and up the Mississippi River as far north as southern Illinois. This unusual tree, which maintains underwater root systems, has the distinction of being a deciduous conifer. It drops its needles each winter, hence the name "bald" cypress. Its closest relative is the California redwood, which, like the cypress, evolved approximately 100 million years ago. The cypress is remarkable any way you look at it. Cypress heartwood can outlast most other materials; cypress shingles are known to still be strong and watertight after 250 years. Hollowed cypress logs used in early New Orleans water pipelines laid down in 1798 were showing no signs of decay when removed in 1914.

Certainly one of the most interesting stands of cypress is along North Carolina's Black River, which flows into the Cape Fear River 16 miles above Wilmington. In the middle section of the well-named Black River, whose waters are stained nearly black with tannic acid, stand the second oldest living things in America. Only the 4,500-year-old bristlecone pines of California's high desert are older! A core sampling study conducted in the early 1980s by University of Arkansas dendrochronologist David Stahle revealed

"Methuselah"—the ancient baldcypress with ecotourists in canoes in foreground.

that individuals of this cypress community were as old as 1,700 years. Stahle believes that other, yet unfound trees may be more than 2,000 years in age. The Nature Conservancy has acquired approximately half the 1,900 acres of old-growth cypress swampland along the Black River and is working to obtain conservation easements from private landowners to protect the remaining virgin cypress.

The best, and in fact the only, way to reach this section of the **Black River** is by boat, and since Stahle's discovery it has become a popular canoeing destination. There are two strategies for seeing the Black River's ancient cypress trees. By putting in at the public boating access on the outskirts of the little town of Ivanhoe, North Carolina, south of Clinton on NC 210, you can paddle downriver, see "Methuselah," the 1,700-year-old tree cored by Stahle and access his "take-out" vehicle at Beatty's bridge, all in one day. While this sounds wonderfully simple, it is not. NC 1100 runs over Beatty's bridge but there is no boat ramp, only a small footpath down to the river here. Locate a canoe club with a member who knows where the ancient one stands; otherwise you will certainly miss the particular tributary you must paddle up to find Methuselah. Environmental organizations such as High Point, North Carolina's Piedmont Environmental Center (chapter 16) take a naturalist-led canoe trip to see the venerable tree each year. A second strategy is to take the overnight trip approximately 15 miles downriver from the Ivanhoe boat ramp. This longer, more difficult trip will carry you through the core area of the Black River old-growth cypress and will require an overnight camp on the river. Many of the oldest cypress trees stand in a region known as the "Three Sisters Swamp." Here the Black River splits into numerous braids or small channels. It is a confusing place, and you will likely have to drag your canoe over sandbars and downed trees in the river, especially if the river level is low due to dry weather. It would be prudent to take this trip with someone who has taken it before, for it could be hazardous for the novice. The *Paddler's Guide to North Carolina* by Bob Benner and Tom McCloud may be useful in planning any Black River canoe trip.

Located in South Carolina's Four Hole Swamp, 5,820-acre **Francis Beidler Forest** is said to contain the largest stand of virgin baldcypress and tupelo gum trees in the world. Within this Audubon–Nature Conservancy preserve are 1,783 acres that have never been logged. The preserve contains many trees

Kayaker silhouetted against the reflection of the sky on the surface of the Black River.

more than 1,000 years old and some as old as 1,500. A true biodiversity preserve, Beidler Forest is being expanded to include upland habitat within the floodplain of Four Hole Swamp. A 1.5-mile-long boardwalk through this classic swamp-riverine ecosystem makes seeing this cypress stand a simple matter. Canoe trips, night walks and other activities are available in season and by reservation only. For information call (803) 462-2150. To reach Francis Beidler Forest, take Exit 177 off I-26 east, just south of the intersection of I-26 and I-95. Next, go south (right) on SC 453 to US 178, turn left (east) and pass through Harleyville on US 178. Follow signs to Beidler Forest from Harleyville to the sanctuary.

Reelfoot Lake, Tennessee (chapters 1 and 40), is another splendid example of a baldcypress community. In fact Reelfoot is an "oasis" in the middle of a large agricultural area of the baldcypress ecosystem that was once a dominant feature of the Mississippi River biosphere as far north as southern Illinois. Although cypress still occur in the entire former range, no better example exists of the cypress community web of life that is so important to the Mississippi River system. A boardwalk behind the main visitor's center, on the south end of the lake, allows you to walk through part of the cypress forest that stands in the fertile waters of Reelfoot.

Another interesting way to experience Reelfoot's cypress forest is to rent one of the famous Reelfoot "stumpjumper" boats, which feature unique forward-facing oars. These slow-moving, low rpm motorized boats are designed specifically for Reelfoot's shallow, stumpy waters. They are available for rent at most of the boat docks on the south end of the lake.

Finally, **Merchant's Mill Pond State Park** in the northeast corner of North Carolina also offers an outstanding example of the baldcypress ecosystem.

23

April Shorttakes

Flowering Trees

The Jurassic period, according to the *Unabridged Edition of the Random House Dictionary of the English Language,* was "a period characterized by dinosaurs and conifers." Flowering trees did not appear for roughly another 30 million years. As with wildflowers, the trees' strategy of attracting pollinators to fertilize seeds represented a new level of complexity in the floral community. A species-poor forest such as the Alaskan spruce forest, with only a handful of species, contrasts sharply with the southern Appalachian forest with 159 species (see chapter 69). The three-state region is one of the great flowering tree centers in the temperate zone of the world. Yet each year flowering trees such as the yellow poplar, Fraser magnolia, catalpa, maples, apples, cherries and a host of others scarcely make a head turn as wildflower enthusiasts file through the forest, heads down. Surely a yellow poplar, or tulip tree with many hundreds of "tulips," or a Fraser magnolia with an 8 to 10-inch diameter flowers high in the forest canopy, or a catalpa tree with 6-inch heart-shaped leaves and clusters of white flowers much like those of the mountain laurel, is as great a masterpiece as a tiny dwarf iris wildflower. The flowers of the broadleafed, deciduous trees are as anatomically perfect and as aromatic as the tiny wildflowers at their feet.

The "Other" Rhododendron

The rhododendron family has a large and enthusiastic following in the three-state region. Around the peak blossoming date of June 20th, the Catawba rhododendrons of Roan Mountain attract many thousands people from as far away as Japan, Europe and Canada. The rosebay, or white, rhododendron is prized as an ornamental and grows wild in profusion along the streams and rivers of the southern Appalachians. This species blossoms in late June and early July. Yet unknown to most fanciers of this ancient floral family, a third, almost unknown rhododendron also exists in the Southern Appalachians. The Carolina rhododendron has leaves that resemble the mountain laurel, more so than the rosebay or the Catawba rhododendron. This member of the heath family blossoms in mid-April, the earliest of any of the southern Appalachian rhododendrons. All three of our rhododendrons are unusal in that they are broadleafed evergreens, thus never losing their leaves. The easiest place to see the Carolina rhododendron is **Chimney Rock Park** (see chapter 26). You may wish to have it pointed out on a naturalist-led wildflower walk.

24

A Closer Look:
Eno River Yellow Lady's Slippers

Across the piedmont sections of the Carolinas, nearly the entire landscape has been severely disturbed by humans. These disturbances were brought about not only by cutting much of the forest but also by first annually exhausting and then artificially rejuvenating the soil with fertilizer. Eventually, the microbial and bacterial communities within the soil were destroyed. Even when rested for decades, soil abused in this manner remains unable to re-create its original floral ecosystems. In locations like the Uwharrie Mountains in North Carolina's piedmont, which appear intact, soil depletion from generations of soil-exhausting agricultural practices still persists.

However, along the Eno River, in spite of its urban setting the soil retains its natural composition and fertility. This 2,000-acre state park is an oasis for an astonishing floral community, a "Noah's ark" for the floral biosphere that once stretched from the coastal plains to the foothills of the Carolinas. Although 30 mills operated along this 33-mile river during the American Revolution, it returned long ago to a nearly pristine state, in spite of its proximity to Durham and Chapel Hill. The rich soil of the river bottomlands, the surprising wildness and elevation of Occoneechee Mountain, the number of disjunct species and the riverine ecosystem of the Eno form a tiny island of undisturbed Carolina piedmont, representing many of the original natural community types found across the region.

Although part of the park actually borders on I-85, you can still find beaver, otter, wild turkey and deer—all thanks to restocking efforts by wildlife agencies. The Eno, unlike most mud- and silt-bottomed rivers of the piedmont, flows over a gravel-bottomed, boulder-strewn riverbed in specific places in the park, and looks much like a smallmouth bass stream in western North Carolina. The water quality of this small river is probably better than it was during the 1700s, when mills used it as a dump site. This fact is illustrated by the Eno's freshwater mussel fauna, which includes 10 species, 5 of which are state-listed protected species. Eno River State Park offers canoeists class I, II and III rapids and 18 miles of hiking trails.

Occoneechee Mountain, on the east end of the park, stands 360 feet over the Eno River and is largely responsible for the number of relic and disjunct species (chapter 38) in the park. Here one finds species more commonly associated with the southern Appalachian mountains, such as mountain witch alder, rosebay rhododendron, mountain laurel, as well as many common and some rare ferns. Parts of the forest within the park have surprisingly old-regrowth mixed hardwood forest. The forest ecosystems range from a healthy river birch, ash and sycamore community along the river, to a southern hardwood forest along the slopes, to a dry Virginia pine–chestnut oak community on top of Occoneechee Mountain. In early April Eno River State Park begins to come to life. Through-migrating warblers are one of the first signs of the awakening biodiversity here. Yet it is the variety of wildflowers that is most remarkable. The Eno's wildflower fauna never slows down but continues to produce species after species, long after the early spring ephemerals have vanished. Among its indigenous species are bluets, annis, windflowers, cranefly orchids, rattlesnake orchids, colonies of jack-in-the-pulpit, acres of May apples, wild geraniums, Catesby trilliums, pinxster azaleas, Solomon's seal, clusters of atamasco lilies, galax, foamflowers, trout lilies, bloodroot, Dutchman's breeches, several violet species, the orange and black speckled Carolina lily and the uncommon wild bleeding heart.

The reclusive yellow lady's slipper orchid, or moccasin flower, may be the single species that finds conditions approaching perfection in the Eno River bottomlands. On wildflower walks in Great Smoky Mountains National Park, or at Roan Mountain, a single yellow lady's slipper orchid brings forth oohs and ahs from pilgrims, photographers fall to their knees and pencils feverishly work. Yet on a good day on the Eno, around April 20, George Pyne, the "keeper" of the park, may point out dozens on a single hillside. Pyne knows individual orchids that have blossomed each year for over a decade. In fact these yellow lady's slippers may owe their very existence to George Pyne, for he and a handful of others have saved the Eno River bottomlands from assorted unhappy fates, including belt thoroughfare, city landfill, sewer system and municipal reservoir.

In the "disturbed" piedmont of the Carolinas, cornfields, monoculture "set-out" pine forest, pasturelands sown with non-native grasses and acres of Wal-Marts, McDonald's and shopping malls comprise the new "natural order." Sadly most people, having known nothing else, know no better. In spite of the preciousness of Eno River State Park, it is threatened on every side by development. The park needs all the friends it can find.

Two of the best hikes for seeing wildflowers in April are the Pump Station Trail and the area of Willard Duke Bluff. Not 20 feet from the old brickwork or the Pump Station dam is an amphibian breeding pond. This pond will contain egg clusters during April and May, when wildflowers are most prominent along the Eno. To reach Eno River State Park, travel east on I-85 through Durham, North Carolina. Take Exit 170 (NC 751), cross over the interstate and go west on NC 70. At Pleasant Road turn right and go 2.1 miles to Cole Mill and turn left. Go 1 mile and turn right at the sign for the park office, which is open weekday afternoons year-round but only sometimes on the weekends; pick up a map here. For information on wildflower walks along the Eno, call Eno River State Park at (919) 383-1686.

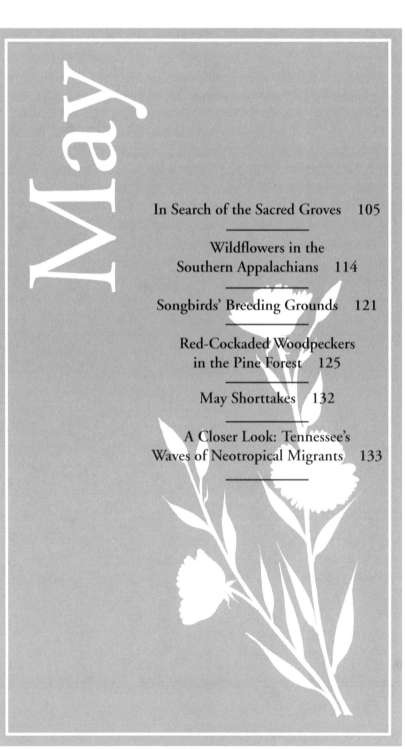

May

Notes

25

In Search of the Sacred Groves

The eastern hardwood forest is the principal ecosystem of the three-state region. Mid-May is the premier time to see the groves, for this month offers the first opportunity to see fully leafed-out hardwoods in the southern Appalachian Mountains. The leaf color will never again be as fresh and light during the yearly cycle.

In North America the broadleaf, deciduous hardwood forest finds its culminating expression in western North Carolina and eastern Tennessee. With 500 endemic species of plants and animals, this region is one of the most biologically diverse forests in the temperate (nonequatorial) zone of the world. The southern Appalachian region, where northern and southern species of trees, flowers and flowering shrubs mix, is truly a large-scale biodiversity center, as opposed to the small-scale species diversity of the longleaf pine–wire grass savanna ecosystem. Supporting more than 3,000 species of vascular plants or 20 percent of the flora in America, this region was the only "reservoir" from which northern species could repopulate once the ice sheets retreated from Pennsylvania and New York state. The botanical importance of this ecosystem is difficult to overstate.

Before the original northern supercontinent Laurasia broke up to form North America, Europe and Asia, the fabulously diverse northern hardwood forest stretched across most of the consolidated northern landmass. Today the northern ancestral forest is maintained in only two floral communities across the entire Northern Hemisphere. One of these is the southern Appalachian forest of the United States. The other "Noah's ark" of the original northern hardwood forest is located in southern Asia, within the boundaries of present-day Burma, northern Thailand, Laos, Vietnam and southeastern China. The forest communities of these two regions are so similar that George Constance, in his book

Hollows, Peepers and Highlanders, was moved to write, "Here's a claim that may surprise you: The forests of eastern Asia and the southern Appalachians are so similar that if you were swept from one to the other, you would be hard pressed to tell them apart."

Everywhere else, across the American West, Europe, the former Soviet Union and much of Asia, climatic conditions became too cold or too dry and the ancestral northern hardwood forest could not survive. It was replaced by the less diverse ecosystems of modern times, such as the coniferous forest of the northern plains states of America, the Alaskan forest and the sparse eastern European steppes. Only in the southern Appalachians and southern Asia did sufficient rainfall, mild temperatures and absence of glaciation allow the original northern forest to survive.

Remarkably, the forests of the eastern United States have regenerated to the point that they are as extensive as at the time of the American Revolution. In the words of author Bill McKibben, "This unintentional and mostly unnoticed renewal of the rural and mountainous East—not the spotted owl, not the salvation of Alaska's pristine ranges—represents the great environmental story of the United States, and in some ways of the whole world."

When the first settlers of the original 13 colonies began to arrive in the 1600s, about three quarters of America's forests were located in the East. Once again, to the astonishment of everyone, the balance has returned to the same proportions. Today about three quarters of our forests are located in the eastern third of the nation. The eastern forest, with its high species diversity, is capable of rejuvenating itself much more quickly than the forests of the American West.

In locations just west of Yellowstone Park, seedlings planted three decades ago in clear-cut areas have attained only about 30 feet of height. It is now suspected that in some of the more arid regions of the American West, these clear-cuts may be exceedingly slow in healing themselves. In contrast, areas heavily logged as recently as the late 1930s in Great Smoky Mountains National Park are completely reforested. Through what McKibben calls "ecoporn," the American public has been led to believe that the landscape of the American West is a hardy, "macho" environment. Nothing could be further from the truth. It is the eastern forest that is hardy and resilient because of high species diversity. Some forested areas in a state such as Montana, with its sporadic rainfall, its nearly nonexistent topsoil in many areas and its short growing season, may be horribly scarred for a century or longer by the large-scale clear-cut logging practices of the last three decades. Because the thin soil present in some of these sites has been severely eroded, reforestation will be all the more difficult.

In the region covering New York, New Hampshire, Vermont and Maine are 26 million acres of eastern hardwood forest. In contrast, Yellowstone National Park contains only 2.2 million acres. When recent white oak pollen counts are compared with pollen counts of the early 1700s obtained from deep core samples taken from swamps of the Cape Cod area, it is apparent that the eastern hardwood forest now approximates its original, pre-Columbian dimensions.

The Appalachians are unimaginably old. They started forming approximately 600 million years ago, before plants had even begun to evolve. These mountains contain the only part of America that has never been flooded by an ancient ocean nor scoured by continental glaciation. This region represents the oldest "continuously available" habitat in North America. In addition, the topography of the Appalachians, with its myriad isolated valleys and unconnected watersheds, gave rise to more speciation than other areas in the country.

Another major factor contributing the rich floral and faunal diversity of the Appalachian range is the north-south orientation of the valley corridors of the mountain range. This geological feature allowed easy southerly migration of northern plant and animal species during the three million years of the Pleistocene ice ages. By contrast, most of the mountain ranges of Europe are oriented in an east-west direction and acted as insurmountable barriers during the ice ages, preventing southerly migration of plant and animal species. Many European species became extinct for this reason, which explains why European forests are so species-poor compared to the southern Appalachians.

The highest peaks of the Appalachian range are in the three-state region. Simply stated, greater elevation range gives more temperature and moisture increments or "bands," each of which supports a unique forest configuration. All along the highest points of the spine of the Appalachian range one finds many of the same boreal forest species that dominate much of southern Canada. This is primarily an evergreen forest and includes balsam fir, black and white spruce, yellow birch and northern white cedar. This northern plant community "invaded" the southern Appalachians with the help of the last glacial age.

The frigid temperatures of the ice sheets that stopped approximately 500 miles to the north in New York and southern Pennsylvania pushed a subarctic climate into the higher elevations of North Carolina and Tennessee. The Canadian boreal forest, through nature's marvelous transport systems, hitched a ride south. When the glaciers retreated, they were marooned and are now "islands in the sky." Other species, such as the New England cottontail rabbit, northern shrews, flying squirrels and scores of northern wildflower species, rode the same transport system south and are also marooned above the clouds, far south of their original range, above 4,500 feet elevation.

Below the boreal (evergreen) forest, the northern hardwood forest community takes in members of both the northern boreal forest and the southern hardwood forest. In this altitude band, a flora more common in New England is found. Here, primarily yellow birch, yellow buckeye and mountain ash occupy the zone that is too cold for most broadleaf deciduous species, yet is too low in elevation for the Canadian spruce-fir forest. This zone is readily visible on Roan Mountain, for instance, for there is a clear line where the dark evergreen forest of the 6,285-foot summit stops and the stunted yellow birch and yellow buckeye begin. The upper range of Roan Mountain's northern hardwood forest is known as a "boulderfield forest" and is considered uncommon in the southern Appalachian region.

Using Roan Mountain as the quintessential model for forest transitions due to elevation changes, it is easy to recognize when one has reached a classic hardwood forest as the highway continues to spiral its way down the mountainside. On the northern end of this altitude band is the mixed mesophytic hardwood forest,

Hiker looking up at giant poplars of Joyce Kilmer Forest.

which supports several dozen species of trees. The primary species you see while driving through this region of the Roan Mountain State Park are beech and maple. Yet other species such as white basswood, red and white oak, hemlock, magnolia, white ash and black cherry are also present.

Finally, as you approach the Roan Mountain State Park visitor's center, you enter the familiar "cove" hardwood forest, or what most people think of as "eastern hardwood forest." Here, many more dozens of species of trees find the temperatures and moisture that allow them to collectively achieve the great biodiversity the area is noted for. A southern Appalachian giant like Roan Mountain, with its altitude bands supporting five distinct forest communities of mixed northern and southern species as well as one of the most extensive highland heath–grass bald systems in America, can claim a biodiversity rivaling some areas of the tropics.

The ultimate thrill for the eastern hardwood forest enthusiast, however, is to walk into the few remaining groves of virgin, never-timbered hardwood forest. These are truly "sacred groves," for they take you back in time to the forest primeval. These groves preserve the genetics of the northern supercontinent ancestral forests, and must be approximately 1,000 years old to have reached the climax stage.

Hot Spots

Some virgin hardwood groves are harder to find than others. The **Grotto Falls Grove** in Great Smoky Mountains National Park is one of the easiest to reach. On this moderately easy 3-mile hike, you will see primarily giant hemlocks. It is best to make this walk early in the morning, for it is popular with tourists from Gatlinburg. To reach Grotto Falls Trail, take Airport Road south out of downtown Gatlinburg, Tennessee. Turn onto Cherokee Orchard Road, which turns into Roaring Fork Loop. The drive through the forest is as beautiful as the hike. You will see huge beeches and hemlocks along Roaring Fork Creek as the road follows it. Look for the parking lot for the Grotto Falls hike. Both the Roaring Fork Loop traffic and Gatlinburg can be hectic; Gatlinburg is very commercial.

The walk into **Ramsay Cascade Grove**, also in Great Smoky Mountains National Park, is a moderately strenuous 4-mile hike through a "sacred grove" to a 60-foot waterfall. It is considered by many who know the park intimately to be one of the most satisfying hikes in the entire 800-square-mile biome. House-sized, lichen-marked, water-streaked granite boulders, spring warblers and wildflowers are all added attractions if you hike it in mid-May. But the most remarkable feature is several black cherry trees along the trail. Each is wider than 4 feet in diameter and more than 500 years old. Since cherry trees have been sought out for their beautiful wood, these trees prove beyond any doubt that the remote Ramsay Cascade region of the park was never reached by loggers.

To reach this trail, take US 321 east from Gatlinburg to the Greenbriar entrance into the park, approximately 6 miles east of Gatlinburg. Take the gravel road that follows the Little Pigeon River into the park for about 4 miles. Look for signs to Ramsey Cascade.

The **Gregory's Bald Trail** sidehills along the mountain, rather than around the bases of the trees of the Gregory Ridge Trail Grove giving the hiker an unusual bird's-eye view of these forest giants. This grove is composed of huge poplars, hemlocks, buckeyes and wild cherry trees, representing an unusually large number of species where no single species has gained dominance. Once the trail climbs out of the creekbed, the virgin timber gives way to less remarkable pine-oak forest. Unless you intend to complete the difficult hike to Gregory's Bald, which is known for the best display, in mid-June, of flame azalea in the park, it is best to stop here. This trail becomes steep and challenging once it climbs out of the watercourse.

To reach this grove, go to the Cade's Cove visitor's center in Great Smoky Mountains National Park. Take the Forge Creek–Parson's Branch Road. In recent summers, however, this road has been closed. You may have to begin this hike at the Cade's Cove visitor's center. After approximately 2 miles, the Parson's Branch Road turns to the right; stay on the Forge Creek road. The trailhead is at the end of this gravel road. You will begin to see the virgin timber approximately 1 mile after leaving the parking area. If you wish to begin this hike early in the day, it might be worthwhile to camp in the Cade's Cove campground.

The **Albright Grove** is located approximately 15 miles east of Gatlinburg, near the town of Cosby, Tennessee, and can be reached by taking US 321 east of Gatlinburg past Yogi's Jellystone Campground. At DJ's, turn right on Laurel Springs Road and travel for 1.5 miles. Bear left until you reach a small, plywood sign for Albright Trail and drive 0.1 mile to the trailhead. This grove is made up primarily of hemlocks and poplars. You will walk through second-growth forest on an old logging road for 1 mile before reaching the virgin timber.

The **Joyce Kilmer Memorial Forest** contains probably the most visited virgin timber grove in the region. It is reached via Route 129 north out of Robbinsville, North Carolina. Follow signs to Joyce Kilmer National Forest. From the parking lot an easy 15-minute hike takes you to the metal plaque commorating Sergeant Joyce Kilmer, who wrote the poem "Trees," and was later killed in World War I. Do not take the trail that turns right at the metal plaque. Walk forward another 20 feet and take the trail marked "Poplar Grove Loop." This hike has the feel of a rain forest and the size of the poplars is stunning.

Great Smoky Mountains National Park contains the best preserved, temperate-zone hardwood forest in the world, as well as the most extensive virgin hardwood timber stands in the United States. Although logging was conducted here as recently as 1937, the park includes more than 100,000 acres that were never cut. These acres of virgin forest contain ancient red spruce, eastern hemlock, northern red oak, Carolina silverbell, Fraser magnolia, basswood and yellow birch. For listings of additional hikes to old growth and virgin timber, buy a copy of the "Hiking Map and Guide to Great Smoky Mountains National Park" published by Earthwalk Press. It is available at the Sugarlands visitor's center at the Gatlinburg entrance to the park.

Other regions of the cove hardwood forest of western North Carolina and eastern Tennessee such as Big Ivy, north of Asheville, are being inventoried for old-growth forest to be protected from logging. Big Ivy may hold the largest stands of undiscovered virgin forest in the southern Appalachians. Surprisingly, blocks of remnant old-growth forest are being discovered by those who search for them in the most inaccessible watersheds and ridges, in the interest of protecting them. In Nantahala and Pisgah National Forests, as many as 100,000 acres hold trees more than 300 years old, and are being considered for protection as old-growth forest. West of Lenoir, North Carolina, 800 acres of old-growth hardwood forest has been discovered by virgin timber sleuths in the last two years. The search for the sacred groves continues.

Great Smoky Mountains National Park

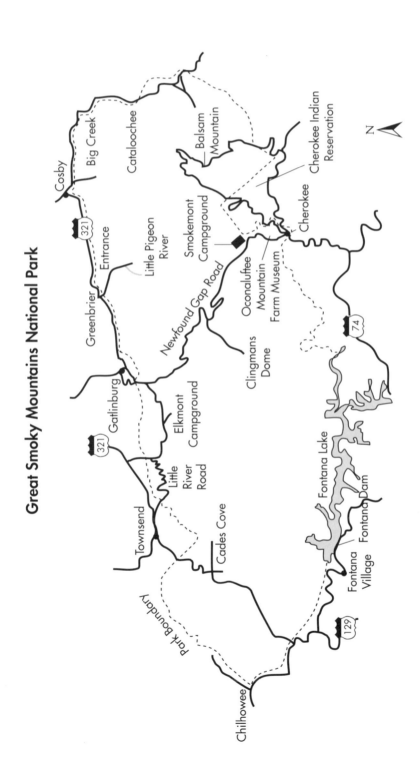

26

Wildflowers in the Southern Appalachians

The list of visitors who have been drawn to the unique mixing grounds for northern and southern wildflower species in the southern Appalachians reads like a who's who of world-renowned botanical authorities of the eighteenth and nineteenth centuries. Beginning in 1789, André Michaux was sent several times by the French government to the southern Appalachians to collect trees, wildflowers and shrubs to adorn the gardens at Versailles. Michaux was fascinated by such southern Appalachian giants as Roan Mountain and Grandfather Mountain. Harvard botanist Asa Gray, for whom the prized Gray's lily is named, studied the flora of Roan Mountain extensively. In 1840, he called it, "without a doubt, the most beautiful mountain east of the Rockies." The list of other historically significant botanists drawn to the Appalachian mountain range includes John and William Bartram; the University of North Carolina's famous mathematics professor, Elisha Mitchell; the Scot John Fraser, for whom the Fraser fir is named; Charles Sprague Sargeant; Moses Ashley Curtis and John Kunkel Small.

What has drawn botanists to the southern Appalachians for centuries? Perhaps Arthur Stupka, for 25 years the park naturalist of Great Smoky Mountains National Park, stated it best: "Vegetation is to Great Smoky Mountains National Park what granite domes and waterfalls are to Yosemite, geysers are to Yellowstone and sculptured pinnacles are to Bryce Canyon National Park." Great Smoky Mountains National Park alone has 130 species of trees, more than all of northern Europe, as well as more than 1,500 flowering herbs and shrubs, and many hundreds of species of mosses and lichens. It is considered one of the great regions of the world for both trilliums and ferns.

The southern Appalachians are very ancient mountains. During the 600 million years of this region's history, its jagged peaks and craggy contours were rounded off by time and bacterial action into a rich layer of topsoil. The composition of the topsoil in these mountains is completely intact, unlike the soils of the piedmont and coastal plains of the Carolinas. As mentioned in chapter 24, the soil of the piedmont and coastal plains was annually plowed, sprayed and artificially fertilized, neutralizing the organic composition of the topsoil layer. In contrast, the wildflowers of the southern Appalachians have a topsoil environment that is virtually pristine in many locations. Only at the highest elevations has acid rain altered the natural chemistry of the topsoil.

Relic species from warmer epochs linger here. Cold-weather northern species, pushed this far south during periods of glaciation, also survive. The names of some of the northern species on Roan Mountain, such as the Greenland sandwort, reflect just how far south they have journeyed. Other northern species are Clinton's lily, wood sorrel, witch hobble and dwarf alder. On the balds of Roan Mountain alone are more than 300 species of flowering plants, many of them northern species. Among these are some of the rarest and most critically endangered species, including the Gray's lily and the Appalachian avens. Roan Mountain's green alder community is the only occurrence of this species south of Pennsylvania.

Wildflowers, like songbirds, are interesting on many levels. The study of the interaction of grasses, sedges and flowering herbs gives one an appreciation of the nearly incomprehensible array of survival mechanisms and interdependencies employed on this biotic level. Flowers are beautiful to the eye because their survival depends upon attracting pollinators such as bees, butterflies and hummingbirds. Color and design are the key. Yet the sedges of Roan Mountain's grassy balds depend upon wind pollination. Some wildflowers have backup systems in case the pollinators do not find them. The dogtooth violet produces seeds with a tiny bump called an "eliasome." This tiny capsule of protein is irresistible to ants, who carry the seeds hither and yon, widely dispersing them. Biologist E. O. Wilson has stated that half the wildflowers in America are inadvertently planted by ants.

Interesting interdependencies are present as well. Wild orchids cannot survive without certain fungi. The Canada violet is white until it has been visited by a pollinator, and then turns pink. By changing color, the Canada violet tells the bee not to waste time repollinating unnecessarily, but rather to visit other, more needy violets. This unselfish strategy keeps the violet gene pool at optimum levels, indirectly benefitting the unselfish individual violets.

There are two periods of particular abundance for wildflowers in the southern Appalachians: mid-April to mid-May and mid-June to mid-July. During these times wildflower pilgrims gather at Roan Mountain, Grandfather Mountain, Chimney Rock and Great Smoky Mountains National Park. The largest wildflower event is the Spring Wildflower Annual Pilgrimage into Great Smoky Mountains National Park at Gatlinburg, which occurs on the last Thursday, Friday and Saturday of April. See chapter 67 for more information on the groups that organize this popular event. Each year hundreds of people, some from as far away as the Upper Midwest, New England and even other countries, form convoys of carpooled wildflower enthusiasts and disperse on nearly 40 different naturalist-led wildflower walks.

In addition to wildflower walks, there are walks to study ferns, salamanders, birds, spiders, mosses, virgin timber, bats and other entities. Some enthusiasts are silver-haired veterans of decades of pilgrimages to attend this event, and come from areas that possess nothing to compare with this 800-square-mile biosphere. Some bring their entire families and plan their year's vacation around the event. Still others come a week in advance and take hikes on their own, in order to determine which areas of the park are peaking on the weekend of the big event. All who come to the southern Appalachians are walking in the footsteps of the botanizing pioneers. Miraculously, the sense of discovery never seems to diminish from generation to generation. For information on the Annual Wildflower Pilgrimage, call Don DeFoe at (423) 436-1262.

Wildflower pilgrims on the grassy balds of Roan Mountain in early May.

Hot Spots

Great Smoky Mountains National Park, 54 miles long and 15 miles wide, is one of the great centers for wildflowers in the nation. Wildflower enthusiasts, sometimes refer to this park as "The Wildflower National Park." As early as late March, certain spring ephemerals and other wildflowers begin to appear. Some of the more accessible locations for these early wildflowers are Noah Bud Ogle Place, Cove Hardwood Trail, Round Bottom Trail, the walkway above Elkmont and many other trails at the lower elevations of the park. From mid-April through mid-May, the majority of species appear. Some of the more popular trails at this time are Buckeye Trail, Ramsay Prong Trail, Cucumber Gap Trail, Cove Hardwood Trail near Chimneys Picnic Area, Chestnut Top Trail, Deep

Creek Trail, Ash Hopper Branch Trail, Ramsay Cascade Trail, Porter's Creek Trail and the Appalachian Trail. Most of these trails are near the Gatlinburg, Tennessee, entrance to the park. Gatlinburg could be considered the wildflower headquarters for the entire park. Purchase a copy of the "Hiking Map and Guide of Great Smoky Mountains National Park" by Earthwalk Press at Sugarlands visitor's center, near the Gatlinburg entrance, as a reference tool. Also for sale is the book *Great Smoky Mountains Wildflowers,* by Campbell, Hutson and Sharp, which is useful for describing where and when to find many wildflower species within the park.

Roan Mountain is composed of three different regions: **Roan Mountain State Park**, where the campground and visitor's center are located; the grassy balds directly across from the Carver's Gap parking lot and the spruce-fir forested summit of the mountain. The famous rhododendron bloom here (see chapter 26) takes place on the grassy highland balds across from Carver's Gap parking lot, as well as in the wild rhododendron gardens on the summit of the mountain. The grassy balds come to life around the first week of May, with the first splashes of bluets. At the same time, the patches of blooming trout lilies can be so thick on the grassy balds, that in places they cover the ground.

On the summit, a 1-mile trail leads to the Roan Mountain overlook. The most interesting areas for spring wildflowers are the grassy balds, the openings around the rhododendron gardens on the summit, the area around the campground and the cove hardwood forest all around the state park restaurant (O'Delly's). To take advantage of this biodiversity gold mine, Roan Mountain State Park has two naturalist's weekends. These events, which examine every aspect of Roan Mountain's flora, fauna, geology, air quality, as well as botanical medicine, plant taxonomy and other subjects, take place on May 7 and 8, and again from September 9 to 11. For information call (423) 772-3303.

Another superlative southern Appalachian wildflower location is **Grandfather Mountain,** near Boone, North Carolina.

This mountain also has sufficient elevation and age to host both northern and southern relic species. This floral biodiversity hotspot is privately owned, and an admission fee is charged. Grandfather Mountain rises 4,000 feet above the surrounding landscape and 5,964 feet above sea level. Grandfather contains rock over a billion years old, some of the oldest in the world. It has been called "a summary of the Blue Ridge Mountains" by noted wildflower author Ritchie Bell of the North Carolina Botanical Gardens of Chapel Hill. Grandfather Mountain is an important biological preserve and possesses three rare and endangered species: the Appalachian avens, the Blue Ridge goldenrod and Heller's blazing star. For information call (704) 733-4337 or (800) 468-7325. Naturalist-led wildflower walks are conducted here each year. To reach Grandfather, take NC 105 south out of Boone. Go 10 miles to the village of Foscoe. After 1.5 miles, look for signs for the entrance to Grandfather.

A destination offering a mix of northern and southern wildflower species is **Chimney Rock State Park**. Like Grandfather, this preserve is privately owned and an admission is charged. For both preserves a very reasonable year's pass is available. Chimney Rock has ongoing programs and workshops on such subjects as ferns, wildflowers, hummingbirds and a peregrine falcon watch. Chimney Rock mails out *Views,* an excellent seasonal publication with updates on wildflowers, birds and other natural events within the 1,000-acre park. This park is blessed with thick stands of Carolina rhododendron, not to be confused with the rosebay, and the catawba rhododendron. Like Grandfather, this nature preserve has several rare and endangered species, as well as many miles of hiking trails. Chimney Rock's granite domes are an excellent location for viewing migrating raptors (see chapter 50). For information on Chimney Rock Park, call (800) 277-9611 or (704) 625-9611. This preserve is located 25 miles southeast of Asheville on US 74.

This chapter has pointed out a few "superlocations" for wildflowers. It is difficult to find a place in the southern

Appalachians where wildflowers are not present. Any National Forest, natural area or riverbottom will harbor a community of them. Check along limestone streams like eastern Tennessee's **South Holston River,** below South Holston Dam, south of Bristol, Tennessee (see chapter 34). Around the third week of April, limestone-loving species such as bluebells can be thick here. Any trail in the southern Appalachian region that traverses creekbottoms in hardwood forests will be claimed by wildflowers. If you are a novice, take a naturalist-led wildflower walk in one of the locations mentioned. Soon you will be ready to discover your own "secret gardens."

27

Songbirds' Breeding Grounds

The return of the songbirds from Central and South America, the Caribbean and the extreme southern United States is a yearly spring event, an in-migration on a scale that few of us can readily grasp. In the three-state region, the neotropical migrants begin to arrive in the South Carolina Lowcountry in late March, increasing in number as April and May progress. Moving upcountry to the foothills of the Carolinas, one sees warblers, thrushes, vireos and others peaking in early May. By the second week of May, the in-migration of neotropical migrants is at its peak at even the highest elevations.

Springtime is without a doubt the best time for birding, for all species are in their bright courtship plumage and the woods ring with their courtship songs. An accomplished birder can hope to identify as many as 100 species in a day by the peak of the breeding season. In contrast, by midsummer the forests of this great region will be essentially still once pairing has been accomplished and the young are demanding food. The neotropical migrants are not ones to rest on their laurels after their young are raised. They feel the stirrings of restlessness almost immediately. Remarkably, as early as July some of the shorebirds, martins and kites begin to congregate to head south for the winter. Late fall and winter are even more frustrating times for birders because songbirds will not only be essentially silent, but will also be in their drab winter plumage, making identification more difficult.

In the mountainous region of the Carolinas and Tennessee, there is no more delightful way to spend a spring day than a leisurely walk down a mountain trail, enjoying wildflowers as well as lustily singing neotropical migrants. Certainly the best environment for wildflowers is North Carolina and Tennessee's Roan Mountain and Great Smoky Mountains National Park. As birding areas both of these locations are excellent choices, for mixing of northern and southern species occurs here, just as it does within the floral community. Twenty-four of the 36 eastern warblers nest here; the other 12 species continue north to nest in the boreal (spruce-fir-larch) forest of Canada and the northern tier states.

In the spruce-fir forests that cover the highest ridgetops of the southern Appalachians, one finds a biosphere much like the forests of southern Canada, 1,000 miles to the north. Here many northern species of birds and plants terminate their southern range. Avian species such as the northern saw-whet owl, Canada warblers, winter wrens, veeries, dark-eyed juncos, ravens and others are commonly seen. The northern hardwood and cove hardwood forests that claim the slopes below the cloud-shrouded spruce-fir summits attract southern species such as Carolina chickadees, wood thrushes, red-eyed vireos, hooded warblers and others. In this altitude band, other northern species such as rose-breasted grosbeaks, black-throated blue warblers and black-capped chickadees mix freely with southern species.

The middle and lower elevations attract yet another complement of southern species, essentially the same birds common across the coastal plains and piedmont sections of the three-state region. This group includes kingfishers, blue jays, eastern screech owls, Carolina wrens, bluebirds, cardinals, song sparrows, American goldfinches and many others.

It is clear that the forests of the southern Appalachians, Roan Mountain and Great Smoky Mountains National Park, in particular, offer the widest range of possible species within the region. The forested slopes of such giants as 6,684-foot Mount Mitchell, 6,642-foot Clingman's Dome and 6,285-foot Roan Mountain give the birder a unique opportunity. Here one can move from a true Canadian life zone to a southern hardwood riverine biosphere, with the appropriate complement of songbirds in each altitude band.

Moving upward 1,000 feet in elevation transforms the environment as if one had moved 300 miles northward in latitude and lowers the temperature by 3 degrees. Thus, by leaving from the 2,800-foot elevation at the Roan Mountain visitor's center on Doe River and driving to the 6,285-foot summit, you have accomplished the same change in environment as a 1,000-mile drive north to James Bay in central Ontario, Canada. You can achieve the same geographical alchemy by taking the 14-mile drive from Sugarlands visitor's center, just inside the Great Smoky Mountains National Park's Gatlinburg entrance, to Newfound Gap. Also, by getting on the Blue Ridge Parkway just east of Asheville and continuing north past the Folk Art Center, Craggy Gardens and Mount Mitchell State Park, you can pass through some of the same vegetation zones. No other location on the East Coast has both the elevation and the overlapping ranges of northern and southern species that allow this to happen. Be sure to start early in the day, for the songbirds are most active in the cool of the morning and again late in the afternoon. By 10:00 A.M. it may become necessary to move to higher, cooler elevations.

By the first week of May, warblers and other songbirds are peaking—in terms of singing and other territorial behavior—in the valley floors of this region. Warbler singing slows down by the first week of June at lower elevations and by the first week of July at higher elevations. Learn to recognize which types of habitat the specific warbler species prefer. Yellow-winged warblers seek out partially cleared hillsides with locust trees interspersed among shrubs. Look for American redstarts among grapevines. These very active warblers snatch flies in midflight; they are nearly as quick and deft as hummingbirds. Go to the higher elevations, above 4,500 feet, to find black-throated blue warblers and Canadian warblers. On the grassy balds of Roan Mountain, at approximately 5,500 feet elevation, the dark-eyed junco and the veery are among the predominant species. On high-elevation grassy balds, you may find as many as 75 pairs of juncos per 100 acres. In the spruce-fir forest of the region's highest elevations, look for golden-crowned kinglets, pine siskins, red-breasted nuthatches and brown creepers.

From the summits of Roan Mountain and the other patriarchs of the southern Appalachians, you can stand along the roadway and see where the spring zone stops and the trees are still budding out, even as songbirds compete for territories in woodlands that have completely leafed out less than half a mile down the mountain. Over a period of weeks, you can "bird" the leading edge of the new spring season as it moves up the mountain. In addition, even after courtship song has stopped on the valley floor, it continues into July on the high grass balds of Roan Mountain. Many weeks after the cove hardwood forest at the foot of Roan Mountain has fallen silent, the bell-like song of the dark-eyed junco and the self-harmonizing, downward-spiraling call of the veery continue on the heath balds near the summit of Roan Mountain. In these unique mixing grounds of northern and southern species, you can walk down a mountain trail under the giant white flowers of Fraser magnolias while attempting to identify the jewel-like superstars, the tiny, agile warblers, up from the tropics, as well as the delicate, colorful wildflowers adorning the forest floor. On such a walk you will begin to grasp the concept of biodiversity and how many converging strands create a web of life both beautiful and resilient.

Hot Spots

Some of the best places to see warblers are in large blocks of old-growth hardwood forests, and as was mentioned in chapter 25, especially in **Great Smoky Mountains National Park.** By taking any of the hikes described in chapter 25, you will place yourself in prime warbler nesting habitat. But don't limit yourself to only old-growth forest in Great Smoky Mountains National Park. Moderately old-regrowth forest, as found in much of Great Smoky Mountains National Park and **Roan Mountain State Park** (chapters 25 and 30), will also attract warblers and the other songbirds of the region. Look and listen very closely along streams and watercourses. Try to join some of the naturalist-led bird walks offered by the Smoky Mountains Field School in late May (see chapter 67). Equally productive naturalist-led bird walks are offered by Roan Mountain State Park the first weekend of May. For information on the May Roan Mountain Naturalist's Weekend, call (423) 772-3303. An excellent guidebook for birding in both Great Smoky Mountains National Park and Roan Mountain State Park is *Birds of the Smokies,* by Fred J. Alsop III. Alsop has birded the park and surrounding area for more than 30 years and is a recognized authority.

28

Red-Cockaded Woodpeckers in the Pine Forest

The red-cockaded woodpecker has been called the snowy owl of the East. Just as the snowy owl coevolved with the Pacific Coast coniferous forest, so did the red-cockaded woodpecker coevolve with the longleaf pine (*Pinus palustris*) forest. Yet few people consider the longleaf pine forest to be in the same class as the old-growth forests of the Pacific Northwest; it is the least appreciated and least understood forest configuration in the region. The longleaf pine forest and associated grass savanna once dominated the landscape of the southeastern United States, stretching from Virginia to Texas. This forest community encompassed some 70 million acres, or 60 percent of the upland region of the coastal plain of the Southeast. The following impression was recorded in 1791 by William Bartram in *Travels through North and South Carolina, Georgia, etc.*: "We find ourselves on the entrance of a vast plain which extends west sixty or seventy miles … . This plain is mostly a forest of the great long-leaved pine, the earth covered with grass, interspersed with an infinite variety of herbaceous plants, and embellished with extensive sanannas, always green, sparkling with ponds of water."

The ecosystem described by Bartram may support well more than 100 species per square yard, making the longleaf pine natural community type the most biologically diverse in North America. It is no coincidence that the four areas containing the greatest diversity of floral species in the temperate zone of the world all occur in longleaf pine–wire grass savannas.

No other tree species could tolerate the excessive heat, extended drought, poor sandy soil and, uniquely, the sweeping fires that helped give the thick-barked, fire-insulated longleaf pine the competitive edge over the hardwood forest. So long as free-ranging fires, set either by lightning or Native Americans, occurred every two to seven years, the hot, sparse, nutrient-poor ecosystem and its coevolved tree species, the longleaf pine, could hold off the encroaching stunted hardwoods. When the colonists arrived in the eighteenth century, however, this forest more than any other became the focus of relentless commercialism. During the Age of Sail, the demand for tar, pitch and turpentine for waterproofing the hulls of oceangoing sailing vessels was insatiable. North Carolina had 1,500 turpentine distilleries by 1880 and produced one third of the world's turpentine. Its nickname, "The Tarheel State," is thought to have come from the ubiquitous tarred boot heel tracks that once led into every doorway and public place in North Carolina. Ships coming into the port of Wilmington often had to wait a week for a docking space. Such was the importance of the naval stores industry, generated at the expense of the longleaf pine forest. When the demand for tar and other naval stores diminished at the end of the nineteenth century, the longleaf pine forests were cut down for lumber. The dominant tree species in the region—in fact, the greatest single species–dominated forest in America—was nearly extirpated. Today fewer than 1,000 acres of virgin longleaf pines remain. Of the nine percent of the original forest still here, virtually all is regrowth. But, in spite of the abuse suffered by the longleaf pine forest of the region, it still dominates over all other forest community types, if only fire is allowed to play its natural role.

More and more, each unique biosphere is regarded as irreplaceable and intrinsically valuable. The fire ecosystem of the longleaf pine forest is coming to be recognized as the most dynamic, quickly regenerating, ecosystem in North America. Only a few days after a burn, new greenery sprouts up through blackened acres. Red-cockaded woodpeckers, chattering busily, are often seen "barking" trees even as fires smoulder nearby. The entire ecosystem is virtually a tinderbox, ready to be scoured clean of competition from the hardwood forest just hours after a driving rainstorm. Because the white sand topsoil is extremely permeable, rain simply percolates through nearly as quickly as it falls.

The Carolina Sandhills and coastal plain are a textbook example of an ecosystem evolving to fit a specialized environment. Since the longleaf pine forests are located within 100 miles of the coast, the Bermuda high-pressure ridges just off the coastline lock out any moisture-laden, low-pressure weather systems that might bring rain. The entire white sand–dominated region bakes in the sun for weeks. The coevolved partner of the longleaf pine, the turkey oak, is the only other tree species that flourishes in this heat. It has the remarkable ability to turn its leaves on edge, with the edges facing the sun, thus avoiding the peak hours of direct sun. When the Bermuda highs finally move off the Carolina coastline, the white sand of the Sandhills and coastal plains may be so hot that the rains of the first low-pressure cell to boil over the southern Appalachian mountains will actually evaporate in midair. The accompanying lightning storms are "invited" by the ecosystem to set fires.

For the naturalist who understands the unfairly named "pine barrens," there is no more beautiful sight than well-spaced, mature longleaf pines with their fire-blackened trunks and a ground cover of pine needle duff and wire grass *(Aristida stricta)*. While the groves of old-growth hardwood forest in Great Smoky Mountains National Park suggest great natural cathedrals where time stands still, here in the longleaf pine forest–wire grass savanna, one has a sense of standing in the middle of a huge, baited trap waiting to catch fire. Yet the wild creatures within this biosphere are perfectly adapted to the harsh, almost desert-like conditions that often occur here. There are many interesting interdependencies. The gopher tortoise is a keystone and a threatened species; more than 80 species of vertebrates and invertebrates depend on its burrows. Other uncommon species, such as the fox squirrel, the pine barrens tree frog, the northern pine snake and pixie moss, are present as well.

No species in this ecosystem is more genetically, behaviorally and organically linked to the longleaf pine forest than the red-cockaded woodpecker. This endangered species has come under tremendous scrutiny in recent years, and has the dubious distinction of being the most studied bird population in the world. The red-cockaded woodpecker, a docile little chatterbox, can live nowhere else but in mature longleaf pine forest. Once the hardwood forest begins to encroach on the longleaf pines, more aggressive woodpeckers, such as flickers, red-bellied woodpeckers and pileated woodpeckers, move and displace the red-cockaded woodpecker. There is great concern over losing the very symbol of the greatest single-species forest that America has ever possessed.

The best time of year to observe the red-cockaded woodpecker is during May and the first week or so of June, when the adult birds are actively working the mature longleaf pines in search of insects for their young. Unlike most other woodland species of birds, this species is very social and lives in clans numbering from two to nine birds. The nucleus is the pair of nesting adults, who are helped by an extended family of nonbreeding adult males. These helpers actually incubate eggs, bring food to the young, defend the territory claimed by the nesting pair and help create new nesting cavities. The clan occupies as many as a dozen cavities in a grove of mature longleaf pine trees. It is a most unusual social arrangement, a veritable model of social cooperation for the common good.

The red-cockaded woodpecker pecks cavities, rendering no harm, into the heartwood of a mature longleaf pine tree. The entrance to the nesting cavity is quite sticky with sap and pitch, which is thought to be a means of deterring predators such as the tree-climbing black rat snake. Red-cockaded woodpeckers will not use nesting cavities once the understory of shrubs and competing hardwoods becomes taller than 15 feet. It is easy to see that this woodpecker is just as dependent on fire as the pine forest itself. On the 45,000-acre Carolina Sandhills National Wildlife Refuge near McBee, South Carolina, between 10,000 and 15,000 acres are burned each year. The burn management plan is working. This large refuge now has 75 active pairs of red-cockaded woodpeckers. As controlled burning becomes more accepted as the way to preserve this important biosphere, the gene pool of the red-cockaded woodpecker is expected to enlarge and stabilize itself, along with the longleaf pine forest. Perhaps someday this unique forest community type will once again blanket much of the southeastern United States.

Weymouth Woods Sandhills Nature Preserve, 1 mile southeast of the town of Southern Pines, North Carolina, is reached by heading out of town on Connecticut Avenue (SR 2033). This 676-acre preserve offers no camping or recreational activities. It is dedicated entirely to protecting the ecosystem, and is actively burned. Miles of walking trails traverse both grass savanna and bog habitat. Some of the remnant old-growth longleaf pine forest here, as well on the nearby 165-acre Boyd tract, is between 250 and 400 years old. Many of these trees have turpentine scars dating back to the Age of Sail, when pitch and tar were harvested from these groves. This preserve offers an excellent classroom for schoolchildren to see nature's regenerative powers as green shoots appear only days after a fire has scorched clear the underbrush.

Nearby **Ft. Brag–Camp MacKall** possesses perhaps the most actively burned longleaf pine ecosystem anywhere, for it is regularly set afire by exploding artillery shells. As a result the diversity of herbaceous plant species here is considered remarkable, and is being studied and documented. This important military base is becoming known as an important biodiversity preserve as well. Although Ft. Bragg–Camp MacKall is a public military base, you should work with Erich L. Hoffman, the base naturalist. For information on gaining access to Ft. Bragg–Camp MacKall's longleaf pine ecosystem, call him at (910) 432-5325. Or write: Department of the Army Headquarters, XVIII Airborne Corps (DPWE attention: Rob Harris), AFZA-PW-DS, Ft. Bragg, NC 28307-5000.

A good example of fire-managed longleaf pine forest occurs in The Nature Conservancy's **Green Swamp Preserve.** To reach this site, which is open to the public, take NC 211 for 5.6 miles north of the little town of Supply, just southwest of Wilmington. Pull into the white sandy parking area next to the small pond. Look for the resident gator. On foot, follow the jeep trail that goes past The Nature Conservancy sign. In 100 feet, the trail forks; bear to the right. Follow the jeep trail through set-out longleaf pines for a quarter of a mile. Stay on the raised boardwalk trail through a classic pocosin thicket.

After emerging from the thicket, you will be standing in a classic longleaf–wire grass savanna. Continue straight ahead on the footpath, winding through the pines. In May and June look for pitcher plants as well as tiny Venus's-flytraps near the end of this grove of pines.

Another easily accessible longleaf pine ecosystem is located near the town of **Havelock,** just north of Morehead City, North Carolina. To reach this site, begin in Havelock at the intersection of US 70 and NC 101. Here, go west on Miller Boulevard. After 0.8 mile, at the railroad tracks, turn left onto Lake Road at the Exxon station/convenience store. From this point drive 6.7 miles, and turn right into an unmarked road. After 100 yards, pass a radio antenna. In a quarter mile you will enter **Millis Swamp Road Flatwoods.** Here trees with red-cockaded woodpecker nesting cavities are circled with blue paint. Look for pairs of bobwhite quail running down the sandy lane during the breeding season. Return to Lake Road and drive 0.9 mile, then continue straight on Nine Foot Road. In slightly over 1 more mile, turn right onto Millis Road and drive about 1.5 miles to **Millis Road Savanna.** This handsome longleaf pine forest is a variation on the pine–wire grass savanna, and is actually called a "wet pine flatwoods" ecosystem. Look for trees encircled with blue paint. Not all trees with nesting cavities are used by woodpeckers.

Yet another splendid example of longleaf pine habitat is found in South Carolina's **Wambaw Creek Wilderness.** Located in Francis Marion National Forest, this little gem of a wilderness area contains not only a classic longleaf pine flatwoods community but also limestone sinkholes, known as "karst topography," and is one of the best places to observe the red-cockaded woodpecker. Look for pine trees with double rings of white paint indicating woodpecker cavities. To reach this site, turn west at the blinking yellow light at the Texaco station/convenience store on US 17 at McClellanville, south of Georgetown. Go approximately 4 miles. Turn right at the brown National Forest sign that reads "Elmwood Hunt Camp." Proceed down this lane. You may wish to go to the U.S. Forest

Service office in McClellanville to get a copy of the Francis Marion National Forest map to help you explore this extremely productive region.

One more location for a longleaf pine ecosystem is **Santee Coastal WMA**, formerly the Santee Gun Club, in South Carolina. The drive into the refuge carries you through a burn-managed longleaf pine forest (see chapter 8). The **Cape Fear Museum** in downtown Wilmington, North Carolina, has an excellent exhibit on the longleaf pine forest. To reach the museum come into Wilmington on US 17 south, which turns into Market Street. The address of the museum is 814 Market Street. Wilmington has no bypass, and traffic can be hectic so plan any trip through Wilmington accordingly. You can call the museum at (910) 341-4350.

29

May Shorttakes

A Short Life for the Ancient Groves?

Chapter 25 points out that the virgin timber groves of the southern Appalachian Mountains preserve genetics that date back to the time of the original supercontinent, which broke up to form North America, Europe and Asia. The 100,000 acres of moist virgin forest in Great Smoky Mountains National Park have the eastern hemlock as a primary species. Yet the eastern hemlock's existence is now threatened by an aphid. A scenario similar to the demise of the American chestnut may unfold again. In case a short life is all that remains for the hemlocks within these 1,000-year-old groves, you should make a special effort to see them while they are still with us.

30

A Closer Look: Tennessee's Waves of Neotropical Migrants

Simon Thompson, an international birder and well-known birding authority in the Carolinas, recently wrote in the FENCE newsletter, "The Carolinas offer some of the finest birding in the country." Few would argue the veracity of his claim. Yet birders of the Carolinas who wish to explore new frontiers should look west to Tennessee. While birdwatchers of North and South Carolina take little notice of their common border and regularly hopscotch from North Carolina's Outer Banks, Lake Mattamuskeet and southern Appalachians, to South Carolina's superlative Lowcountry, Beidler Forest and Congaree National Monument, trips to their neighboring state to the west are few and far between. Most birders from the Carolinas, many of whom travel to exotic destinations such as Costa Rica, Belize or Alaska on a fairly regular basis, have never been on a birdwatching trip to Tennessee.

A comparison of the interiors of the Carolinas with Tennessee's interior reveals two very different environments in terms of disturbance at human hands. Chapter 24 points out that the coastal plain and piedmont of both North and South Carolina have been intensively farmed as well as logged and developed. In sharp contrast, Tennessee's interior has been altered far less. The reason is simple: Instead of the soil that blankets the interior of the Carolinas, Tennessee's interior is underlain by limestone. Intensive agriculture as well as pine plantations simply were not an option in many areas of eastern and central Tennessee. After the original forest was cut, this land could not be converted to farmland, because there was hardly enough soil to plow. Once regions like the Cumberland Plateau, the Highland Rim and the Central Basin

Hatchie National Wildlife Refuge

reforested themselves, they were essentially returned to their original condition. Scattered throughout the tens of thousands of acres of hardwood forest underlain by limestone are unusual geological features. Gorges, such as those of the Obed River and Savage Gulf; sandstone "rockhouses," such as those of Standing Stone State Rustic Park and Pickett State Rustic Park; the cedar glades south and east of Nashville and some of the most extraordinary karst topography in North America are just a few of the geological jewels in the relatively undisturbed interior of Tennessee. In addition, on Tennessee's western border is North America's greatest river, the Mississippi. Warblers and other neotropical migrants use all the large blocks of riverbottom hardwood forest here. Although some of these warblers are passing through on their way to northern breeding grounds, this area is also heavily used by nesting neotropical migrants, including the threatened cerulean warbler. All these features combine to make an exceedingly interesting landscape for the birder to explore.

For a birder who lives in an urban center such as Charlotte or Raleigh–Durham–Chapel Hill, a birding trip to
the Mississippi River offers a change of scene on the same
level as a trip to another country. Considered one of the
world's great rivers, the Mississippi adds an element of excitement and awe to this unique ecosystem. The Mississippi Flyway is one of the principal North American migratory routes
for neotropical migrants such as warblers, thrushes, vireos,
flycatchers and kites, not to mention waterfowl and shorebirds, headed for northern breeding grounds. The large areas
of old-growth hardwood forest contained within Tennessee's
Ft. Pillow State Park, Chickasaw NWR, Hatchie NWR and
Meeman Shelby State Park (chapters 2 and 3) form the core
area for the most important high-density nesting area for warblers in the North American interior. Hatchie NWR is considered by western Tennessee birders to be a warbler hotspot
during the spring migration from early to mid-May. For information on Hatchie NWR, call (901) 738-2296.

The forest bordering **Reelfoot Lake** (chapter 40) in the
northeast corner of Tennessee offers an oasis of rich habitat
for neotropical migrants moving up the Mississippi River corridor. An interesting bird walk here is the nature trail at the
Air Park Inn. To reach this location, proceed north out of
Tiptonville for 7.7 miles on TN 78. Turn right into the Air
Park Inn, park and walk to the north end of the parking lot,
where the nature trail begins. Another productive area here is
the **Walnut Log Road**. This dead-end, 2.5-mile road through
lowland forest is an ideal location for finding neotropical migrants. To reach the Walnut Log Road, proceed through the
little town of Samburg. Drive 5.4 miles north of Samburg,
then bear left on TN 157 north. Go 2.1 miles and turn left on
Walnut Log. After 0.9 mile, the road turns to gravel and enters a swampy ecosystem. Begin birding here. This road runs
another 2.4 miles, all of which is excellent warbler habitat. It
is also a very good place to call up barred owls at night.

Tennessee's waves of neotropical migrants know that even
urban settings may contain niches of productive songbird

habitat. Knoxville's **Sharp's Ridge** may be the best natural land bird "trap" in Tennessee, and warblers and other migrants are not deterred by the clutter humans have put there. If you can ignore the radio and TV towers standing along the spine of this ridge, you might be able to identify as many as 28 species of warblers in a short time during mid- to late May. Across from the TV antennae is a wooden observation platform where spring warblers and other migrants as well as fall raptors can be observed. Park at the observation deck or the small picnic area and walk the road, looking in the adjacent trees. Although this little park is not pristine, it is certainly productive. To reach Sharp's Ridge, stay on I-40 through the main part of Knoxville (as opposed to taking the bypass). Take US 441 north and proceed approximately 1.5 miles north. As you drive north on this busy street, you will notice a number of communication towers on a ridge looming prominently on the horizon several miles ahead. This ridge is your destination. Turn left on Ludlow, go 0.4 mile and bear to the right. Follow signs to Sharp's Ridge Park.

Another destination for observing neotropical migrants is the riverine ecosystem of the **Hiwassee River**. This clear, cold-water, gravel-bottomed river flows through a region that was once the heart of the Cherokee Nation. It is also one of the premier trout habitats in the eastern United States. If Hiwassee Dam is not releasing water, the river will be low and wadable, providing an excellent opportunity to turn over stones and observe tiny mayfly, caddis fly and stone fly nymphs. The upper end of this splendid river is sheltered by large hardwoods and provides cool and shade for nesting warblers as well as migrants passing through. The upper Hiwassee River is a place of great beauty.

To reach the Hiwassee River, proceed east on TN 40 out of Cleveland in the southeast corner of the state. This highway turns into US 64/74. Near the little town of Archville, head north on TN 315. At the town of Reliance, turn east and begin to follow the Hiwassee River Road toward the powerhouse. At Webb Brothers Texaco, cross the river. Here you

Norris Dam—Songbird Trail

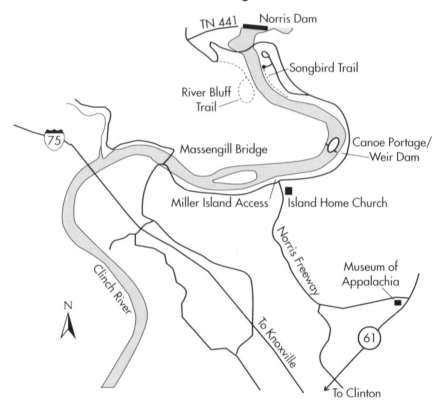

can pick up the John Muir Trail and proceed on foot. To continue up the river, after crossing the river turn right at The River–Medical Clinic. Follow signs to the powerhouse. Park in the numerous pullouts along the river and proceed on foot.

The forest below the Norris dam along the **Clinch River** is another destination for enjoying Tennessee's waves of neotropical migrants. This splendid limestone-based cold-water ecosystem is quite beautiful and illustrates that the marriage between nature and technology can be a happy one. Two trails, the Songbird Trail and the River Bluff Trail, wind through the forests below towering Norris Dam and regularly draw local birding groups.

To reach the birding trails take I-75 north out of Knoxville, Tennessee, to Exit 122 at Bethel and head north on TN 61.

Follow signs to Norris Dam on the Norris Freeway (TN 441). Just before TN 441 reaches the dam, take the turn that leads to the parking lot at the foot of the dam; this is where the Songbird Trail begins.

June

Notes

31

The World's Showiest Display of Purple Rhododendron

The great rhododendron centers of the world are cool places of great moisture year-round. Often such places have heavy snow cover in the winter. The world offers perfect environments for this truly cosmopolitan shrub in only a handful of locations. The greatest rhododendron center is western Yunan, in southwestern China, where 200 species of rhododendron can be found in a relatively small area. Here trunks of individual plants may be over 2 feet in diameter. Areas of the Himalayas, the Malay Peninsula, New Guinea, Burma and even the tropical woodlands of the East Indies are all rhododendron centers. Another world-renowned center is much closer to home. It too provides a perfect environment for this splendid shrub misnamed by the ancient Greeks, who called it the "rose tree." Indeed, no member of the rose family would ever be as extravagant as the rhododendron thickets, which can cover more than 500 acres or a whole mountainside.

The rhododendron is from a truly ancient order of plants. Its extravagance seems to represent an earlier age, when dragonflies had 3-foot wingspans and nature molded all things on a giant scale. To witness the Catawba, or purple, rhododendron bloom on eastern Tennessee and western North Carolina's Roan Mountain in a peak year is to understand, in an instant, the extravagance of that earlier age. The three-state region has the world's greatest, showiest display of purple rhododendron. It is completely natural and unmanipulated by human hands.

Although rhododendrons occur in all regions of the Appalachian range, the highest expression of this acidic soil–loving species is in the mountains. Here rhododendron thickets frequently cover entire mountainsides. Three species occur in the southern

Purple rhododendron—Craggy Gardens near Asheville, North Carolina.

Appalachians: purple rhododendron, rosebay rhododendron and the lesser-known Carolina rhododendron. The traditional date for the purple rhododendron blooms in the premier locations, Roan Mountain and Craggy Gardens, is June 20. The watermelon-colored blossom of the Catawba rhododendron can be seen in early to mid-May at lower elevations of the Blue Ridge Parkway. In areas where the purple rhododendron occurs in the piedmont of North Carolina, such as on Occoneechee Mountain in Eno River State Park, the date is pushed back even further. The rose-bay, or white rhododendron, which unlike the purple variety, favors forested streamcourses and has larger leaves and blossoms later in the summer, in late June and early July. The Carolina rhododendron, whose leaves resemble those of the mountain laurel, blossoms in mid-April. A primary location for the uncommon Carolina rhododendron is Chimney Rock Park, near Lake Lure.

More than 100,000 people may come to **Roan Mountain** to see the purple rhododendron blossoms in a good year. More than 600 acres are dominated by the 8- to 12-foot-tall shrubs. Two different concentrations of this species are present here. The lion's share of those who come to see the purple rhododendron drive to Carver's Gap, turn at the sign that reads "Cherokee National Forest–Roan Mountain Gardens" and then drive to the summit of the mountain. Here the Rhododendron Gardens offer gravel paths that wind through the maze of rhododendron shrubs. An information booth is located here during the peak of the blooming season.

The second concentration is located across from the Carver's Gap parking lot, in the more open grass bald system that continues for miles across Round Ball, Jane's Bald, all the way to the Cornelius Rex Parke plaque and far beyond. The more adventuresome blossom enthusiasts are usually drawn to the wild, moor-like heath bald, even though the rhododendron shrubs are less concentrated there than in the gardens. Here the **Appalachian Trail**, the world's longest continuous footpath, winds for miles across a meadow-like bald system peppered with clumps of rhododendrons. Remarkably, no less spectacular are the less abundant flame azaleas of Roan Mountain's grassy balds (see chapter 37). Their orange sherbet–colored flowers compete effectively for the throngs of buzzing pollinators as well as the eye of the blossom pilgrim. There are only a handful of these shrubs on the balds, and they are located primarily in the second half of the hike to the Cornelius Rex Parke plaque, which is mounted on a cluster of large boulders visible on the horizon, as you toil your way up the trail. Roughly two thirds of the way to the Parke plaque, the Appalachian Trail bears off to the left. Here, stay to the right and head for the large boulder cluster visible on the highest point of the grassy bald. Allow a third or a half day to reach the Cornelius Rex Parke plaque. You do not have to hike this far over the grass bald to see many rhododendron shrubs. In fact, most people stop on the first level of the grassy bald, at Round Bald.

Not every year produces the same fecundity of blossoms. In some years, much of the energy of the early growing season goes into new growth of stems and leaves, rather than the purple flowers. It is as if the Roan Mountain heath balds save their energy for great performances only. If you arrive only a few days after the traditional peak date of June 20, you may see dried clusters of shriveled blossoms and petals scattered over the ground. Timing is critical. There are people who live in the very shadow of the Roan who have never hit the display at its absolute peak. You might consider coming a week or so early both to avoid the crowds and to garner extra moments during this brief window of opportunity. A wind-driven rainstorm may crash the event on the big weekend. The weekend closest to June 20 sees Roan Mountain State Park hosting the Annual Rhododendron Festival.

In the event of an electrical storm, get off the high, exposed knobs and ridges at once. In fact get off the mountain altogether, and wait in your vehicle if you see the sky turning black and hear the thunder beginning to roll. Roan Mountain can be very dangerous during lightning storms, for it is a lightning rod. Take a jacket and a light raincoat even if the temperature is mild. Weather can change quickly here. Part of the charm of this mountain is that it plainly does not recognize the dominion of humans. Roan Mountain is located southeast of Johnson City, Tennessee, in the northeast corner of the state. The simplest way to get there is to take US 421 out of Boone, North Carolina, then turn onto US 321, and cross into Tennessee. At the little hamlet of Hampton, follow US 19E toward Linville, North Carolina. Follow signs to Roan Mountain State Park. Once inside the park, drive past the visitor's center and campground. Several miles beyond the visitor's center, you will pass through some private inholdings. Continue up the mountain until you reach Carver's Gap parking lot.

Another superb location for purple rhododendron is the well-named **Craggy Gardens,** on the Blue Ridge Parkway. To reach Craggy Gardens, take Business 70 out of Asheville for

Roan Mountain

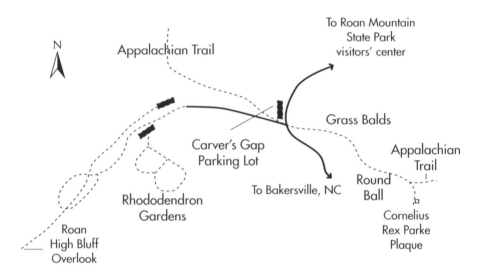

several miles headed east. Get on the Blue Ridge Parkway where it crosses Business 70. Head north toward the Folk Art Center for approximately 18 miles. Craggy Gardens has its own small visitor's center. For information on the progress of the Craggy Gardens rhododendron bloom, call the Folk Art Center at (704) 298-0495.

The rosebay rhododendron is just as handsome in bloom as the purple variety. This white-blossomed shrub is actually more prevalent than its famous cousin, and is the common rhododendron growing along streamcourses, creating thickets called "hells" by mountain folk. The rosebay has larger leaves and blossoms a little later, around the end of June and early July. Rosebay rhododendron can be seen along the **Roaring Fork Motor Nature Trail** near Gatlinburg, Tennessee (chapter 25). **Newfound Gap Road**, in Great Smoky Mountains National Park, is another good choice.

In your search for rhododendron, you should not ignore the splendid mountain laurel. Its delicate, trumpet-shaped blossoms hang in clusters along most trails in the southern Appalachians. The bloom of this shrub lasts from mid-June until well into the summer, depending on the elevation.

32

Colonial Nesters
Along the Coastline

Species of waterbirds such as royal terns, least terns, sandwich terns, common terns, gulls and black skimmers offer excellent opportunities to observe social behavior among birds. On lonely stretches of beach, natural islands and, more recently, "dredge spoil" islands created by dumped sand from dredging operations, these species can be found nesting in colonies. To watch the excitement, the behavioral eccentricities and social interaction in these colonies is a privilege that occurs in June, tapering off as July progresses. Renesting after a storm wrecks a colony is fairly common, and may cause a particular nesting community to remain intact well into July. But normally these large groups disperse fairly early in the summer.

Dredge spoil island colonial nesting sites are harder to reach than those on beaches, for a boat is necessary, but they are often the most dynamic of all. Colonial nesters benefit from the numerous spoil islands along the coastline. These islands first appeared in the 1920s and 1930s, as the Army Corps of Engineers began dredging the estuarine area of the Carolinas, and the colonial nesters immediately began to make use of them. Now there are 400 of them in North Carolina's coastal waters alone. They are helping to slow the overall decline in numbers of colonial nesting species. Species such as herring gulls, black-backed gulls, cattle egrets, glossy ibis and white ibis have all extended their range, both from the north and from the south, to include this region.

As you approach a dredge spoil island colonial nesting site, if you are downwind, you will know immediately if it is in use by the smell. Terns, gulls and pelicans occupy these habitat niches, often in dense concentrations. They are busy places, and during nesting season most are off-limits to people on foot, who might alarm the birds. Yet, from a boat, you can watch the various species transporting food for their young.

Dredge spoil islands evolve with age. A recently created dredge spoil island is essentially bare and unvegetated. Royal terns, sandwich terns and least terns find these islands most appealing. After five years, grasses appear and black skimmers, gull-billed terns, pelicans and laughing gulls begin nesting. After 30 years a dredge spoil island will support a youthful maritime forest, and will be primarily a heron-egret-ibis rookery, such as Battery Island or Bird Island in South Carolina's Lake Marion (chapter 33).

Hot Spots

Some nesting colonies, such as the one 100 yards east of the old Coast Guard station at the north end of **Pea Island** (chapter 57), are exclusively occupied by terns. In the roped-off sections of beach here, terns can be seen incubating eggs that rest directly on the sand. Here you can watch the most graceful in flight of all the colonial nesters, the least tern. This 9-inch sprite has wings like scyths, and is all swept-back lines and light-boned slimness—a veritable little wind dart. Least terns dip, dive and hover for hours at a time in the winds that blow ashore from the ocean, while their mates incubate the eggs. This is one of the most accessible colonial nesting sites.

Other colonies are far more diverse in composition. Just south of **New Inlet,** on Pea Island, is a much larger colonial nesting site. Here you can observe several very different species at once. On this lonely stretch of beach, with the houses of Rodanthe just visible far to the south, hundreds of black skimmers, common terns and others nest from just beyond the high tide line all the way to the grass tussocks of the dunes. Perhaps the best way to see all that transpires here is to bring a lawn chair, sit and watch from a discreet distance with binoculars. If a tern dives toward you, go no closer, for your presence is beginning to alter their behavior. These birds need no additional stress.

From your observation post you will see skimmers go past, often several flying together in such a perfect unison of wingbeats that they resemble a triple-decker oriental kite moving in the wind. A single skimmer may fly by in the peculiar head-down, hangdog attitude characteristic of this species. The male often carries a small fish in his beak, which he may offer to his mate, incubating on the bare sand. You will hear the slow "bark" of the black skimmer. You may see a head-bobbing shouting match break out among the oystercatchers, whose beaks are red as blood. They are tolerated by the other species here, for they are not known to eat chicks or eggs.

Before making the 1.5-mile hike down the beach from New Inlet, it is prudent to check with the naturalist at the Pea Island visitor's center to see if the colony has set up house-keeping for the summer. To reach the tern-skimmer nesting colony across from New Inlet, drive approximately 3.5 miles south of the Pea Island visitor's center. Park at the boating access marked "New Inlet." Walk across the sand dunes to the ocean, then down the beach (south) for approximately 1.5 miles. Once the colony is present, the roped-off section of beach, as well as terns and skimmers in flight and nesting on the sand, will be evident. This is one of the few secluded beaches where these birds can successfully raise young. Do not be intrusive. The phone number for the Pea Island visitor's center is (919) 987-2394.

Finally, a colony similar to the one near the old Coast Guard station is found just east of the **Cape Hatteras Public Campground's Loop C.** Go to Cape Point Public Campground located near Cape Hatteras lighthouse, and obtain permission from the ranger to park. Then proceed east from Loop C in the direction of the ocean. A footpath winds through the dunes. Immediately turn right on the four-wheel-drive sandy lane, and proceed 100 feet. Turn left here and proceed down another sandy four-wheel-drive lane through stunted juniper forest. This area comes alive with lightning bugs after dusk (chapter 42). Just before reaching the ocean, you will see roped-off areas where terns nest, on your left as you face the ocean.

By asking around at the Oregon Inlet Marina, just south of Nag's Head, North Carolina, on the north end of Oregon Inlet, you should be able to find a waterman, who will give a birder an unobtrusive look from a boat, at the colonial nesting sites in **Wanchese Channel.** A final dredge spoil island site is located in Charleston Harbor. **Crab Bank Island**, located off the mouth of Shem Creek in Mt. Pleasant, is too far offshore for a sensible canoeist to attempt. Call Coastal Expeditions, located nearby at Sullivan's Island, at (803) 884-7684 to organize a sea kayak trip to this site.

33

Lake Marion's Rookery

Two of the most dynamic waterbird nesting sites in the Carolinas are located on relatively accessible islands. One is Battery Island, in the mouth of the Cape Fear River near Southport. More than 6,000 pairs of white ibis nest here. The other is Bird Island, on South Carolina's Lake Marion, 40 miles north of Charleston.

Lakes Marion and Moultrie, still often referred to as "Cooper-Santee," have been famous since their construction in the early 1940s as productive fisheries. The reason for the success of these large impoundments is simple: No other lakes on the East Coast, with the possible exception of Florida's Lake Okeechobee, can match their fabulous food chain. Because these lakes are within 30 miles of the ocean, they have a climate similar to the semi-tropical Lowcountry around Charleston. A run of blue-backed herring migrates yearly up the Cooper River and is given access to the lakes by the Santee Fish Lift (see March Shorttakes). Few other significant east coast inland fisheries have direct links with the ocean. This is part of the reason for Moultrie and Marion's year-round fertility. A blue catfish caught in March 1991 in the Tail Race Canal below Lake Moultrie was only about 15 years old, yet weighed 109.4 pounds. This world-record catfish gives some idea of the amount of food available for all species in this food chain.

While canoeing the waters of Lake Marion, which has more diversity of habitat than the lower lake, Lake Moultrie, you will see wildlife of every description. A half day's paddle will place you in an environment that could support certain fish-eating species of dinosaurs today, if they could somehow be reintroduced. Other primitive species, such as alligator gar, bowfin or blackfish, alligator snapping turtles and American alligators, thrive here. Because all these species made it through the mass extinction, yet were contemporaries of the dinosaurs, it is reasonable to assume that the same environment supporting them today would support the "terrible lizards" as well.

As you paddle through these fertile waters, minnows will jump out of the water, fleeing the prow of the canoe at times. Schools of gar, carp and bowfin bask along the edges of millfoil beds and charge away explosively as your canoe approaches. Alligators are commonly seen swimming across arms of the lake or sunning on logs. Yellow slider turtles, a favorite food of gators, are common as well. The anhinga, or "snake bird," may pop its tiny head above the surface near your canoe as it swims with the rest of its body submerged. If you paddle close enough to alarm it, a large, reptilian-looking bird may erupt from the water and fly laboriously to a snag. Sometimes, if they are alarmed while drying themselves in the sun, they will plunge into the water like a snake or turtle and swim away underwater, rather than fly away.

The upper end of Lake Marion has a sunken baldcypress forest where there are nesting cavities created by the now extinct ivory-billed woodpeckers. Ospreys and bald eagles find good hunting here. Handsome cottonmouth moccasins grow fat. Always observant, great blue herons wade with an attentiveness bordering on paranoia, knowing full well that gators lie in wait for them with a patience that surpasses their own. In fact Lake Marion supports such an expansive population of great egrets, cattle egrets and great blue herons that these birds have learned to linger at boat landings and eat the scraps thrown to them by anglers cleaning catfish, crappies or stripers.

But of all the natural wonders within the environment formed by this sprawling half lake, half swamp, perhaps the most unusual one is Bird Island. This small island of several acres has become one of the most important waterbird rookeries in the three-state region. As mentioned in chapter 20, many biologists believe that this nesting colony was formed mostly by birds fleeing raccoon predation in a large rookery formerly located in Charleston Harbor. From a boat just offshore of the island at dusk, you can watch thousands of cattle egrets, great egrets, white ibis and other species converge on this spot to roost, joining those already there attending their young. Individual trees are filled with scores of ibis, and small groves hold hundreds. A great joyful clamor issues from this location, which seems tiny because of the vastness of the surrounding water. Since bad weather can blow up quickly on these large bodies of water, attempting to paddle a canoe across the 2 miles of open water to Bird Island is not recommended. To reach the island via a fishing guide or an ocean kayak is far safer. The trip may be possible in a 17-foot canoe with a 3-horsepower outboard motor, for the outboard can power the canoe against the wind should it blow up quickly, whereas the average paddler cannot. (See chapter 56.)

Hot Spots

A good place to start this trip to **Bird Island** is Santee State Park (chapter 20). From this park, follow SC 6 south, bearing north to cross the canal connecting Lake Marion and Lake Moultrie. After crossing the canal, head toward Pineville. Proceed into Eadytown and **Harry's Heart of the Lakes fish camp.** From Harry's, Bird Island is visible across several miles of water due north. Have someone at Harry's point it out to you. A reasonable fee is charged for launching a canoe or camping here.

In order to see the sunken baldcypress forest where the old ivory-billed woodpecker nesting cavities are, call Fisheagle Tours, which offers wildlife tours departing from Santee State Park, at (803) 854-4005.

Another interesting side trip is the **Dennis Wildlife Center** in nearby Boneau, on SC 52 between St. Stephen and Monck's Corner. The William Elliott Bird Egg Collection is considered remarkable on the East Coast.

34

The Dance of the Mayflies

Beneath the surface of a cold-water, gravel-bottomed brook or river of the southern Appalachian region exists a food chain and a micro-ecosystem as intricate and interconnected as the vast cove hardwood forest towering above it. Living among the pebbles, cobbles and boulders and within the aquatic vegetation are orders of streamborn insects that fill every niche in the aquatic environment. Indeed, this same scenario could be applied to every ecosystem, from intertidal sandy beaches on the coast, salt marsh mudflats and a roadside barrow pit full of rainwater and cattails, to a grassy highland bald on a mountaintop. Each of these environments constitutes a tiny universe teeming with specialized life-forms.

To comprehend the concept of the "micro-environment," you might start with the cold-water mountain stream, because the components are pleasant to handle and each has its own distinctive beauty. When you "graduate" from this thorough biodiversity appreciation curriculum, you will be able to see beauty and value in a sulfurous-smelling salt marsh mudflat; a cold-water, gravel-bottomed mountain brook and every micro- and macro-environment in between. For this "degree" you need no textbooks or diplomas. The only prerequisites are curiosity and owning your own time.

A mottled streambottom, with its orange, yellow and brown pebbles, some sporting black periwinkle snails, interacts constantly with sunlight passing through moving water. By picking up stones and carefully examining them, you will see the nymphal and larval forms of mayfly, caddis fly, stone fly, crane fly, water striders and others, some only a quarter inch long, others nearly an inch. Here these insects graze in different "pastures" on the riverbottom, as they grow toward emergence into the vast world just beyond the mirrored surface of the river. Some eat algae, some weave underwater nets to catch plankton, while still others are predators that feed on their fellows. All are eaten opportunistically by trout and other fish. The diversity among the aquatic, lakeborne and riverborne insects is astonishing. More than 1,200 species of caddis fly alone exist in the freshwater habitats of North America.

To find caddis fly larvae, pick up flat stones and look for ingeniously constructed cases, made of tiny bits of sand and rock cemented together. Other caddis flies build their houses, generally about a half inch in length, out of twigs. The head and front legs of the insect may be visible at the front of the case. No other order of aquatic insect has elevated architecture to this level. The horizontal winged adult caddis, which can be brown, tan or black, emerges to resemble a small moth.

Put an aquarium net several inches below medium-sized stones in moderately strong current. Gently turn the stones over and allow the current to wash whatever is living under the stone into the net. Be sure to place the stone back in its depression on the riverbed. You may catch a stone fly nymph, or it may cling to the underside of the rock. This handsome nymph measures less than an inch long in most mountain streams. Stone flies are the predominant aquatic insect in many of the free-flowing streams and brooks of Great Smoky Mountains National Park and the surrounding area. If you are fortunate enough to be present during a hatch of little yellow stone flies, the air above the stream will be filled with hundreds of flying sulfur-yellow insects. They are quite beautiful, both as nymphs and as adults.

Yet, in terms of beauty, both in the appearance of the vertical-winged adult flies, or "duns," as they ride on the surface of the river, and in their behavior as they "dance" in the corridor over the river, the mayfly is the undisputed queen of streamborne insects. As mayflies emerge from their nymph cases, they are vulnerable to trout. If you are present during a mayfly hatch, you will see trout "rises" as they pluck the emerging as well as fully emerged adults riding on the surface of the river. Perhaps the mayflies are able to sense their vulnerability to trout, for as soon as they are able, they rise almost magically into the corridor above the river.

The adult mayflies spend the next day, or perhaps two, among the leaves of the forest along the river. Here mayflies undergo one more molt, shedding the exoskeleton for the last time. Finally, on the day of their death the male mayflies emerge from the trees along the river's edge and form swarms over the tails of long pools in the river, where they "dance," by flying vertically and then dropping. As the males bounce over the river, the females emerge from the foliage, drawn to the spectacle of the bouncing swarms of males. When a female flies into the swarm, she is met at once by a male, who deposits his sperm on her egg sac. She then lights on the surface of the river and drops her fertilized eggs into the river. Her energy spent, she collapses on the water surface, losing her erect, dignified carriage, and floats helplessly on her side with splayed wings. Trout feed actively on the female mayflies at this time. Fly fishermen have artistic, hand-tied flies that imitate the nymph, the dun and the spinner, or spent-wing mayfly.

The morning after a heavy evening spinner fall, the side channels, backwaters and eddies of the river may hold the lifeless forms of thousands of spent wings the trout were unable to eat. The males never return to the river but die quickly in the riverine environment, caught in spiderwebs or captured by swallows, cedar waxwings or other predators. Each year a new generation of mayflies emerges from the riverbed, briefly and dimly experiences the vastness of the greater world and then dies. No species summarizes life's ephemerality more poignantly.

Hot Spots

All the streams of **Great Smoky Mountains National Park** have populations of aquatic insects. The little yellow stone fly is the predominant species here. Heavy hatches can occur on the **Little Pigeon River** along the road leading to the trailhead of Ramsay Cascade Trail (chapter 25). The **Doe River,** where it runs through Roan Mountain State Park, has an aquatic insect fauna similar to that of the Little Pigeon River.

The best location for seeing a mayfly hatch in the three-state region is the **South Fork of the Holston River.** This river has the ideal combination of perfect water pH, almost no sediment and minimum flows regulated by an oxygen-infusing weir dam. A limestone bedrock boosts the fertility of this river, unlike others in the region. Hatches peak in late May and June. Holston River is best experienced on low water, which is to say when the TVA is not releasing water to generate electricity. In fact, on high water the river becomes a raging torrent. If you are in the river, turning over stones or examining aquatic vegetation for nymphs, and the water begins to rise, get out immediately! To learn the generation schedule, which varies each day, call (800) 238-2264, press 4, then press 01 and then press the pound key. Phoning in this code will give you the number of generators releasing water on a particular day. The river is only wadable when zero generators are in operation. The TVA tends to release less water during the weekend, when demand for electricity is lower.

To reach this superlative river, take US 421 west out of Boone, North Carolina. Cross into Tennessee on crooked US 421 through Mountain City. Cross the green iron bridge over Holston Reservoir and, after traveling 6 miles, look carefully for a green sign on the south side of the highway for TVA South Holston Dam. Here turn left onto Emmett Road. Travel 0.4 mile, then bear right at a fork in the road. Drive 0.3 mile to the parking lot at the weir dam. If the weir happens to be in operation, watch it, for it is impressive. Continue another mile past the weir dam to catch the view from the top of Holston Dam. Look for black vultures riding the thermals that rise from the sun-heated rocky face of the dam. The mayfly fauna for 6 miles downstream from the weir dam is excellent most years, although it is cyclical. Nymphs live in the aquatic vegetation growing on the stones of the riverbottom as well as under the rocks. This river is unusual in that it contains a freshwater shrimp, or "scud," an important factor in its fertility. Scuds are approximately a quarter of an inch long. For a more detailed, illustrated explanation of aquatic insects, pick up a copy of *Hafele and Roederer's Aquatic Insects and Their Imitations* at any fly-fishing shop, such as the Holston Angler in Piney Flats, near Johnson City.

Two other nearby picturesque freestone (undammed) mountain streams also possess outstanding aquatic insect faunas. To reach **Beaverdam Creek,** backtrack out US 421, cross the green iron bridge over Holston Reservoir and continue east on US 421 toward Mountain City, Tennessee. Several miles after crossing over Holston Reservoir, enter the idyllic little village of Shady Valley. You may wish to return on the first Saturday of October for the Cranberry Festival, or to explore a very uncommon habitat niche in the southern Appalachians, a cranberry bog. This high elevation valley (2,800 feet) is a biodiversity hotspot. Endangered bog turtles, as well as nesting bobolink, are found in Shady Valley—one of the most southerly occurrences of a cranberry bog. Remarkably, here the brown thrasher nests on the ground, in the manner of thrashers in New England. To reach Beaverdam Creek, take TN 133 out of Shady Valley toward Damascus, Virginia. You will drive along Beaverdam Creek as you head to Backbone Rock Recreation Area. Just before entering Virginia, you will see a hole through a 100-foot-high rock wall, where TN 133 passes through it. Park either in the parking lot at Backbone Rock or in any of the turnouts along the river before reaching Backbone Rock. This section of Beaverdam Creek has caddis flies, little yellow stone flies, mayflies and the huge green drake mayfly, better known as the "coffin fly." Look for the nymphs of these insects under the rocks of the riverbed. If you are fortunate, during the month of June or the last two weeks of May you may catch a hatch. During such an event, the air over the river can be filled with as many as half a dozen different aquatic insect species. You will be lucky indeed if you witness the hatch of the uncommon green drake.

To see another splendid river rich in aquatic insect life, drive several more miles into **Damascus, Virginia.** This fetching little hamlet is unique for both its beauty and tranquillity, and because the Appalachian Trail goes down the main street of town. Here, through hikers pick up mail, eat the junk food they have fantasized about for days and enjoy a truly civilized town. Yet, even with all these assets, Damascus, Virginia, desperately needs friends who value its rare quietude. The forces of unbridled development are pushing hard for diverting a heavily traveled truck route through Damascus. Pick up VA 58 in Damascus, heading east, and drive approximately 5 miles until you see signs for the Virginia Creeper Trail (see chapter 16). **Whitetop Laurel Creek** is very similar to Beaverdam Creek in terms of its beauty and its aquatic fauna. Inspect the river for its tiny mayflies and stone flies as you enjoy the splendid Creeper foot and mountain bike trail.

One final destination with a superlative aquatic food chain is the sister river to the South Holston, the Clinch River below Norris Dam (see chapter 30). The Clinch River, like the South Holston, is a limestone stream with a newly installed oxygenating device in Norris Dam. The Clinch River may now be the most fertile cold-water river in the East. The Clinch is a large river with 300 cubic feet per second of water released during off-generation. Call (800) 238-2264, then hit 4, then 17, then the pound (#) key to get the water-release schedule for the Clinch River. The Clinch is only wadeable when zero generators are in operation. Mornings are the best time to catch the Clinch River when it can be waded. Due to generation schedules, the best access is often near Songbird Trail area.

35

June Shorttakes

Cerulean Warblers from the Blue Ridge Parkway

During the early weeks of June, you may be presented with an easy opportunity to observe the increasingly uncommon cerulean warbler. In the cool hours of the early morning, cerulean warbler males often call from the locusts and other hardwoods of the **Bull Creek Valley Overlook**. This overlook along the Blue Ridge Parkway is just north of the Folk Art Center, which is reached by getting on the Blue Ridge Parkway east of Asheville, from Business Route 70. Look for a blue-backed wood warbler (without any yellow plumage), which sings like the northern parula warbler. Do not fail to notice the many fine specimens of wild cherry trees along the parkway for a quarter of a mile in either direction from the Bull Creek Valley Overlook.

The Ospreys of Lakes Marion and Moultrie

One of the best locations for watching the osprey, or fisheagle, at work is the Lake Marion–Moultrie complex. Here fish are so plentiful that the ospreys have adopted a more relaxed fishing style. In less fertile waters, ospreys often dive into the water's surface much like brown pelicans. Yet the concussion from such an entry must be unpleasant for the osprey. The Lake Marion–Moultrie ospreys hover, as do other osprey, until they are certain of their prey. They drop swiftly until they are just above the water and then fly parallel to the surface so that they are able to simply pluck the fish from the lake without pausing. It is a far more civilized method of fishing because the ospreys know that if a fish is missed, another will soon be spotted. There is no need for the "kamikaze" technique here.

One of the best locations for seeing these birds is **Angel's Landing** on Lake Moultrie. Here nesting pairs of osprey claim many of the smaller baldcypress trees that grow in this shallow arm of the lower lake. Often several ospreys fish one area at the same time. After a fish is snatched from the water, the osprey quickly turns the fish in its talons so the head is facing forward, thus creating less aerodynamic friction. Watch closely with your binoculars or you will miss this deft footwork. This location provides the canoeist or the shore-bound observer with an excellent birding opportunity from mid-April when osprey pairs are nest-building, through mid-June when the adults are actively feeding their young. At Angel's Landing there is a nominal fee for launching a boat or canoe. Fisheagle Tours conducts naturalist-led tours on Lake Marion, the upper lake. Ospreys are always seen on these trips. Fisheagle Tours departs from Santee State Park boat ramp (see chapter 33).

To reach Angel's Landing head south from Columbia, South Carolina, on I-26. Take Exit 98 for Eutawville and then SC 6 through town. After approximately 4 miles outside Eutawville, turn north on SC 45 and drive over the diversion canal. One mile beyond the canal, take the blacktop road to the right to Angel's Landing. Al Jones, the proprietor of Angel's Landing will happily direct canoeists and ecotourists to interesting destinations. Angel's Landing, with showers and grills, is an excellent place to camp while enjoying the wildlife of Lakes Marion and Moultrie.

36

A Closer Look:
Mysterious World Travelers

Perhaps no creature inhabiting the coastal waters of the Carolinas stirs the imagination as much as the great sea turtles that ride the Gulf Stream up from the tropics. These world travelers range as far north as the British Isles, Newfoundland and Nova Scotia and as far south as Argentina in their wanderings. The placid sea turtles that navigate the coastline of the Carolinas symbolize, as well as any species living, how little we really understand the effect of currents, interacting climatic forces and the overall global equation. In truth, the sea turtles move in harmony with all these things.

Very little is known about the five species—the green, the Ridley, the loggerhead, the leatherback and the hawksbill—that travel through this maritime region. We know only that the hatchlings enter the ocean and that the females return as adults to deposit their eggs. In the case of the green turtle, the nesting females return to precisely the same beach where they themselves were hatched. The males are never seen again except randomly on the open ocean. Because tracking devices are quickly ruined by the corrosive action of saltwater, knowledge of where the sea turtles go and what they do during most of their lives is largely a void.

Yet the coastline of the Carolinas is a decidedly friendly place for the sea turtle community. Sea turtles nest primarily from North Carolina's Ocracoke Inlet southward. Although five of the world's eight marine turtles make use of these waters, almost all the nesting effort is made by the most common sea turtle in the region, the loggerhead, which weighs from 170 to 500 pounds and is the largest of the hardbacked sea turtles. In May, when the waters of the Atlantic are just beginning to warm, all five species arrive off

Turtle Project volunteers move a threatened loggerhead sea turtle nest.

North Carolina's coast to feed on jellyfish. At this time a flight down North Carolina's 26-mile-long Topsail Island can reveal as many as a dozen feeding leatherback turtles, even though it is thought there are fewer than 1,000 females worldwide. Also at this time, the turtle patrols swing into action, and no adversity keeps them from swiftly completing their appointed rounds. The first full moon in June is the peak laying time for loggerheads. Any morning from late May through August, however, can present the new turtle volunteer with his or her first look at the tractor tire–like tracks of a female that has emerged from the ocean, crawled beyond the high tide line and dug her nest. August is actually the busiest month of the turtle season, for this is when the greatest number of nests hatch, and nesting females are still coming ashore. By being involved with the turtle project in August, one may have the opportunity to see a turtle nest hatch as well as discover a new nest.

All along the coastline of the Carolinas is a network of turtle projects in which volunteers are assigned sections of beach to walk. Devoted, serious-minded volunteers working under licensed leaders, locate the nest sites, "adopt" nests and then stand guard over them as the incubation period nears its end in approximately 60 days. When the 2-inch-long baby turtles emerge from a nest and head pell-mell down the beach, the proud and excited "nest parents" are there to clear a path, making sure no tire tracks will entrap them, no predator will eat them before they reach the water and no floodlights from beachfront homes will confuse them. The hatchlings, which nearly always emerge at night, are guided to the surf by moonlight or by flashlights borne by volunteers. Because baby turtles instinctively head for any light, one of the most important duties of the volunteers is to persuade beachfront homeowners to extinguish floodlights when they hatch.

Many nests on some of the more altered beaches must be moved. A naturally overwashed and migrating beach has a gradual slope, but a beach anchored by planted sea oats, sand fences or a sea wall defies the ocean, and will always be short and steep. Most egg clutches deposited on such a beach must be moved, for they will be underwater at high tide and the developing baby turtles will drown inside their eggs. On some of the more developed beaches, relocation is required for as many as half of all new turtle nests.

Volunteers keep a logbook, recording the date each nest is found. After 55 days, hatching is imminent and the "nest-sitters" take up their vigil around nests that are ready.

An evening nest-sitting on the beach is always full of sensory impressions. The moon slowly sinks into the ocean. The lights of shrimp boats bob far offshore. Flashes of lightning pulse over the ocean in the distance. You may recognize members of the turtle patrol walking the lonely strand early in the morning and again at dusk. The turtle motifs on their T-shirts distinguish them from the other walkers at dawn. You might ask them how to get involved, for they welcome any interest. You may get to watch them carefully remove more than 100 white, golfball-sized eggs from a threatened nest site, carefully place them in a white pail and then rebury them in a safer place where the dunes gradually merge with the beach strand. With a success rate of nearly 80 percent on all nests, including relocated ones, the turtle project volunteers have a tremendous sense of purpose. The patrols are active until early October.

Virtually any stretch of coastline or barrier island beach south of North Carolina's Ocracoke Inlet can be visited by nesting sea turtles. Most of the coastline of the Carolinas is covered by the turtle patrols. Yet prospective volunteers need to know that working within the turtle project network is essential. There is ample space for any and all serious-minded volunteers who want to walk a beat of shoreline or protect nest sites. All efforts must be coordinated through licensed leaders. Untrained volunteers working on their own can actually frighten off turtles attempting to nest. Following is a list of phone numbers for some of the turtle projects covering the coastline of North and South Carolina.

- North Carolina state sea turtle coordinator Ruth Boettcher (pronounced "Betzer"): (919) 729-1359
- Pea Island, North Carolina: (919) 473-1131 (ask for Bonnie Strasser)
- Holden Beach, North Carolina, Turtle Project: (910) 842-7242
- Sunset Beach, North Carolina, Turtle Project: (910) 579-6559
- Ocean Isle, North Carolina, Turtle Project: (910) 579-9513
- Long Beach, North Carolina, Turtle Project: (910) 278-5518
- Hilton Head Island, South Carolina, Turtle Project: (803) 686-0904 (ask for Ed Drane)
- Pritchard's Island, South Carolina, Turtle Project: (803) 521-4110 or (803) 521-7432 (ask for Lynn Corliss)
- Edisto Beach, South Carolina, Turtle Project: (803) 869-3134 (ask for Glenda Chumney)
- Edisto Beach, South Carolina, State Park: (803) 869-2756 (ask for Rob Achenberg)
- Botany Bay Island: (803) 889-6432 (ask for Patty Kusmierski)

July

Notes

37

The American Chestnut:
Echoes in the Forest

An article appeared in the February 5, 1994, issue of *Science News* magazine that was widely discussed in scientific and ecological circles. Working from a plot of relic short-grass prairie in the American West, researchers proved that prairie with a large number of species of forbes, wild grasses and flowering herbs healed from disturbance more quickly than that with fewer species. Researcher and ecologist David Tilman was moved to say, "Biodiversity is really an insurance policy against catastrophe" upon completion of the experiment. Although this concept may seem unremarkable to the uninitiated, it proved conclusively what ecologists and botanists had long known: A natural system with rich biodiversity heals itself more quickly than a system with low biodiversity. Yet this experiment was conducted on a tragically huge scale, and with consequences understood only by those living individuals who knew the eastern hardwood forest when its keystone species was present.

The American chestnut was the keystone species of the eastern North American hardwood forest ecosystem, dominating a forested region that stretched from Mississippi to Maine, covering 1,500 miles north to south and 500 miles east to west. The first recorded reference to this forest monarch was made by the Spanish explorer de Soto as he passed through the southern Appalachian region in 1520: "Where there be mountains, there be chestnuts: they are somewhat smaller than the chestnuts of Spain." He was almost certainly referring to the small nuts, rather than the tree itself, for American chestnuts reached 120 feet in height, 13 feet in diameter, and 500 years of age. In fact they were so fast-growing and tolerated shade so well that they usually made up 25 percent of the forest, a percentage that climbed to 85 percent of the forest biomass on mountain slopes of the southern Appalachians.

In 1896, Charles Sprague Sargent said of the American chestnut in *Silva of North America:* "Always beautiful with its massive trunk, its compact round-topped head, and slender dark green leaves, in early summer, long after the flowers of its companions have disappeared, the Chestnut covers itself with great masses of spikes of yellow flowers, and is then the magnificent object in the sylvan landscape."

The narrow, round-topped upper canopy of the chestnut allowed a rich understory of hazel, holly, dogwoods, huckleberries, redbud, mountain laurel and rhododendron to grow. The chemical makeup of the soil and the water that seeped through the mat of living material was influenced by this keystone species. Wild game flourished in numbers we cannot grasp today, for the forest floor was literally black with the small chestnuts. Bears, turkeys, squirrels, humans and passenger pigeons all knew that this one-mast crop never failed. Because the flowers of this tree blossomed long after the last killing frost, the fruit of the chestnut was dependable, unlike the fickle mast-producing oaks and hickories of today's forest.

Bear populations were fabulous, for there were unlimited numbers of hibernating dens in dead chestnuts. Chestnut and corn, ground together, were used to make a delicious bread. Chestnut wood made roofing shingles and split-rail fences that refused to rot because of its high tannin content. To a large degree, a way of life for both human and beast revolved around this remarkable species.

But in the 1890s, disease-bearing Oriental chestnut nursery stock was imported into New York. By 1893 chestnut trees on Long Island were dying. By 1950 nearly every chestnut tree on the eastern seaboard was dead. And herein lies the crux of this story. In one of the greatest biodiversity resiliency demonstrations in recorded history, the chestnut-dominated hardwood forest became the oak-hickory forest. The enormous niche vacated by this keystone species was immediately filled by other species with similar habitat proclivities. The forest continued to hold soil, create rain and filter and oxygenate the air, as well as support its dependent fauna. With more than 130 species of trees in the southern Appalachians, other species with similar or overlapping habitat requirements were able to fill in and keep the forest biomass intact. Remarkably, the eastern hardwood forest continued to function smoothly, even with the keystone species gone. Many wildlife species declined in number but as far as is known, extinction of any regional, forest-dependent faunal species did not occur because of the chestnut blight.

If one were to take this same nightmare scenario and move it to the Alaskan forest, which has low species diversity, the outcome might be very different. Here seven species of trees—the Sitka spruce, white spruce, Alaskan birch, balsam poplar, western hemlock, black cottonwood and quaking aspen—constitute most of the Alaskan coastal and interior forest. If an important species such as the Sitka spruce or white spruce were to collapse, it is doubtful that any combination of the other six species could fill the empty niche successfully. The dependent wildlife species, as well as the forest itself, certainly would not recover from a blight as well as the species-rich southern Appalachian ecosystem did.

Yet the chestnut did not become extinct. The genetic blueprint for this species is still alive and well. Sprouts continue to issue from still-living underground root systems of old chestnut trees in the southern Appalachian region. Many reach a height of 30 feet, but then the blight attacks and kills the sprout. The *Endothia parasitica* fungus is a tough and determined foe of the chestnut. A few American chestnut trees survive within the original range along the eastern seaboard states. Included among these blight survivors are the Gault Tree in Ohio; the Floyd Tree in Virginia; "Yancey" in Yancey County, North Carolina, and "North Carolina Champ" in Wilkes County, North Carolina.

There is hope that the American chestnut will once again be an important part of the forest of the region, perhaps within the lifetime of persons living today, for the chestnut is a fast-growing tree. Deer and bear populations, currently light in the southern Appalachians because of the undependable nature of the yearly acorn crop, might make a fabulous comeback. Chestnuts, a nearly perfect food, could once again become an important cash crop for the southern Appalachian region. Chestnut is very close to brown rice in terms of nutrition, but brown rice contains 100 times as much sodium. Chestnuts contain three times as much protein as fat, unlike most other nuts. The small black nuts have no cholesterol and high amounts of the three essential amino acids required for daily nutrition. Chestnuts were once called "the grain that grows on a tree." On the Mediterranean island of Corsica, where chestnut trees are still cultivated, a 1-acre grove will produce 3,000 pounds of nuts per year. With the present price of $6 per pound for European chestnuts, the American chestnut forests region could provide a stable economic cash crop with no maintenance and no negative impact on the land.

Two recent developments have given renewed hope and enthusiasm to those who live in hopes of a eastern hardwood forest once again dominated by the American chestnut. The first is the natural evolution of a less virulent, or "hypovirulent," strain of Endothia. Some trees in Connecticut were inoculated with hypovirulent Endothia 10 years ago and appear to have some degree of blight resistance. In essence, the blight disease itself has a disease, which weakens it. In recent years across the region, chestnut sprouts have been growing with a robustness not seen before, perhaps due to this weakening of the blight disease.

Another glimmer of hope comes from work done at the University of Minnesota and at The Research Farm of the American Chestnut Foundation in Meadowview, Virginia, just north of Abingdon. Here American chestnut stock has been hybridized with the blight-resistant Chinese chestnut. By "backcrossing" the blight-resistant hybrid with pure American chestnut stock for three generations, a blight-resistant American chestnut may result. For more information on this research, as well as on where to purchase seedlings, call the American Chestnut Foundation at (802) 447-0110.

A final strategy being tried at certain clear-cut sites in North Carolina's Pisgah National Forest is the removal of all competing young trees of other species, in order that young chestnut sprouts can live long enough for the blight disease itself to be attacked by the pathogen that weakens it, thus rendering the blight virus too weak to kill the trees. Yet for every step forward, humankind seems doomed to take two backward. In 1975 a grower of Asian chestnuts in Georgia once again brought in Asian nursery stock without inspection or quarantine, thus introducing the Oriental chestnut gall wasp to America. The gall wasp now attacks both the introduced

Asian chestnut trees and the American chestnut sprouts.

Many people have never known the American chestnut. To them the eastern hardwood forest is fabulously rich and diverse. Yet it is only a shadow of what it was, without its keystone species. The oak-hickory forest we know today could lose another keystone species, the oak, with the gypsy moth encroaching. Widespread across Europe and Asia, the gypsy moth was introduced by humans to the northeastern United States in 1868. The caterpillars, or larval form of this moth, defoliate oak trees, thereby killing them. The gypsy moth has spread as far south as Virginia's Shenandoah Valley. The oak-hickory forest may become a shadow of a shadow, and so on, until biodiversity is reduced to a myth.

> *Poem of Preservation and Praise for the*
> *Hemlock/Canadice Watershed*
> —Stephen Lewandowski

Here is the land where trees have a vote.
Watch how they are cast. White pine votes for clean air.
Black willow votes for water. Young poplars loitering in a crowd
Vote for a flowing spring. Tribes of chestnut and elm
Are sadly diminished: Their once great pluralities
Silent.
Shagbark hickory votes in a hail of nuts.
Sugar maple and black cherry cast a sweet ballot.
At the marsh edge beech, birch, maple and ash
Gather to discuss issues. Scotch pine plantations vote
In a block like a union. Here and there lonely idealistic hemlocks
Hang against a shady bank still voting against gravity
Again this spring with flower, leaf, root, branch and bole,
Trees vote unanimously to bask in sunshine,
To hold soil and drink water. And to return us breath.

Hot Spots Learn to recognize the oblong, 5- to 9-inch, toothed leaves with long points on the ends. The Audubon Society Field Guide to North American Trees is useful for this purpose. The most striking field marks are the teeth along the edges of the leaf blade and the parallel veins. The sprouts that carry them are fairly common throughout the mountainous region of western North Carolina and eastern Tennessee. Some of the sprouts have reached heights of 30 feet, and can be 4 to 6 inches in diameter.

Some chestnut sprouts are reaching the forest canopy now, in **Great Smoky Mountains National Park** and in other areas. Some of the sprouts are producing chestnuts before the individual trees are killed by the blight fungus. Nature may be working out this biodiversity impediment, cleaning up the mess caused when humans imported this foreign pest, to which native species had no immunity. Look along the ridge of **Holston Mountain** near Holston Lake (chapter 19), for the American chestnut. To get there, take TN 91 from the east side of Elizabethton, Tennessee, toward Shady Valley. After passing A. D. Fletcher's Amoco, drive 1.2 miles until you reach the sign for Blue Hole–Low Gap. Turn left onto a blacktop road, which turns to gravel after 0.6 mile, and travel for 5.2 miles. Pass a red and white radio tower on the right. Begin looking closely for the distinctive leaves of the American chestnut seedlings along the side of the road. In 0.4 mile you will reach the FAA Airplane Communications tower; park here. Look next to the telephone pole with transformer near the gate. This American chestnut tree is 40 feet tall. The blight has killed one stem of this tree but two others are alive and healthy. Continue on foot a quarter mile toward the television relay station at the end of the uphill gravel road. Under the power line that goes to the station are many dozens of healthy American chestnut sprouts, many of which are 20 feet tall. Flame azalea, in both yellow and orange sherbet, grows here as well.

Unhappily in June 1996, maintenance crews cut down the 40-foot chestnut next to the telephone pole, as well as most of the sprouts under the power line. Yet the sprouts will come back quickly. There is a second, smaller chestnut 10 feet beyond the stump of the 40-foot tree, which apparently did not threaten the power pole.

38

Relic and Disjunct Species and Ecosystems

"Landscape-level ecology," an increasingly popular concept, means viewing a forest, a seashore or a prairie not as a single monolithic block, but rather as a mosaic of interacting environments. Some of the pieces of this mosaic are specialized ecosystems that have evolved to meet specific, regional environmental factors such as extreme weather or fire. Within a large region such as the southern Appalachians, there may be "break points" where northern and southern species terminate their range or even overlap. In fact a large ecosystem such as the southern Appalachians might be considered a living museum of natural history, for some of the most interesting pieces of this vast mosaic are relic species and ecosystems left behind by warm epochs as well as the ice ages, and disjunct species and communities existing far outside their core areas.

Relic and disjunct ecosystems and species are, most simply stated, "out of place." The New England cottontail rabbit, the northern flying squirrel and the northern shrew are all examples of disjunct species continuing to survive in a relic ecosystem, the spruce-fir forest. This type of forest configuration is found in western North Carolina and eastern Tennessee on Mt. Mitchell, Clingman's Dome, Roan Mountain and Unaka Mountain. Neither the spruce-fir forest nor the animals mentioned can escape from their out-of-place location. The spruce-fir forest and all its dependent faunal species would be more centrally located in central Ontario, Canada. But this island of spruce-fir forest is unable to transport itself over the thousands of miles of hardwood forest that claims and resolutely defends much of the territory between eastern Tennessee and western North Carolina and central Ontario.

Shrubs and wildflowers are often left behind after epochs of cold weather. The grassy balds of Roan Mountain provide a perfect example: Here more than 300 species of wildflowers and shrubs flourish, among them many relic northern species (see chapter 22). Bear in mind that the raven, another northern species, lives on Roan Mountain and in other islands of spruce-fir forest, but it is not considered a relic or disjunct because it stays by choice.

How did the spruce-fir forest get to the southern Appalachians? The glaciers so transformed the weather of the higher elevations of the region that in places it was subarctic, even though the ice sheets stopped in New York and Pennsylvania. The spruce-fir forest was able to "outcompete" the southern hardwood forest, for it was coevolved and genetically tailored to fit this brutally cold, harsh weather. The spruce-fir "army," in its blue uniforms, invaded the south at the head of the glaciers. When the glaciers retreated 10,000 years ago, the spruce-fir forest was unable to hold its territory in the "war between the forests." The gray-barked southern hardwood forest took the sunlight away from the northern invaders everywhere except above 5,500 feet, where the spruce-fir trees are held prisoner. Yet even today, the "front lines" between the hardwood forest of the higher slopes of Roan Mountain and the spruce-fir forest of the summit "seesaw" back and forth. A few mild winters will see hardwood species such as the yellow birch, yellow buckeye and mountain ash encroach hundreds of yards into the dark spruce-fir forest, which in turn will reclaim this territory as soon as a cold winter kills the seedlings of the hardwoods. It is an old story.

Hot Spots

The last great glaciation left behind many relic species and tiny ecosystems that gamely fight off encroaching indigenous species and systems. The largest, most robust relic ecosystem in the region is the spruce-fir forest mentioned; yet hundreds of miles away from the spruce-fir strongholds on Roan Mountain and Mt. Mitchell, on the edge of the coastal plain near Cary, North Carolina, south of Raleigh, a tiny hemlock forest survives within the southern hardwood forest on a cool, well-shaded, north-facing slope of a ravine. In Cary's

Hemlock Bluffs City Park, fewer than a dozen of the hemlocks are large, for most were cut down or dug up and transplanted. Still, this little community of evergreens survives and produces new seeds yearly, left over from a much colder period when hemlocks were common across the piedmont of North Carolina.

In nearby **Eno River State Park,** near Durham, relic communities of mountain laurel and Catawba rhododendron are able to survive in moist, cool, shaded pockets because their genetic material makes them the fittest in this micro-environment. Like the hemlocks of Cary's Hemlock Bluffs Park, this community of laurel and rhododendron are survivors from a time when these two species were found in most cool, shaded, rocky, thin-soiled environments across the now temperate North Carolina piedmont.

To reach the rhododendron thickets of Eno River's **Occoneechee Mountain,** take Churton Street north through Hillsborough, North Carolina. Turn left on King Street, passing the Colonial Inn, and turn left on Nash Street, which becomes Dimmock's Mill. Turn left on Allison Street, cross the Eno River and drive 100 feet and park on the right. Walk on the footpath 0.75 mile to the Bluffs of Occoneechee Mountain. Many mountain laurel bushes can also be seen along the **Pump Station Trail** of Eno River State Park.

Some relics and disjuncts in the region, however, are left over from warmer epochs. Near **Highlands, North Carolina,** southwest of Asheville, more than 100 waterfalls over 50 feet high are found. The tiny "spray cliff" ecosystems behind and adjacent to these waterfalls provide unique micro-environments where tropical disjuncts further enrich biodiversity composition. Here is found the vitalis fern, a critically globally endangered species and Caribbean disjunct located nowhere else in North America except behind **School House Falls,** in a stunning example of a disjunct far, far from home. These Transylvania County waterfalls are home to other disjunct species such as the filmy fern, northern beech fern (an Alaska disjunct), club mosses and the lampshade spider. The southern

Appalachian spray cliff–waterfall micro-ecosystems form a "Noah's ark" for five tropical ferns and 30 species of tropical liverworts and mosses.

Sufficient rainfall is essential to maintaining the spray cliff environment. Because reduced forest biomass means reduced rainfall, the existence of these tropical disjuncts depends upon a vast, uncompromised, rain-producing forest ecosystem. Some of the southern escarpments near Highlands, North Carolina, receive 90 to 110 inches of rain per year, making them the wettest places east of Washington state's Olympic Peninsula. The "Land of Waterfalls," Transylvania County, North Carolina, lies on either side of US 64, which winds between Brevard and Highlands.

In addition to northern and Caribbean disjuncts, a prairie component exists in the region. Within the barrens of **Buck Creek Serpentine** in Clay County, North Carolina's **Nantahala National Forest** is a plant community with a strong floral kinship to the midwestern prairies.

The Nature Conservancy has recently purchased a small plot of land 25 miles south of Charlotte, a fragment of one of the world's rarest ecosystems: piedmont North Carolina prairie. This 11.6-acre floral ecosystem is one of the few remaining pieces of an extensive prairie that once covered parts of piedmont North and South Carolina. This fire-dependent eastern prairie was kept open by grazing bison and elk, both of which were extirpated by the time of the American Revolution. The prairie ecosystem was able to flourish in the heart of the piedmont hardwood forest because of the presence of poorly drained, rocky soil, which trees could not utilize, thus allowing the colonizing of prairie grasses and plants such as the disjunct Schweinitz's sunflower.

Another area with a strong prairie disjunct community is the cedar glade area of middle **Tennessee's central basin.** Here soils developed from cherty limestone were quite acidic compared to others of the region. The acid soils, the exposed limestone and the associated gravelly glades together kept the area from becoming heavily forested, in much the same manner that the piedmont prairie of the Carolinas was kept open. No doubt fire and the grazing of large herbivorous mammals also played a role. These small, scattered, middle Tennessee prairies were once physically connected to the vast tall- and short-grass prairies of the Midwest and northern plains. Both of these huge, sprawling grass ecosystems have been plowed under and turned into the corn belt and the grain belt. Yet, like the blighted American chestnut, the genetic material for many species of the grass prairies is still alive and well, preserved in disjunct communities as well as a few undisturbed plots of prairie grasslands.

Midwestern prairie disjuncts are well represented in the middle Tennessee cedar glades among grass, sedge and forb communities. In addition to a healthy wildflower fauna that represents the regional indigenous species, the cedar glades has the most diverse prairie disjunct wildflower community in the three-state region. Here are such species as the prairie coneflower, the rough blazing star, the endemic Nashville mustard and the Tennessee coneflower, which is found nowhere else but in a three-county area of middle Tennessee. Here one also finds the remarkable Missouri evening primrose, whose core range is between Missouri and Texas. This flowering herb, which slowly springs open in the weak light of early evening, is found in the cedar glades near Murfreesboro, Tennessee.

Middle Tennessee's cedar glade region has, as its geographical center, the town of Murfreesboro. **Cedars of Lebanon State Park,** approximately 20 miles north of Murfreesboro on TN 231, contains many cedar glades. The wildflowers here blossom from May through September. To see one of the extremely rare Tennessee coneflower communities, go to the Bryant Grove Unit of **Long Hunter State Park,** just east of Nashville, where coneflowers have been planted on the roadside. Another coneflower population near Cedars of Lebanon State Park is the **Vesta Glade** coneflower population, one of the largest and most robust populations. Call (615) 532-0431 and ask for Bryan Brown, who will give you directions to this location. In some cases flower enthusiasts must be accompanied by Tennessee Natural Heritage Foundation or Nature Conservancy personnel, for coneflowers must be protected from poachers. Some locations are not readily given out.

Another ecosystem with a strong prairie disjunct community is Tennessee's grassy bends of the Mississippi River. This habitat niche benefits both from windborne seeds from remnant prairie ecosystems to the west and from floodborne seeds carried downstream from the upper Midwest by the Mississippi River. The grassy bend ecosystem of Nebraska Point in **Chickasaw NWR** (chapter 3), is being inventoried by botanists.

Remarkably, there is even a small African disjunct community on **Bull Island** in South Carolina's **Cape Romaine NWR** (chapter 69). Before 1989, when Hurricane Hugo essentially deforested this island, much of its interior was shaded by live oak and palmetto palm. After Hugo, most of this semitropical island was converted to open barrens where only heat-tolerant species could survive. Almost immediately, seeds and spores carried from Africa by Hugo germinated and began to colonize.

39

High Arctic Nesters
on the Outer Banks

Einstein need not have looked to deep space or equations on the chalkboard for proof that time is relative. He could have come to the beaches and mudflats of Pea Island and Hatteras Island, where the behavior of shorebirds would have given him all the verification he needed. Late July may be the dog days of summer to vacationing families on the East Coast, but for certain high Canadian arctic nesting species of shorebirds it marks a critical point in one of the most remarkable of global migrations.

By the last week of July, shorebird species such as the red knot, whimbrel, semi-palmated sandpiper, white-rumped sandpiper, stilt sandpiper and Hudsonian godwit have already flown up from Argentina and southern South America to the Canadian arctic, paired off, produced broods and are a third of the way back to Argentina. For these species the hot, lethargy-filled days of late July are both precious and numbered.

To the high arctic breeding shorebirds, Pea Island, Hatteras Island and Cape Hatteras are hallowed ground. Sandy Cape Hatteras protrudes 20 miles out into the Atlantic and is apparently unique even to these world travelers. In contrast to the densities of migrating shorebirds here in late July, noted birding locations such as Huntington Beach State Park, South Carolina, are nearly devoid of these species at this time.

On North Carolina's Outer Banks, the migrants pause to rest, feed and replenish fat stores, even as their children in the Canadian arctic prepare for their first global migration, instructed only by information encoded in their genetic material. It is thought that these adult shorebirds leave the arctic well in advance of their young so that they will not be in competition with them for the limited protein there. For whatever reason, the adults arrive on the Outer Banks in their drab winter plumage many weeks in advance of the birds of the year. The fall migration down the Atlantic Coast to the southern wintering grounds is a drawn-out affair. It begins in late July and may continue, in dribs and drabs, through late November, as different groups of shorebirds work their way south. In contrast, the spring migration of shorebirds headed north, dressed in courtship colors, is short and sweet, beginning in early May and essentially over by the end of May.

Hot Spots

The behavior of the vanguard of the high arctic nesters when they arrive in late July differs from that of the local birds. As you walk the nature trail on the west side of **North Pond,** across from the **Pea Island** visitor's center, you will see ospreys, snowy egrets, oystercatchers, white ibis, tricolor herons and local passerine species. The reverie of the local birds is palpable compared to the frantic behavior of the migrants. All along the exposed shorelines of **North Pond** and **South Pond of Pea Island,** the saltwater pond at **Cape Point** and the large freshwater pond at **Bodie Island** in front of the lighthouse, the high arctic breeders probe the aromatic mudflats in search of tiny crustaceans, insects, mollusks, worms and vegetable matter. Meanwhile, across NC 12 on the beach strand, the legs of hundreds of other frantically feeding shorebirds move in a blur as they chase the waves, probing deeply into the wet sand with their bills. Within every 100 yards of beach not occupied by sunbathers, swimmers or strollers, flocks of shorebirds work the sand for tiny isopods and marine invertebrates. Farther south, on the deserted beaches of **Hatteras Island,** many hundreds of semi-palmated sandpipers, willets and whimbrels per mile glean every available bit of protein from the wet sand. Be sure to search both beaches, as well as the freshwater ponds, to see the full complement of early migrating shorebirds. Tidal flats and inlets can be productive too.

Even though all the migrating shorebirds are in their drab winter colors in late July, certain species, such as greater and lesser yellowlegs, willet and dowitchers, are unmistakable. The whimbrel, with its long, downward-curving bill, looks like a mosquito from hell as it skims along just over the surf after being flushed from the beach. This is a challenging but interesting time to learn how to differentiate the many species of sandpipers collectively referred to as "peeps." It is best to walk down the beach in search of high arctic breeders at low tide, for the hard sand at this time is much easier to walk on. Look for pullouts or parking lots with few cars on Pea Island and **Hatteras Island.** You may have an entire undisturbed beach to yourself.

All summer long, until Labor Day, the Pea Island visitor's center offers bird walks at 9:00 A.M. on Tuesday, Wednesday, Thursday and Friday. After Labor Day, the bird walks are on Saturday morning only. To reach the Pea Island visitor's center, take NC 12 south from Nag's Head across the Oregon Inlet Bridge. Continue south to the visitor's center; North Pond is directly behind it. South Pond is off-limits to birders. To reach the Bodie Island lighthouse freshwater pond, turn into the Bodie Island visitor's center just before crossing the Oregon Inlet Bridge. To reach the ponds at Cape Hatteras Point, follow signs to Cape Hatteras Lighthouse and Campground, approximately 40 miles south of the Pea Island visitor's center. Follow signs to the Cape Point Campground, but drive 50 feet past the campground entrance, park on the left side of the road and walk toward the ocean on the four-wheel-drive sandy road. The large pond is on the right, 100 yards before reaching the ocean.

A Birder's Guide to Coastal North Carolina, by John Fussell III, is the definitive guide to birding the Outer Banks and describes many additional side trips in this region.

Interesting floral events take place on Pea Island and in the Cape Hatteras area during the last week of July. Look for gerardia, the rust-colored flowers with yellow-tipped petals, along the road. The arrowleaf morning glories are at their peak then as well, and are much in evidence between the district office and the Cape Hatteras Public Campground. In the marsh immediately behind Pea Island visitor's center, colorful marsh mallows are peaking during this week.

Three years ago the Park Service began allowing pedestrians to walk to the top of Cape Hatteras Lighthouse once again. The walk to the top platform is equivalent to walking to the top of a 20-story building, but the view is worth it. There you can see the unique composite of ocean, barrier island, salt marsh and brackish water sound ecosystems, which all converge here. The Cape Hatteras Lighthouse is open from 9:30 A.M. until 4:00 P.M. On crowded days during the summer, 45 people are allowed to walk up at a time.

Mosquitos can be fierce on the Outer Banks on calm, windless days. Wear light-colored, long-sleeved cotton shirts and pants. Carry bug repellent for your hands, wrists, face and neck.

40

Midsummer Events
Along the Mississippi

During July, the Mississippi River offers the ecotourist several interesting spectacles. You may want to combine these events with a canoe exploration of the Mississippi River environment (see chapter 51). The premier floral event in the Reelfoot Lake ecosystem, located several miles east of the Mississippi River in northwestern Tennessee, is the annual blossoming of the American water lotus. These huge yellow blossoms fill up some coves and shorelines of the lake. They are actually an indication of the reclamation of this long, shallow, earthquake-created depression by the surrounding landscape. The filling of Reelfoot Lake with sediment would normally be a natural process, but it is taking place at an accelerated pace because of regional agricultural practices and the cutting down of the buffering forest that once surrounded the lake. The flourishing of the American water lotus, pickerel weed, spatterdock, fragrant water lilies, rose mallows and other species that thrive in shallow water is actually part of the natural process of the reclaiming of all shallow lakes by the surrounding landscape. Reelfoot presently has 13,000 acres of water and an average depth of 5.2 feet. Although it is still Tennessee's largest natural lake, it was twice its present size 50 years ago. This filling may diminish the lake's water pool, but it benefits wildlife in many ways. The shallow, vegetation-filled lake produces not only game fish but also "rough" fish species such as carp and gar, which are easy prey for the large overwintering bald eagle population. In addition, the shallow-water ecosystem provides ideal habitat for the large puddle duck and goose populations that winter here.

A blossom of Reelfoot Lake's American water lotus.

Hot Spots

The yellow blossoms of Reelfoot Lake's American water lotus can be 6 to 10 inches in diameter. These striking blossoms, as well as the rose mallows that bloom concurrently in the wetlands adjacent to the lake, constitute a floral event best observed from a canoe. If your timing is right, you will see acres of yellow blossoms in some areas of the lake. The week of July 16 is the peak of the yellow blossoms. Call (901) 253-9652 to check on the progress of the bloom.

Begin this trip with a visit to the **Reelfoot Lake's visitor's center,** reached by taking TN 21/22 east out of Tiptonville. To find the greatest profusion of yellow blossoms, continue east on TN 22 to the little town of **Samburg.** Locate The Pier restaurant, which stands at the edge of the lake. If your timing is right, the arm of the lake immediately behind the main lake will be filled with yellow blossoms. Buy an inexpensive daily-use pass for the lake at the restaurant-motel complex and launch your canoe at the little dock next to the restaurant.

Paddle north, following the shoreline across acres of blossoms, for approximately one half mile. Look for a cut through to another large bay of Reelfoot Lake. Paddle through the cut and explore this large section of the lake, looking for large family groups of purple martins massed in the tops of baldcypress trees. Be careful when paddling under overhanging limbs; cottonmouth moccasins are part of this ecosystem, and one could drop into your canoe. Preclude the occurrence of this unhappy but spectacular event by being observant. There are no alligators here, although both French and Spanish explorers cited them as present all the way north to southern Illinois. Ecotourists may wish to rent one of the small, comfortable cabins by the night at Boyette's in Tiptonville, Tennessee.

Just west of Reelfoot, the area around **Island 13** of the Mississippi River hosts an interesting avian event. Here, in mid-July, the Mississippi kites are feeding very actively, putting on fat for their migration to the tropics for the winter. These birds are strictly summer residents and will be gone by mid-September. During the time of the yellow blossoms on Reelfoot Lake, the Mississippi kites are often found in large groups; sometimes as many as 100 can be seen working a dragonfly hotspot. The area around Island 13 is one of the premier locations to see these consummate fliers.

The principal food of this species is the dragonfly, and kites often drop hundreds of feet to pluck one out of the air. After a successful dive, the kite does not land, but instead "roller-coasters" back into the sky, dismembering and eating its prey on the wing. Watching these graceful and adroit fliers through a pair of binoculars as they work a pod of dragonflies is an extremely interesting birding spectacle. An adult Mississippi kite looks like a cross between a small white-headed eagle and a falcon. The juveniles are gray.

Along the sandbars of the river at Island 13, look for thousands of rough-winged swallows massing for their southerly migration flight. Also look on the power lines, as you drive through the entire region, for purple martins massing for migration. Another excellent location for martins is **Chickasaw NWR**, between the Ed Jones boat ramp and the parking area for Nebraska Point (see chapter 3); look on the power lines. Like the Outer Banks of North Carolina nearly a thousand miles to the east, the Mississippi River corridor is already buzzing with migration activity.

To reach Island 13, drive to Wynnburg, Tennessee, just south of Reelfoot Lake. Find the grocery store with the wonderful chocolate soldier painted on the south wall of the building; you cannot miss it. From this store, proceed due west for 1.1 miles and turn left. Drive for 1.3 miles, then turn right. Proceed 50 yards and turn left. In 0.7 mile you will see the Mississippi River in the distance. After making the last left turn, in 1.2 miles the blacktop goes to the left, but do not take it. Continue straight over the levee on a gravel road. Look for Mississippi kites working the groves of trees along this stretch. After driving 3.3 miles on the levee road, bear right off the levee and drive 0.6 mile toward the river. Park in the large grove of cottonwood trees, and walk 100 yards to Island 13.

41

July Shorttakes

Ballooning Spiders

The atmosphere surrounding the earth is filled with life including "planktonic" bacteria, seeds, spores and a host of insects. One of the most interesting of the wind-borne insects is the ballooning spider. From the spinnerets at the end of its abdomen, the spider emits a long strand of silk, which becomes an elongated "sail" that, once it catches enough wind, launches the spider on a flight that can cover many hundreds of miles. Ballooning spiders have been caught in sampling filters suspended from hot air balloons miles above the earth's surface. Since they have no control over where they land, many drown in the earth's oceans. In this way, however, new life is constantly dispersed over every square foot of the earth's surface.

When you are on top of **Grandfather Mountain**, **Chimney Rock Park**, **Hanging Rock State Park** or any rocky, windswept promontory in the region watching for migrating hawks in the fall or enjoying a view, watch for the sunlight to glint momentarily on the silken sail of ballooning-spiders. Look closely for the spider, riding the wind to its random destiny.

42

A Closer Look:
Great Evening Performances

As any ocean sailor knows, the night can be a time of life as much as the day. In the three-state region, the night is a time of great activity, for nature is far too creative to leave so large a period unfilled and unused. Beginning at dusk, a close observer will see signs of nocturnal activity.

One of the most evocative and mysterious birding events in the region occurs early in the year, in mid-February. At this time male woodcocks perform their courtship flights, spiraling upward as their wings produce a twittering, tinkling music over the late-winter landscape at dusk. The courtship flight of the woodcock awakens in the beholder an awareness of nature's astonishing musicality as few other events in nature can do. The FENCE center, near Tyron, North Carolina (chapter 16), conducts woodcock walks around February 20 each year.

As early as late April and early May, nighthawks begin their courtship flights at dusk and continue into the night. The males dive, often from great heights. As they pull up at the end of a dive, their deeply cupped wings form a nearly complete circle, and certain primary feathers vibrate or buzz with great effect. The roar of the courting nighthawks can be heard for great distances and has been compared to the sound of an elephant trumpeting in the far distance. Learn to identify this slow-flying, long-winged, erratically flapping bird. Not a true hawk at all, it eats large quantities of insects. When actively feeding, groups of 50 or more may boil up on the horizon like so many chimney swifts and work a large open pasture. You will hear their nasal "peent" as they fill the sky over a large field, a lighted football field or a city park.

Also beginning their courtship vocalizations at dusk are two true nocturnal virtuosos. The whippoorwill and the chuck will's widow are definitely birds, but they don't sound like most diurnal birds. Natural selection apparently favored a lower-frequency vocalization in the cool, humid, still nocturnal atmosphere. The voices of these two nightjars are quite different, although few people—even mountain folk who have heard both species all their lives—realize that there are two different species calling.

The whippoorwill's call is fairly quick and rolling and has a flutelike quality, while the chuck will's widow song is slower, deeper and has less of a rolling quality. To become familiar with these calls, buy a copy of the *Peterson's Field Guide: Birding by Ear— Eastern/Central* tape series.

Another "first-chair" musician of the night is the screech owl. This tiny owl, unlike the other birds in this chapter, can be moved to song any season of the year, even on the coldest nights of January. The screech owl has two primary vocalizations: a high "whinny" and a sustained whistled tremolo. Once again, the *Peterson's Birding by Ear* series will help you become familiar with this call. By playing this tape on a still evening, you may elicit responses, even a chorus of responses from several owls.

The most venerable night musicians of the region are the tree frogs, cricket frogs, chorus frogs and toads. Theirs was actually the original music of the landscape, for they existed long before the first birds. To stand in the stillness of night and savor the fluttering song of the bird-voiced tree frog, the plunked string calls of a green tree frog or the "rattling pebbles" of the cricket frog is to go back in time and enjoy the earliest music on earth. Nor has the music of these amphibious "Perlmans" been eclipsed by the sophistication of the more recently evolved diurnal songbirds. Indeed, the tree frogs are the warblers of the night. American toads descanted and achieved harmony long before Benedictine monks, and green tree frogs plunked the banjo string long before humans in Africa. The great pity is that these musicians, are like "full many a flower … born to blush unseen, And waste its sweetness on desert air," and go unappreciated by the human ear. Few people have any idea of the music rising from the wetlands of the region.

"Herping by ear" is a sport that is beginning to attract a following. These creative people stalk the wetlands of environments such as Walnut Log Road (chapter 30) near Reelfoot Lake, or the South Carolina lowcountry freshwater marsh, and identify by ear the various tree frogs. Then they locate these living gems of color in a flashlight beam. An excellent guide for this discipline is the tape *Voices of the Night,* prepared by the Cornell Laboratory of Ornithology. The tape can be ordered by bookstores directly from the Cornell Laboratory of Ornithology.

One great evening performance is remarkably, completely visual. Many people who grew up in the region remember childhood evenings when lightning bugs, or fireflies, appeared over the pastures, fields and village greens. Yet in places like Greensboro, Raleigh and Charlotte, this spectacle is no longer part of the once magical experience of being a child. Loss of habitat, insecticides and, perhaps most detrimental to the lightning bug, light pollution have all but eradicated this species from urban centers.

In diverse locations, however, lightning bug populations are as robust as ever, and it is worth the trip to see them. The stunted juniper forest between the Cape Hatteras Public Campground and the last dunes before reaching the beach (chapter 32) blinks off and on as if draped by Christmas tree lights during June and July.

One of the major strongholds of lightning bugs is the southern Appalachian region. All the public campgrounds in Great Smoky Mountains National Park contain the combination of forest and grassy fields that lightning bugs require. Both Elkmont and Smokemont, the public campgrounds on either end of US 441, which bisects the park, are prime lightning bug habitats. In fact Elkmont, the public campground on the Tennessee end of US 441, is the site of a lightning bug study. Cade's Cove, also on the Tennessee side of the park, is another prime location for this pyrotechnical beetle. Below South Holston Dam (chapter 34) in the large grassy meadow, lightning bugs have a truly beautiful setting for their courtship and mating rituals. By the end of July, the peak of the firefly light show is over.

There is more to the lightning bug story than the incandescent beauty that meets the eye. In truth the web of intrigue spun around this magical creature that talks in flashes of light demonstrates nature's use of deceit, trickery and general amorality for survival. This insect is an astonishing model of aggressive mimicry.

Each species of firefly has its own language of light flashes that vary in color, intensity of light, number and duration, rate of flash and rate of repetition of sequence. Yet, according to the studies of Dr. James E. Lloyd of the University of Florida, the complexity only begins here. Once the Photuris versicolor female firefly has mated, she is chemically transformed into a predator. At this point she not only continues to signal to males of her own species, but also mimics the light patterns of other species, hoping to lure them in as well. The females of some Photuris species are capable of mimicking, nearly perfectly, 11 other firefly species. The poor male Photinus collustrans firefly has his own light signal answered five times more often by predatory Photuris females than by fertile females of his own species. The Photinus male, knowing this, lands a safe distance from all advertising females and advances with great caution. Photinus males try to do most of their courting before total darkness so the larger silhouette of the Photuris female, literally waiting with open jaws, can be detected.

To counteract the increasingly cautious behavior of the Photinus males, some species of Photuris females then switch over to aerial predation, striking males in flight, as they mimic male light patterns. Photuris females consistently misflash the signal of the advertising Photinus female pattern, adding one extra flash. Therefore Photinus males, once they have located an actual Photinus female, then imitate the incorrect pattern of the Photuris predatory female, knowing that other male Photinus will veer off, giving themselves more time to copulate without interruption. This is an example of mimicry of mimicry.

These are some of the simpler firefly strategies and counterstrategies. They continue to increase in complexity but become so byzantine that the explanations break down under their own weight. Yet it all makes perfect sense to the lightning bugs, which recalls the axiom quoted once before in this text: "Nature is not only more complex than Man thinks, but she is more complex than Man can think." So the next time you imagine you are seeing the stars of the heavens, which have fallen into the forest and glow from the branches and leaves, know that you are right. These are the "stars" of deceit and trickery.

There is also innocence in the forest. Consider, even as you watch the fireflies whom George Constantz calls the "femmes fatales" of the night, the katydid. These gentle, leaf-green insects are the voice of the southern hardwood forest. In the southern Appalachian forest, their ratcheting voices often merge to form a chant that reverberates across the ocean of blue ridges and valleys. "Katydid, katydid, katydid, katydidn't." It repeats itself until it becomes a mantra, as Oliver Wendell Holmes illustrates in his poem, "To an Insect."

August

Notes

43

Dolphins in the Estuary

Whale watching takes people to Alaska, California and Baja California. Unknown to many whale watchers, however, North Carolina has a small but stable population of sperm whales that hunt squid along the edges of the continental shelf off Nag's Head. Both humpback and fin whales are sighted with regularity on pelagic birding trips to the Gulf Stream from North Carolina's Outer Banks (see chapter 49). Yet there is a much easier way to see whales in the three-state region.

The bottlenosed dolphin is a true toothed whale. This steel-blue whale can weigh up to 500 pounds and should not be confused with the smaller Atlantic Harbor porpoise, which ranges from the north Atlantic south to Delaware. The sight of a family group of dolphins working their way up a tidal creek in search of mullet or menhaden gives even the most experienced waterman pause. To exchange looks with a dolphin from a canoe in a 50-foot-wide tidal creek is a privilege of the highest order. These creatures may have exchanged looks with sperm whales surfacing from a 10,000-foot (nearly 2-miles) dive from the frigid, black, current-torn depths beyond the continental shelf off North Carolina's Cape Hatteras, where the whales go in search of squid. Perhaps the dominant members of the pod have butted and killed large, oceangoing sharks with their heads, as they sometimes do. The dolphins one encounters in the estuary have seen the surface of the ocean overhead lashed by hurricanes, and feel every tide turn around on a level we can only try to imagine. No one who has watched a dolphin riding, just beneath the surface of the ocean, the bow wave of a charterboat returning from the Gulf Stream can doubt their prodigious capacity for pleasure. The dolphin truly knows the meaning of living by one's wits on a daily basis.

Dolphins are land mammals that decided life outside the ocean was too harsh and returned to the sea. They still possess the

A cavorting bottlenosed dolphin in a South Carolina tidal creek.

de-evolving leg bones in their front flippers to prove it. These air-breathing mammals use echolocation to locate prey and to communicate with each other. They are often seen herding bait fish into coves or shallows, where they can be more easily caught. The efficiency of their hunting strategies is so great that prey species such as menhaden or jumping mullet sometimes leap out of the water onto the mudflats in an effort to escape the dolphin, whose sonar clicks track their prey down, even in zero visibility.

For the first several years of life, the adults of a pod or family group teach young dolphins how to hunt. They enter the brackish water estuary year-round, but tend to do so more often after late April, when bait fish begin to enter the salt marsh. Dolphins usually come in with the incoming tide and can go for many miles up tidal creeks. If the fishing is good, they may stay in the salt marsh during low tide, but more likely they will return to the estuary at ebb tide. April and May, August and September and the early fall are good times to look for these small whales in the tidal creeks from a canoe, although there are no hard and fast rules. During periods when the mothers are nursing young, they tend to avoid the vibrations of boat motors and may be harder to approach. Of course, for a canoeist or kayaker this would not be a problem. You may also see loggerhead turtles on high tide, while exploring the salt marsh in search of dolphin pods. Listen for the "whoosh" of air rushing through the blowhole in the top of the dolphin's head and look for fins and disturbances in the water, as well as little waterspouts during exhalations. Pods sometimes allow a canoeist or kayaker to remain in their midst for hours as they work their way up a tidal creek. They seem to be curious and often surface nearby, apparently for a closer look.

Hot Spots

Dolphins often follow shrimp boats in order to eat the "by-catch" thrown overboard by the fishermen. For this reason a small town like **McClellanville, South Carolina,** just south of Georgetown and the home port for several shrimp boats, but with light boat traffic, is a likely choice for a dolphin safari. Dolphins use **Jeremy Creek,** which flows past the boat ramp located in front of the municipal offices of this village.

Paddling against an outgoing tide can be difficult, especially if the wind is also against the canoeist. A three-horsepower outboard mounted on a stern bracket made especially for a 17-foot canoe may be a necessity. Moving at 8 or 10 mph, the quiet, low-rpm motor is not objectionable to dolphins. The kayak is another excellent craft for observing wildlife in the tidal creek and is safer on larger tidal creeks than a canoe, which was designed primarily for use on lakes and rivers.

Be careful not to stray too far in search of dolphins. Either a pod will happen to come in the creek or it won't. You probably have a one in three chance of seeing a group, for the dolphins work a large territory. An extensive search won't turn up anything if a group does not happen to be in the area. Rather than go searching for dolphins, let the incoming tide bring them to you. Wait at a point where you have a good view of the tidal creek. Coastal Expeditions, located in Sullivan's Island near Charleston, has guides who are familiar with the tidal creeks and estuaries of this region and who will increase your odds of seeing dolphins.

Waters rich in marine life attract the greatest numbers of the little cetaceans, which range from Cape Cod to Florida.

The tidal creeks around **Edisto Beach State Park,** about 50 miles south of Charleston, are full of food and attractive to dolphins. Dolphins use **Fishing Creek,** which runs by the large Indian midden mound at the end of the Spanish Mount Trail (see chapter 10). A copy of Coastal Expedition's map is invaluable for locating canoe launch sites. While Fishing Creek is small and relatively safe, other creeks are large. Do not casually go exploring the vast South Carolina tidal zone. It is best to go with an experienced guide, at least the first time. Remember, there is a good chance you will not see a dolphin family group, but a salt marsh is full of life (see chapter 56). You will learn and see interesting sights.

44

Night Skies

Night skies are an endangered perspective. Most people living in mid-sized American cities are accustomed to the night skies seen from a golf course or a backyard. Stars are few and far between. To these millions of people, this night sky is scarcely worth a glance. Children from the inner city, when exposed to the glorious, speckled, vibrant, infinite night sky, have been known to react with fear and disbelief. It is a poignant statement of how far we have separated ourselves from the natural environment.

A single large city will diffuse light pollution for hundreds of miles in every direction. To see an unpolluted night sky, you need to distance yourself from these concentrations of humans and their by-products. Choose a night with no moon, for the full moon floods the night sky with light, obliterating the darkness that brings out the Milky Way galaxy. Even an Alaska, or a Montana night sky has satellites moving slowly across the firmament as well as high-flying airliners with strobes flashing. You should expect this on a planet whose moon has footprints, lost golfballs and golf club divot marks on it.

Yet the night sky, where you can find it, is a thing of great beauty and movement. Constellations slowly rise over the dark rim of the earth and seem to crawl across the void. Of course it is the earth that is actually revolving. The Big Dipper may hold water early in the evening, but it will be standing on its handle by 2:00 A.M. By timing your night skies trip to coincide with the Perseid meteor shower, which occurs from August 11 to 13 each year, you have a chance of seeing shooting stars. Of course, you might see them any night of the year. At locations such as Roan Mountain, with an elevation a mile above sea level, meteors can flash by with such brilliance that you can see a smoke trail in the rarified atmosphere, if your eye is quick. Try to plan a pilgrimage to a location such as Roan Mountain within a days after a storm system has blown the entire region clear of any smog or pollution. Then the night skies pulsate.

From a location such as Roan Mountain, or a pullout along the Blue Ridge Parkway, you can sit and watch that which held our ancestors in awe. When we are no longer stirred by the sight of the universe, when it emerges from behind the cloak of cloud and blue wavelengths of sunlight, we need to ask what we have become.

Hot Spots

Cape Hatteras (chapter 12) combines the night sky with the experience of being 20 miles out at sea. You can have the view without the maintenance of a sailboat. Consider that the stars outnumber the grains of sand on the beach.

Roan Mountain (chapters 31 and 64) offers a splendid, open night sky a mile above sea level. Here you look through much less atmospheric distortion than at lower elevations. The openness of the grass bald adds to the sense of vastness. Make the 20-minute walk to Round Bald, the first "step" on the heath bald opposite Carver's Gap, by flashlight. Sit on the ground beside the Appalachian Trail and imagine that you are on a starship—which, of course, you are.

Finally, the Blue Ridge Parkway could not have been better designed for viewing night skies if the architects of the world's premier scenic drive had been trying to achieve such an end. Drive the most open, elevated ridges, such as the **Craggy Gardens** (chapter 31) ascent or the **Doughton Park** area (chapter 19), and park at one of the scenic overlooks. Place your lawn chair by the vehicle, sit down and enjoy the greatest show on earth, a nightime view of the universe.

45

A Comparison of
Three Spruce-Fir Forests

Roan Mountain, Mt. Mitchell and Grandfather Mountain provide a textbook study of three spruce-fir forests, before acid rain and after. As explained in chapter 32, spruce-fir forests are ecological islands in the sky, left behind when the glaciers retreated 10,000 years ago. These evergreen forests represent the southern terminus of this forest configuration. Yet the fact that the evergreen keeps its needles year-round condemns them to be ravaged by pollution 12 months of the year. Many people who walked through the spruce-fir forest of Mt. Mitchell as children remember the footpath that wound its way to the concrete tower as surrounded by a forest so thick and robust that it blocked out most of the sunlight. This forest created an environment of great coolness, even in the summer. The summit of Mt. Mitchell, the highest mountain east of the Mississippi River, often created its own small snow squalls, thunderstorms and lightning storms.

Now the path to Mt. Mitchell's tower winds through an open area of struggling seedlings. The skeletons of the spruce-fir forest known by so many Tarheels in the 1950s, 1960s and 1970s stand row after row, mile after mile, going out of sight down the tallest mountain in the East. Mt. Mitchell has the misfortune of being in the path of the prevailing winds from the Ohio River Valley. Oil- and coal-fired electrical generators in Dayton, Cincinnati, Louisville and Indianapolis burden the easterly wind with an acid mist of sulfates and nitrates. More than 200 pounds of acidic sulfates per year are precipitated out of these poisonous clouds passing over Mt. Mitchell. During the worst single episode of acid rain deposition, rainwater falling on Mt. Mitchell registered as halfway between lemon juice and battery acid on a water pH scale. Other coal- and oil-fired generators from Birmingham, Atlanta,

The dying spruce-fir forest on the summit of Mt. Mitchell.

Memphis and Nashville, as well as cars, diesel trucks and airplanes, contribute to the acid load of the eastward-trending poison clouds. The forests of other patriarchs of the Southern Appalachians such as Clingman's Dome and Mt. LeConte are dying as well. An acid rain study was conducted on Mt. Mitchell by Dr. Robert Bruck; for information, write to: Dr. Robert Bruck, Department of Plant Pathology, North Carolina State University, Box 7617, Raleigh, NC 27695-7617, or call (919) 515-2086.

Hot Spots

Mt. Mitchell is one of the centerpieces of the Blue Ridge Parkway. The path of the parkway was certainly routed to Mt. Mitchell so that motorists could experience the crowning peak of the entire Appalachian mountain range. No one could have foreseen the degradation of the forest here when the parkway was designed and built in the 1930s. To reach Mt. Mitchell, take Business 70 east out of Asheville. Follow signs to the Folk Art Center, and then on to Mt. Mitchell State Park.

Grandfather Mountain (chapter 26), at 5,964 feet elevation, is tall enough that the acid mist and accompanying rain are wrung out as they pass over it. It is an ancient mountain, containing some of the oldest rock on earth. The acid rain is damaging the mountain and the spruce-fir forest there even more than the passage of time. A 1964 photograph of the mile-high swinging bridge on Grandfather shows a healthy spruce-fir forest. A 1990 photograph shows few living trees in the same location, which was never logged. Grandfather's peaks receive 100 pounds of acidic sulfates per year, but the natural ecosystem can buffer out only 18 pounds per year.

On many of the high peaks of the southern Appalachians, acid rain weakens the Fraser fir to the point that the wooly aphid is able to kill the tree. Yet the red spruce, which is immune to the wooly aphid, is dying as well because of acid rain alone. Above 6,000 feet of elevation along the Blue Ridge Parkway east of Waynesville, North Carolina, the red spruce forest at **Richland Balsam** is dying. Silver skeletons speckle the forest. To reach Richland Balsam, drive to milepost 435 of the parkway southwest of Asheville. The destruction of the spruce-fir forest of the southern Appalachians is only one of the casualties of acid rain. In New York state and the upper northeastern United States, many lakes are dead. Quebec is losing its maple trees to acid rain.

The spruce-fir forest of **Roan Mountain** (chapters 25 and 64) is less plagued by acid rain. A few skeletons are in evidence below the Cornelius Rex Peake plaque at the top of the heath bald system. In the forest along the road to the summit are random skeletons, but much of this may be natural die-off. After several days with no wind to move smog off the western horizon, a faint line of yellow crud can be seen in the distance. Overall, though, the Roan Mountain ecosystem and its evergreen forest are blessed with excellent air quality. The spruce-fir forest of the summit of Roan Mountain is at the level that those of Mt. Mitchell and Grandfather Mountain were 30 years ago. The same robust, sky-blocking thicket of evergreen boughs creates a tunnel over the footpath leading to the Roan Mountain Overlook. Try to make all these trips on the same day, to get a sense of the price of 3 percent annual economic growth.

46

Cade's Cove: Spotted Fawns, Black Bears and Red Wolves

The extensive grass meadow ecosystem of Tennessee's Cade's Cove in the heart of Great Smoky Mountains National Park is one of the important game sanctuaries of the southeastern United States. These meadows are managed in such a way that they closely approximate the grasslands once kept open by buffalo, elk and fires set by the Cherokee Nation, in precolonial times. The Cade's Cove ecosystem supports a large white-tailed deer population, black bear, wild turkey and, most recently, red wolves. Until the wolves were reintroduced, no large predator existed at the top of the food chain here to cull weak animals and prevent overpopulation. The deer herd in Cade's Cove began to suffer. The animals increased in number until there was not enough grass and acorns to support them. The individual deer became stunted because it evolved for small body mass and small antlers.

Cade's Cove became the second location in the nation, after North Carolina's Alligator River Preserve, to receive pairs of red wolves, released into the ecosystem. They are thriving, perhaps in part because heartworm is not as prevalent in the southern Appalachians as it is within the coastal plains of North Carolina, where Alligator River is located. There, each red wolf must be captured and treated for heartworm yearly. Cade's Cove's red wolves live in an essentially unmanipulated state and are successfully holding off coyote intruders.

These wolves are the result of a bold, successful experiment. The wild red wolf population was killed back, from a wide distribution across the southeastern United States, until only a small number of them existed in Texas. All remaining wild red wolves were live-trapped. At this point only several dozen red wolves and red wolf–coyote hybrids, as well as red wolf–dog hybrids, existed in the world. The red wolf gene pool was poised to vanish forever,

A white-tailed deer spotted fawn.

so a total of 14 animals thought to have pure genes were placed in a breeding program. Extreme precautions were taken to maximize genetic diversity by "swapping" partners. From the original population of fourteen, 300 red wolves have issued. Based on the success of this program, all California condors have been live-trapped and are under a similar regimen. Such drastic steps were necessary to prevent the extinction of both species.

The red wolf has reclaimed the Cade's Cove ecosystem. The chorus of howls that sometimes rises on still nights and at the first light of morning has reintroduced an important component of the ethos of Great Smoky Mountains National Park. Once again red wolves hunt the hardwood forest and grassy meadows in pairs or in small family groups.

One of the most interesting times of the year to observe the white-tailed deer of Cade's Cove is during the period of the spotted fawns. The spots on the coat of a fawn are an example of protective coloration when fawns are in the first weeks of life. At this stage of development, the best defense against predators for the nearly scentless fawn is to lie perfectly still. The white spots are thought to suggest sunlight dappling the forest floor. If you come to the Cade's Cove meadows hoping to see does and spotted fawns too early in the summer, your chances will be slim. During late May and early June, the tiny fawns are instructed by their mothers to remain hidden at all times. The only evidence you may find of a fawn, even with a spotting scope, is a doe with red teats and a bag full of milk, as she switches her tail and looks around nervously. By waiting until later in June or even July or August, the fawns, still carrying their spots, will be seen feeding alongside their mothers.

By driving the lanes bordering the sprawling grass meadows late on a summer afternoon of stable weather, you may see 50 to 100 deer feeding out in the open. Some of these will be does with fawns. Bucks with antlers in velvet will be in bachelor groups at this time. Because mornings in Cade's Cove are often foggy and offer poor visibility, late afternoon is usually the best time to observe the deer, when they may appear almost red in color. Since deer in the park have been protected from hunting for generations, no living deer has any recollection of being endangered by humans. You can walk slowly across the meadows and often approach to within 30 feet of feeding deer. Cade's Cove is a photographer's paradise. So long as you don't alarm or alter the natural behavior of deer or other wildlife, this is allowed by the park guidelines. As you glass the extensive meadowlands with binoculars or a spotting scope, look closely along the edges of the forest. Flocks of wild turkeys are sometimes seen feeding out in the open, usually within 100 yards of the forest.

One other important player in Cade's Cove's large mammal fauna is the black bear. In fact Great Smoky Mountains National Park played an important part in saving the black bear of the southern Appalachians in the years following the chestnut blight. After the last diseased chestnuts were logged, black bear numbers plummeted. There were almost no bears left in the region, except for in a few very remote locations. Two of the most important of these were the Thunderhead area and Bone Valley, both within the boundaries of the park. Here enough bears survived to maintain a small but healthy gene pool. Largely from these two reservoirs and a few others, the black bear population has grown to near the carrying capacity for this species within the fickle oak-hickory forest (see chapter 37). Although numbers of black bear will never approach the size of the population sustained by the forest when the keystone species, the American chestnut, was present, Great Smoky Mountains National Park presently supports 400 to 600 bears and is considered a regional stronghold for these mammals. Only Alaska, Maine, Minnesota and Wisconsin have larger populations of this fascinating species.

Hot Spots

Mid-August in **Cade's Cove** is when the fruit of the wild cherry trees becomes ripe. At this time Cade's Cove draws every black bear for miles. Bears move into the cherry trees, displaying their remarkable athleticism, climb out on limbs like squirrels and devour the cherries. While you drive the lanes of Cade's Cove, look in the roadway for small branches and leaf clusters from mature cherry trees. If you see such sign, pull over to determine if a bruin is working a cherry tree along the lane. Bears ignore humans while they are in cherry trees, giving a rare opportunity to observe this often shy and reclusive animal. During early to mid-August, when the cherries are ripe, is probably the best opportunity of the year to observe black bears in the park. Black bears also become concentrated in huckleberry patches at this time. Mid-October through November finds the bears working the white oak groves, foraging for acorns, as they put on fat for hibernation.

Black bears can appear anywhere in Cade's Cove during the cherry season, but some locations have mature cherry trees that consistently attract them. Approximately 1 mile past the Hyatt Lane cutoff, on the Cade's Cove Loop Road, is a large, mature cherry tree that is regularly climbed by bears. Spark's Lane, limited to foot and bicycle travel only, has mature cherry trees that attract bears as well. The area around Elijah Oliver homestead also has cherry trees. To check on the progress of the ripening of Cade's Cove cherries, call (423) 448-2472.

Deer may be seen while you drive the scenic loop around Cade's Cove. You can either take the entire loop or cut the drive in half by taking the **Hyatt Lane cutoff**. Though seldom seen, red wolves can be heard howling throughout Cade's Cove. **Cade's Cove Campground** is a good location for hearing them.

47

August Shorttakes

Hot Weather Travel

Much has been said about dressing properly for cold weather and watching for sign of hypothermia. Yet in the three-state region, extreme heat may be just as great a threat. In the summer of 1995, more than 500 people in Chicago died of exposure to heat. With a simple understanding of how to lower body temperature naturally, these people would have been much better prepared for this crisis. Body temperature can be effectively lowered, regardless of air temperature, by wearing a long-sleeved cotton shirt, a pair of long cotton pants, and a turban that have been dunked in cold water while sitting in front of a fan. Nature has relied on evaporation for cooling for a very long time.

It is ironic that the hotter the ambient air temperature, the more drivers will rely on air conditioning to maintain a comfortable temperature inside their vehicle. The moment they step outside, into 90 degrees of heat and 90 percent humidity, their body is overwhelmed by the unnatural change in the environment. Heat prostration is a serious condition. For the ecotourist or birder who spends time in the salt marsh, the middle Tennessee cedar glades or along the Mississippi River in July or August, heat awareness is absolutely essential.

On hot, sunny days, do not wear short pants, a short shirt and depend on sunblock. Instead, create your own shade by wearing light-colored lightweight long cotton pants and a long-sleeved shirt. As sweat evaporates through the fabric, natural cooling is accomplished. Drink plenty of liquids. A wide-brimmed hat is also a must. In extreme conditions, douse yourself until dripping wet with a jug of water. As the water evaporates you will be amazed at how efficiently your body temperature is lowered.

As you drive to a hot-weather outing, try to maintain a comfortable body temperature the natural way. Wear a wet, long-sleeved cotton shirt. To really get into the spirit of natural cooling, wrap a dripping-wet turban around your head. Drive with the windows down. You'll get some funny looks from other motorists, but just smile at them, content in the knowledge that you're cooler than they are. Naturally!

48

A Closer Look:
The Swallowtailed Kite

"In Florida Everglades where the Miami River rises, I had the pleasure and satisfaction of studying those remarkable birds the swallowtail kites. Gifted with extraordinary wing and tail surfaces they live almost entirely in the air, floating, soaring, and circling with all the buoyancy and dash of their minor prototypes, the barn swallow, to whom they bear a singular resemblance in shape, color, action, and superlative wing power—in fact in nearly everything but size.

The three birds I observed were feeding on small snakes, apparently water moccasins, which were neatly snatched from their lurking places in the reeds and devoured on the wing … . One of the birds carried aloft a small alligator, perhaps a foot long, but the morsel proved to be too obdurate and was dropped. At times they made long downward sweeps like the drop of nighthawks, apparently in a spirit of play.

No other North American bird approaches the swallowtail in the grace and beauty of its flight; the duck hawk alone equals it in speed. The former conveys the impression of lightness in the air; the latter, of power and impetuosity."

These are the words of R. I. Brasher, one of the contributing authors of T. Gilbert Pearson's *Birds of America*. His description of the swallowtailed kite may have captured the spirit of this ethereal bird as well as any. Anyone who watches this larger version of the Mississippi kite will find it hard to deny that this bird defines grace as no other bird can. The great good fortune of the three-state area is that, as the swallowtailed kites have extended their range northward, there is now a reasonably dependable, easily accessible location for seeing this species. In fact swallowtailed kites are being sighted as far north as Cape Hatteras and the Roanoke River near Scotland Neck, North Carolina. But South Carolina's Santee River is without a doubt the most dependable location. Mississippi kites work the dragonflies and rodents of the Santee Delta alongside the swallowtails, yet the great size and, in particular, the black, swallowlike tail make recognition easy. The swallowtail is twice as large as the Mississippi kite. Both species of kite drop vertically to snatch dragonflies, small rodents and small reptiles from the air, ground or water, never pausing in their flight. No other bird has so mastered this technique.

To reach a good location for observing the white-headed, white-breasted kite with the deeply forked tail, drive approximately 10 miles south of Georgetown, South Carolina, on US 17. Immediately after crossing the North Fork of the Santee River headed south, cross over to get on the northbound lane to gain access to the parking area on the east side of the highway, just below the south end of the bridge.

Both species of kite prefer hot weather—the hotter the better—perhaps to gain access to rising thermals. Don't hesitate to look for these tropical species during the hottest part of the day, from 10:00 A.M. until midafternoon. With binoculars, look from the parking lot for a buteolike soaring pattern as the kites gain altitude. If no kites are visible, you may wish to walk south on the northbound lane for a quarter of a mile to a steel gate. Walk out onto the levee, where there is a commanding view of the Santee Delta. With great luck you will see wild hogs here as well, for they are present.

Kites spend much of the year close to the equator. They are gone from the three-state region by early September. Both species nest in nearby Francis Marion National Forest and can be seen anywhere in the broad, grassy delta between the bridges crossing the North and South Forks of the Santee River. However, the area near the bridge over the North Fork of the Santee River seems to be their preference.

September

Notes

49

Pelagic Birding Trips

Brian Patteson, the leading offshore birding authority in the three-state region, states in his 1995 brochure, "The Gulf Stream off North Carolina is arguably the best place in the western North Atlantic for seeing numbers and variety of pelagic seabirds." More species of whales and other marine mammals have been recorded in North Carolina's coastal waters than in any other location in this hemisphere. The reasons are simple: northern and southern species mixing and a bounty of food. These two reasons explain why North Carolina's territorial waters host more species of seabirds than any other state on the East Coast. As the western edge of the Gulf Stream overrides the continental shelf off Nag's Head, dynamic upwelling from the ocean depths occurs, flushing to the surface zooplankton, crustaceans, fish larvae and squid, all food for seabirds.

As one cruises toward the indigo-colored Gulf Stream roughly 20 miles offshore, one passes through what amounts to a dead zone as far as open-ocean bird life is concerned. Upon reaching the most important global current in the world, the sea becomes strewn with sargasso, or "gulfweed." Flying fish, flushed by the bow of the charter boat, skim miraculously over the waves for 50 yards before knifing into a wave wall. Open-ocean birds are seen in flight and in rafts on the ocean's surface. Portuguese man-o'-war jellyfish trail deadly tentacles. Dolphins begin to follow the boat. Fin and humpback whales are seen with fair regularity. Suddenly the boat emerges from the dead zone of gray water into a cobalt-blue ocean full of life. The Gulf Stream passes closer to the mainland at Nag's Head than anywhere else on the East Coast, except south Florida. What makes this location so special is the interaction between cold-water and warm-water species, one that does not occur north or south on this coastline.

Offshore from Nag's Head is one of the most important marine ecotones of the North American coastline. A pelagic birding trip may be the best way to experience this ecosystem. While fishing "headboat" skippers have little time or interest in pointing out seabirds and oceangoing wildlife to paying customers, skippers who take out pelagic birders know that these enthusiastic students of biodiversity are interested in all facets of marine life. A manta ray leaping out of the ocean, a sperm whale waterspout, a rare basking whale shark—nearly any form of marine wildlife will bring the skipper to the microphone, directing the gaze of the several dozen passengers to a point on the endless horizon. Fishing lines are often trolled behind the boat, so birders have the opportunity to see the gamefish species that follow this remarkable river within an ocean.

A day of pelagic birding begins early, with offshore trips leaving at 6:30 A.M. and ending at 5:00 P.M. The Atlantic is not a calm ocean, so be prepared for a bumpy ride. Make preparations for seasickness if you are prone to this malady. Pelagic birding skippers are not normally receptive to suggestions to return to port early.

The different seasons of the year offer varied opportunities to the open-ocean birder. Spring trips are usually scheduled from May 20 through the end of May, when birders have the chance of seeing the greatest number of species. An added attraction is the courtship plumage of most high arctic breeders on their way north. Species to look for on May trips include jaegers, arctic terns, shearwaters, south polar skuas and various petrels. Rarities such as the red-billed tropicbird are always a possibility.

Summer pelagic birding trips offer fewer species but a calmer ocean with fewer cancellation dates. Summer is the best time for band-rumped storm petrels, Leach's storm petrels, black-capped petrels and bridled and sooty terns. Masked boobies and white-tailed tropicbirds are possible on summer trips. Summer trip dates are June 17–July 30 and August 5–27. Fall off North Carolina's Outer Banks offers a chance to see a wide variety of seabirds such as Cory's and Audubon's shearwaters, long-tailed jaegers, occasionally the rare Sabine's Gull and other species. Fall trips are usually scheduled for September 2–3 and September 16–27.

An open-ocean birding trip any time of the year is exciting. Be prepared for the unexpected. Imagine seeing a "great white" heron, a reddish egret, a black-tailed godwit, a curlew sandpiper, an Antillean nighthawk, a Eurasian collard dove or a northern wheatear over the open ocean! All these and many other landbird species were observed in 1994 on pelagic trips off North Carolina. One should take note of the ocean, for ocean-dwelling microbes are primarily responsible for the physical and chemical makeup of our planet. Marine organisms produce dimethyl sulfide, a substance whose production is apparently accelerated or retarded, as needed, to balance the global temperature, thus counteracting the greenhouse effect. The biodiversity in the ocean, as well as on ocean floors, means many millions of species are still waiting to be discovered by science. Coral reefs cover 68 million square miles of ocean floor and may possess as many species per square mile as the rain forest. It is impossible to overstate the importance of the ocean as an ecosystem.

No creatures demonstrate better than the seabirds that nature can fill even the most unlikely habitat niches with flourishing lifeforms. Many pelagic species have evolved special tubes on the top of their beaks, specifically for expelling excess salt. These open-ocean seabirds never leave the ocean except to breed on rocky islands. While watching the very social behavior of flocks of band-rumped petrels or Cory's shearwaters, you will come to realize that the open ocean is actually a very benign environment for those creatures coevolved to live in it. How do they deal with hurricanes? Only the seabirds know for certain the answer to that question. Skippers who have ridden out hurricane-force winds on the open ocean have reported seabirds frolicking in 120 mph winds. For seabirds, remaining airborne for several days while a hurricane passes through is a fact of life. In order to truly understand the biodiversity within the region, an open-ocean trip, designed especially for nature enthusiasts, is a prerequisite.

Hot Spots

Brian Patteson is the most experienced organizer of off-shore birding trips in the Carolinas. His trips are all onboard either the 72-foot *Miss Hatteras* or the 55-foot *Country Girl*. Trips depart from both **Hatteras Inlet** and **Oregon Inlet.** For information, call (804) 933-8687 during the off-season. During the pelagic birding season, May through October, Brian Patteson can be reached at (919) 986-1154. Do not call him after 9:00 P.M. during the pelagic birding season. A brochure may be requested by writing: Brian Patteson, Inc., P.O. Box 1135, Amherst, VA 24521.

50

Fall Hawk Migrations

The first migrating monarch butterflies each autumn serve as a reminder that hawk migrations are under way. From a rocky promontory like Caesar's Brow in Caesar's Head State Park in South Carolina, or North Carolina's Chimney Rock Park, in mid-September a hawk watcher may see a red-tailed hawk soar by. Two of the feisty little accipiters—the sharp-shinned hawks—may engage in a brief mock dogfight almost in front of a hawk-watching platform, much to the delight of hawk watchers. A peregrine falcon, with its unmistakable black cheek patches, may briefly appear like visiting royalty, wings oaring swiftly with shallow strokes, punctuated with a brief glide. Yet the main event for most hawk watchers is the sight of a "kettle" of broad-winged hawks.

The chunky, blocky broad-winged hawk is the consummate wood hawk, although it is considered a buteo, or soaring hawk. The ability of the broad-winged hawk to soar is never more apparent than during migration.

Caesar's Head State Park, on the North Carolina–South Carolina state line, is one of the best locations in the Southeast for observing hawk migrations. Although it does not offer the sheer numbers of Pennsylvania's famous Hawk Mountain, Caesar's Head is certainly the closest thing to it in the region. For kettles of broad-winged hawks, Caesar's Head can positively cook. On September 21, 1994, between midmorning and midafternoon, 2,090 broad-winged hawks were tallied by hawk maestro Irving Pitts. September 21 usually marks the peak of this event.

The broad-wing migrates in flocks, unlike all other species of hawks. Their ingenious method of covering miles over the ground is one of the great spectacles of the birder's year. As hawk watchers scan the northern horizon with binoculars, a kettle of broad-wings often shows up as specks, thousands of feet above the mountains.

Hawk watchers on Caesar's Brow.

The kettle, which may contain hundreds of broad-wings, continues to build altitude by spiraling upward on thermal winds. When the swirling kettle has gained all the altitude it can from a particular thermal, it is as if someone were to cut the string that has pulled them thousands of feet upward. Each hawk sets its wings and coasts downhill, gaining every yard of southerly travel possible over the ground. On a single downhill ride, a kettle, still traveling as a group, will cover enough miles of southerly travel to vanish from sight altogether, even from binocular-aided eyes. To watch several hundred broad-wings suddenly come streaming down from the sky is unlike anything else in the birder's year. After one kettle has passed from view, all eyes turn to the northerly horizon and the watch begins for a new approaching kettle. On a productive day, several kettles may be in sight at the same time for most of the day. Other species of migrating raptors, even monarch butterflies, make a September day spent on a rocky promontory like Caesar's Brow delightful. You can meet the most interesting people here, and have plenty of time to exchange stories of past birding sorties. Remember to take a folding chair or cushion to sit on. Cloudy days with limited visibility generally offer poor hawk watching for the high-flying broad-wings.

Hot Spots

Caesar's Head State Park is reached by taking SC 276, which connects Greenville, South Carolina, with Brevard, North Carolina. At the state line on the South Carolina side, look for signs to Caesar's Head State Park. Park and proceed on foot to Caesar's Brow Rock, 100 yards above the parking lot. Take a seat on the hawk-watching platform, where a splendid view to the south awaits.

Another rocky promontory that lies in the principal north-south migration route of the broad-wings of the eastern seaboard is **Chimney Rock State Park** (chapter 26). There is an entrance fee for this privately owned preserve; the best bargain is the year's pass. This park, long recognized for its view of Lake Lure and granite outcroppings, is becoming known as a naturalists' destination. Spring wildflower walks, bird walks and hawk watching are just a few of the nature activities here. **Sharp's Ridge** (chapter 30) in Knoxville is another premier location for raptor watching.

A vastly different ecosystem, the Outer Banks of North Carolina, also has a hawk migration. Here you will not see kettles of broad-winged hawks but rather solitary migrants, principally sharp-shinned hawks, Cooper's hawks, peregrine falcons and merlins. The two best spots on the Outer Banks are the two wooden observation towers on North Pond, on **Pea Island NWR**. One platform is located on the dike a half mile west of the Pea Island visitor's center. The other is the north dike observation deck at the north end of North Pond. The north dike deck may be the more productive of the two for migrating raptors. From these two platforms you have a good chance of seeing several peregrines in a day. The coastal migration peaks the first week of October.

51

The Mississippi River:
One of the World's Great Rivers

North America's Mississippi River belongs to the set of the world's great rivers: South America's Amazon; Africa's Zaire, Nile and Niger; Siberia's Yenisey and China's Yangtze. The Mississippi's name is from the ancient Algonquin language. It has been called "the lifeblood of the richest river valley on earth." Mark Twain said of it, "It is not a commonplace river, but on the contrary is in all ways remarkable." Disgorging four million gallons of freshwater per second at its mouth, the Mississippi watershed drains roughly half of the continental United States, receiving water whose origin is as far away as Yellowstone Park. Only the basins of the Amazon and Zaire Rivers are larger. The Mississippi River is directly or indirectly involved in generating three quarters of the United States' gross national product in agriculture, commerce and industry.

Once upon a time, the Mississippi River possessed the greatest alluvial floodplain broadleaf deciduous hardwood forest on the planet, extending from Louisiana to northern Minnesota. Its basin drained the greatest short- and tall-grass prairie ecosystems in the world. These prairies supported 60 million plains bison, the largest assemblage of large mammals the earth has ever known.

The hardwood forest of the Mississippi bottomlands is largely gone. The short-grass prairie was converted into the corn belt; the tall-grass prairie was converted into the grain belt. The plains bison was snatched from the jaws of extinction by crossbreeding a few hundred animals, primarily from privately owned herds. No greater metaphor need be conjured up to tally what was traded in order to create the greatest economic power in the world.

Yet the same energy and enthusiasm that once dismantled this great ecosystem are now at work to reconstruct it. Tennessee possesses more large blocks of Mississippi River floodplain hardwood forest than any other state on the lower end of the river's 2,350-mile course. In Tennessee's large tracts of unaltered Mississippi River bottomlands, you can still experience the ambience of this unique ecosystem. Work is already under way to connect the large blocks of remaining riverbottom ecosystem in the lower half of Tennessee's section of the river. When accomplished, this ecosystem will be like Great Smoky Mountains National Park, a true large scale biodiversity sphere. The migratory bird component and the riverine life web would also contribute to the richness of biodiversity found here. Eastern cougars and red wolves might be reintroduced. French and Spanish explorers once cited alligators as present as far north as southern Illinois. Perhaps this species will again populate the many backwaters and sloughs of this mighty river.

"It's lovely to live on a raft," said Huck Finn, as he drifted down the Mississippi. "We had the sky up there, all speckled with stars, and we used to lay on our backs and look up at them, and discuss whether they was made or only just happened." The Mississippi River spawned the prototypical American novel, the tale of a youth discovering a new, self-defining national character, one without the class society of Europe. This great river may have shaped the American character as much as any single entity between the two coasts. Paddle wheelers up the Missouri River, one of the main tributaries of the Mississippi, were the only way young men could follow Horace Greeley's advice and go west. Get to know this great river of the world. The story of the Mississippi, its alteration, use and resurrection is a uniquely American one.

Hot Spots

If you wish to explore the main channel of the Mississippi, it is best to go with someone who knows this very dangerous river intimately. Waves from barges can swamp a skiff. Terrific currents exist behind rock revetments that extend far out into the river and powerful "suck holes" could lie behind these rock revetments during periods of high water. A moving, submerged tree may strike the bottom of the river with its root ball, suddenly stand up and then topple forward in the river, during the spring floods. You can get to know the

Mississippi River ecosystem quite well by exploring the protected backwaters, oxbow lakes and sloughs, especially by canoe. **Coal Creek Chute,** near Ft. Pillow State Park, is a splendid example of an oxbow, or meander of the river that was cut off and left behind as the river wandered within its floodplain. Very large cottonwood trees line Coal Creek Chute. Here you can see interesting fauna, from alligator gar to cottonmouthed moccasins to a diverse warbler and songbird population. To reach Coal Creek Chute, leave from the entrance of Ft. Pillow State Park (chapter 2) and backtrack east for 3.4 miles to Meter's Gulf station and store. Turn left here and go 1.7 miles. You may be surprised to see that roadside dumping of garbage is still an accepted practice here. Cross the C. H. Sullivan Bridge, park in the parking lot and paddle down Coal Creek for a half mile to enter Coal Creek Chute. If the water is high, you may be able to paddle nearly all the way to the Mississippi River, located 1 mile to the southwest. Be very careful to look for cottonmouths as you pass under overhanging limbs. In fact, be very aware of dangerous snakes the entire time you explore this region. The Chickasaw Bluffs of the Mississippi River, with its copperheads, timber rattlesnakes and cottonmouths, has a wonderfully diverse herpefauna.

To reach **Wardlow's Pocket** in **Chickasaw NWR** (chapter 3), take the road past Ed Jones boat ramp and continue straight for approximately 4 miles to the boat ramp at Wardlow's Pocket. This 2-mile-long lake is another easily accessible piece of Mississippi River bottomland ecosystem. Nearby **Nebraska Point** (chapter 3), also in Chickasaw NWR, offers an opportunity to paddle your canoe in a protected arm of the Mississippi River itself. You must portage the canoe for a half mile from the parking area for Nebraska Point to the river. A wheeled canoe dolly, available from L. L. Bean, will make this a simple task.

Another destination for the canoeist who wishes to explore the Mississippi River ecosystem is **Reelfoot Lake** (chapter 40). Even though this large earthquake-created lake is several miles east of the river and is not physically connected to it, it still has an oasis of Mississippi River floodplain species.

52

Shorebirds Along the Mississippi River

Tennessee's segment of the Mississippi River offers to birders of the three-state region an opportunity to see shorebirds in an environment vastly different from Pea Island, North Carolina; Huntington Beach State Park, South Carolina and the strand at Cape Hatteras. The Mississippi River is the greatest flyway in America for waterfowl. Waterfowl and shorebirds using it may be headed as far north as the prairie potholes region of the Dakotas and Saskatchewan, or even the Canadian arctic. Although the number of species seen here in a day will probably not equal the number seen in a location such as Cape Hatteras or Pea Island, birding along the greatest river in North America has an excitement all its own.

The Mississippi River has an openness and vastness, especially in the fall of the year when water levels are low, that may suggest the Outer Banks of North Carolina to birders accustomed to going there. Early September, around Labor Day, is one of the two premier times for seeing shorebirds here. Likely species include black terns returning from the prairie pothole region, Forster's terns, red knot, buff-breasted sandpipers, ruddy turnstones, stilt sandpipers, dowitchers, as well as greater and lesser yellowlegs. The least terns seen at this time may be local birds that nested on sandbars of the river. In the fall the riverine ecosystem is probably the only habitat available for these waterbirds as they migrate south. An extremely rainy fall may fill up the ponds and ditches, but this is unusual. The Mississippi kites are still present early in September, and this is one of the best spots in the southeastern United States to see them. They depart by mid-September. The falling river strands many species of fish in pockets and depressions, and alligator gar and short-nosed gar litter the sandbars and shoreline.

The other time of year for observing shorebirds along the Mississippi River is spring. "Relativity of time" among shorebirds (see chapter 39) occurs here as well as on the Outer Banks, and some species may arrive as early as February and return to South America by July. Yet the heaviest shorebird traffic moves through during the first half of May. An advantage for shorebirds during the spring is the availability of rainwater-filled ponds, sloughs and ditches in the river floodplain. These ponds are important sources of protein for migrating shorebirds. Thousands of pectoral sandpipers may be seen, along with many herons and egrets, feverishly working the edges of ditches and ponds for snails, fish and other small crustaceans and insects. A "drop-out" of several hundred golden plovers or red knot in courtship plumage on the many pits, ponds and sloughs along the river is an exciting possibility. Try to plan a spring shorebird trip to the Mississippi River after a rainy period, when the ponds are full. As on the Outer Banks, a spotting scope will help tremendously here. A spring shorebird trip could be combined with a spring warbler trip to Chickasaw NWR, Hatchie NWR, Meeman Shelby State Park and Ft. Pillow State Park. Of these locations, Hatchie NWR (chapter 30) may be the premier location for spring warblers.

Hot Spots

The shoreline and sandbars of Island 13 (chapter 40), on the Mississippi River, as well as the ponds and pits along the levee on the way to this location, attract shorebirds. The ponds and gravel pits are more important during the spring migration because they tend to be filled with rainwater. The **Phillippi Pits,** just west of Reelfoot Lake, is another shorebird magnet during both the spring and fall migrations. These extensive, excavated barrow pits collect rainwater and provide excellent shoreline habitat. They are easily accessible and can be viewed with a spotting scope from the road. To reach the Phillippi Pits, take TN 78 north out of Tiptonville, in the northwest corner of Tennessee. Pass the turnoff for Air Park Inn and proceed 1.3 miles to the crossroads called Phillippy. Turn west at the abandoned white cinderblock building and head west for 1.4 miles. Do not bear left, but continue west. The Phillippi Pits lie on either side of the road. By turning right just beyond the pits and driving several miles into Kentucky, you may see more red-headed woodpeckers than you ever knew existed. During stable weather conditions, they often fly out of the large cotton-woods along the Mississippi River and perch on telephone lines along the road. Many other interesting birding side trips are outlined for this area of Tennessee in *Bird Finding in Tennessee* by Michael Lee Bierly, available from Michael Lee Bierly, 3825 Bedford Avenue, Nashville, TN 37215, as well as in many bookstores.

53

September Shorttakes

Birder's Hurricane Net

While the hurricane season runs from early June through November, the peak is from September to early November. Hurricanes are of interest to birders because they widely disperse birds. In 1995, Hurricane Opal put unusual birds in out-of-the-way places: A Mississippi kite was reported in Durham, North Carolina; a parasitic jaeger and a black skimmer showed up in Chattanooga, Tennessee. In July 1996, Hurricane Bertha forced many pelagic birds into the Chesapeake Bay. What is unique about these sightings is that, for the first time, they were reported on the Hurricane Net over the Internet. Birders from all over the East Coast reported sightings in this way. If you want to participate and report any bird displaced by a hurricane or learn of sightings by others, you can reach Wallace Coffey by e-mail at jwcoffey@tricon.net. In addition to the Hurricane Net, there is an e-mail network for people who feed birds, as well as the Valley Net. The Valley Net unites electronically birders in the great valleys west of the Blue Ridge Mountains, including the Shenandoah Valley, the Roanoke Valley, the New River Valley, the Holston River Valley and the Tennessee River Valley as far south as northern Alabama. If you want to become part of this network, send your name and address to Wallace Coffey, and he will subscribe you to the Net.

Monarchs Along the Blue Ridge Parkway

In chapter 50 it was mentioned that migrating monarch butterflies are a fairly common sight around the various rocky outcroppings common to migrating hawks. If you want to plan a trip specifically to observe migrating butterflies, try Milepost 415.6 of the Blue Ridge Parkway. Thousands of monarch butterflies pass through the Tunnel Gap in September as they migrate to central Mexico.

54

A Closer Look:
Late Summer Wildflower Strategies

As different as the two worlds encountered by Lemuel Gulliver in Swift's *Gulliver's Travels* are the spring and fall wildflowers. Like the tiny Lilliputians who cabled Gulliver to the ground as he slept are the early spring ephemerals and flowering herbs. The petals of the bluet are studies in tiny perfection, each barely over a quarter of an inch. The entire plant may stand only 4 inches tall. Clusters of violets can carpet the forest floor along trails, but the individual plants are small. The average height for hepatica, creeping phlox, blood-root, many species of trillium, trout lilies, showy orchids and yellow lady's slippers is less than a foot in most cases, and all are less than 18 inches tall. Rather than spending most of the energy allotted to them on height, these species seem to prefer creating masterpieces of color or design. Jack-in-the-pulpit, Dutchman's pipe, Dutchman's britches, pitcher plants and many of the diminutive insectivorous plants have elevated the art of building insect-entrapping chambers to astonishing levels. The insects targeted are sometimes destined to be devoured, and sometimes allowed to escape after being dusted in pollen. Yet even these clever architects have constructed their castles on the same lilliputian scale.

Lemuel Gulliver moves from the island of Lilliput to the mythical peninsula of Brobdingnag, east of the Molucca Islands, where people are as tall as church spires. So, too, the wildflowers move their strategy 180 degrees away from the "small is beautiful" concept. Beginning in midsummer, big is better, and biggest plus most audacious is best.

Many spring wildflowers are able to attract pollinators with color and design before the forest completely blocks out the sunlight. The midsummer group occurs primarily outside the forest in fields, along roadsides, under power line rights-of-way, along riverbanks—anywhere the forest canopy does not block the sun. However, these open areas are always claimed by a tangle of weed, briar and bramble, grasses and struggling seedlings when the late wildflowers begin arriving in midsummer.

The late flowers' strategy may seem preposterous, for flowers are typically thought of as retiring things of delicate beauty. Compared to tiny 4-inch-tall bluets or hepatica, late flowers are truly Brobdingnagian. The joe-pye weed, with its thick, strong stem topped by lavender flowers, may stand 15 feet high. The brilliant purple ironweed is nearly as tall. Along the roadside or in large forest openings and fields, Queen Anne's lace, butterfly weed, goldenrod, asters, black-eyed Susans, farewell summers, chickory and wild phlox attract hordes of pollinators by dominating whole hillsides, growing as tall as necessary to transcend the wild grasses and weeds. By late September, bees by the thousands create a polite roar as they work acres of towering wildflowers moving with the wind. Along the rivers and creeks, cardinal flowers, jewelweed and thistle fight their way through tangles of adversaries that compete for the sunlight, and then advertise for pollinators. These late flowers, though less demure and more insistent, are every bit as fetching as the spring innocents. The sight of a dozen tiger swallowtail or black swallowtail butterflies working a cluster of purple flowers on a pocket of thistles is quite different from that of a showy orchid on a shaded hillside, but is no less miraculous.

Late wildflowers are quite widespread and can be found along pastures, on hillsides and along the roadsides of the region. Upper eastern Tennessee seems to be unusually blessed with late flowers, perhaps because of the limestone component in the soil. Look along the entire length of the South Holston River (chapter 29) on islands, along the river and along the road following the river. Under the power line rights-of-way are hotspots for these flowers. Explore the backroads of Sullivan Country, Tennessee, with an eye out for openings and fields where sunlight is available.

October

Notes

55

The Free-Ranging Wild Ponies

Romantic stories have been woven to explain the origins of the wild horses that have survived on the Outer Banks. Some insist that the ancestors of certain of these herds swam ashore through the surf as Spanish galleons foundered in "The Graveyard of the Atlantic," the treacherous shoals and sandbars of North Carolina's barrier islands. It is entirely possible that some truth lies in this explanation, for ships known to be transporting "livestock" did go down off the Outer Banks during the Age of Sail, and horses would have been capable of making such a swim. Regardless of how they initially got there, two out of three of the herds on North Carolina's Outer Banks are now restrained. The Ocracoke Island herd is kept off the highway by confinement in a large pen. The Corolla herd, numbering 26 animals, is restricted to a small area because they are regarded as a threat to the expensive homes and lawns, as well as to motorists of this newly developed area north of Nag's Head. This represents a great change in lifestyle for this herd, for the Corolla area was a wild and unfettered place until a decade ago, when a divided highway threw the region open to development. Only the herd of Shackleford Banks and the Rachel Carson Estuarine Preserve still survives using its own wits.

Shackleford Banks and the Rachel Carson Preserve's Carrot Island and Horse Island have been used as communal pasture by people from the mainland since the turn of the century. Prior to that time, a town called Diamond City, with a population of 500, tied up the resources of this elongated barrier island behind Cape Lookout. Some of the horses now living on Shackleford Banks may actually be descendants of the animals left behind when Diamond City disbanded after an onslaught of hurricanes and powerful winter storms during the early 1900s. However, with the annual pasturing of horses, goats, sheep and cattle since then, on

Shackleford Banks and the other, smaller islands this may never be accurately determined. What is certain is that in 1988, all species except the horses were rounded up and removed so that the limited vegetation on the islands could go toward maintaining the horse herd.

The wild horses of these islands are actually no more wild than any horses left to fend for themselves for decades. What is different about them is that physiologically they have undergone metabolic modifications to allow survival in a very sparse ecosystem. The horses of these islands have demonstrated a remarkable ability to survive on coarse, rough, wild grasses with low nutritional value. They obtain drinking water by pawing holes in the low-lying areas of the islands, thus obtaining brackish water for drinking. These horses even wade the tidal zone and eat spartina grass.

Yet, with this herd, as with the Chincoteague Island, Virginia, herd and the Cumberland Island, Georgia, herd, overpopulation has led to depletion of the already limited available protein sources. In small herds, such as the Shackleford Banks–Rachel Carson herd, inbreeding has brought out recessive traits, as a small gene pool always tends to do. Because these herds are unable to leave their respective islands, achieving enlargement and diversification of the gene pool, humans have had to intervene. Presently, the Shackleford Banks–Rachel Carson herd has more than 200 animals, but the carrying capacity of the islands is less than half that number. It is estimated that Horse and Carrot Islands can support approximately 30 animals and Shackleford Banks about 60. The surplus horses, according to the management plan contemplated, will be captured and adopted out to families who want them. This intervention has become necessary since some of the horses in the herds are anemic and close to starvation, and others appear to be diseased. Lack of additional habitat has brought about this problem.

That the Shackleford Banks–Rachel Carson Preserve possesses this exotic component in its estuarine ecosystem, in addition to a pristine salt marsh and rich waterbird life, makes it unique in the eyes of many. Paddling a canoe or kayak through a salt marsh,

Beaufort—Rachel Carson Preserve

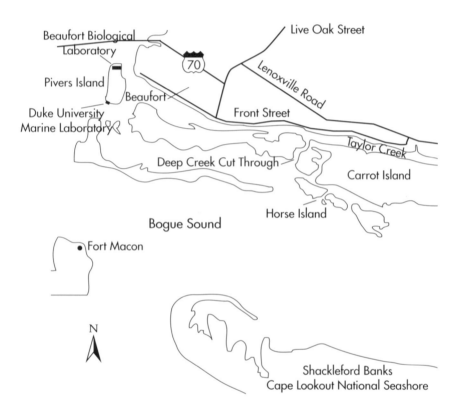

Beaufort Biological Laboratory

Live Oak Street

70

Lenoxville Road

Pivers Island

Beaufort

Front Street

Duke University
Marine Laboratory

Taylor Creek

Deep Creek Cut Through

Carrot Island

Horse Island

Bogue Sound

Fort Macon

N

Shackleford Banks
Cape Lookout National Seashore

observing herons, egrets and shorebirds, as well as the other fauna
present, and perhaps seeing members of one of the last truly free-
ranging horse herds of the seashore of the East Coast, is a special
opportunity.

**Hot
Spots**

The **Rachel Carson Preserve** is best seen from a canoe or
kayak, but the main channel into the preserve, Deep Creek,
is only passable several hours on either side of high tide, so
timing is important. If you attempt to make it through the
channel into the preserve on low tide, dragging your canoe or
kayak will be necessary. Wild ponies can be seen on either
Horse or Carrot Island, often grazing in the edge of the salt

Wild horses in the Rachel Carson Preserve.

marsh itself. At times wild ponies can be observed from Front Street in downtown Beaufort, but a canoe or kayak provides the best means to experience this ecosystem. Canoe access is gained from the north end of Front Street. Park in one of the designated spaces along the waterfront parking area on Front Street, and carry your gear and canoe to the tidal creek.

Reaching **Shackleford Banks** is too dangerous to attempt by canoe. For information on using the Shackleford Ferry, see chapter 8. For additional information on the wild horse herd, call Dr. Michael Rikard or Chuck Harris at Cape Lookout National Seashore at (919) 728-2250.

56

Exploring the Salt Marsh

The two most pristine salt marsh–estuarine areas on the East Coast—A.C.E. Basin and Cape Romaine NWR—are located near Charleston, South Carolina. Yet 250 miles away via I-26 is Great Smoky Mountains National Park, generally conceded to be one of the most splendid examples of temperate-zone hardwood forest in the world. The vast southern Appalachian region is one of the great floral provinces of the world. The three-state region is blessed to have vastly different ecosystems just hours' driving time apart.

The hardwood forest and the salt marsh are truly worlds apart. All the flora and fauna of the cove hardwood forest would quickly die if placed in a salt marsh environment, where the water is approximately 35 parts per thousand of salt. How did nature create a web of life as complex as the one in Great Smoky Mountains National Park in a salt marsh? In the case of marine animals, the answer was to provide them with brinier blood. Whereas salt is approximately 1 percent of the total volume of human blood, marine animals have nearly 3 percent salt content in their blood. Salt spray plant communities have clever mechanisms and designs to protect themselves from the ravages of salt. Some plants, such as the halophytes, have hairy leaves and stems that trap salt before it touches the plant. Others, such as succulent shore plants, conserve moisture and repel saltwater with thick, fleshy leaves protected by thick, waxy, epidermal layers. Study the salt marsh as an ecosystem that is equally complex as, and far more dynamic than, any other in the region.

The salt marsh is where the ocean and the mainland meet. The sea, with a host of organisms, invades this realm twice every 24 hours. This ecosystem is the nursery for most important sport and commercial marine species, and the estuary is the most fluid, changing ecosystem of all. Tides enter the ecosystem and completely submerge the salt marsh. Even a sudden shower can change its salinity. Storm and hurricane surges may bury the ecosystem under 20 feet of raging ocean. In comparison, the freshwater inland marsh is quite static. An acre of salt marsh produces eight times more protein per acre than a highly fertilized acre of planted corn or wheat. The 5-foot-tall spartina grass or cordgrass sustains 90 percent of marsh inhabitants directly or indirectly. There is no more interesting ecosystem to explore than the salt marsh, and the canoe or kayak is the perfect vehicle.

Salt marshes are flooded at high tide by plankton-rich water as well as an army of species. The ebb tide carries out dissolved organic matter, decaying spartina grass and dead and decaying small marine creatures. This "nutrient stew" is traded back and forth, each environment receiving enrichment from the other. The mudflats, once they are left exposed by the retreating tide, are immediately claimed by an army of crabs. As in the altitude bands of Roan Mountain, different denizens of the mudflats claim different ecosystems in the salt marsh. Sand fiddler crabs claim the high ground, while mud fiddlers claim the low ground. Mud crabs eat them both, only to be eaten themselves by snowy egrets, great egrets and green herons. It is estimated that one acre of semitropical South Carolina mudflats will support one million fiddler crabs.

Fiddler crabs and spartina grass are important keystone species. Spartina grass is so successful here that it forms vast grass prairies extending across miles of salt marsh, but this important source of protein must be converted into a form that can be used by species higher on the food chain. The fiddler crab performs this important task by rolling up tiny balls of mud, enriched by organic material from decaying spartina, and sucking out the protein. This protein, when converted into millions of fiddler crabs, can then be used by the many species that cannot eat spartina but can eat fiddlers. Wading birds, diamond-backed turtles, otters, raccoons, spot-tailed bass and a host of others depend on fiddler crabs as a primary part of their diets. The fiddler crab, the locomotive that pulls much of the higher end of the salt marsh food chain, escapes from the midday heat by burrowing deeply into the mud bottom of the salt marsh and then plugging the hole with a round ball of mud.

The salt marsh food chain is multilayered. Zooplankton are eaten by shrimp and filter-feeding fish and insect larvae. Small fish eat the insect larvae. Detritus and decaying spartina grass are eaten by fiddler crabs, oysters and clams. Starfish and oystercatchers eat the bivalves. The wading birds are the towering "Tyrannosauarus rexes" of the salt marsh, as they stalk about in search of fiddlers, small minnows, small eels and even baby alligators.

One of the most interesting wading birds to watch is the green heron. This bird may stand so still on the edge of a mudflat that it seems to make itself into a stick, or a piece of mud, until a school of minnows works its way up the shoreline. Suddenly this block of wood becomes a green heron as it creeps up to the water's edge, with its head, neck and beak held very low so as not to cast a shadow. Having crept to within a few feet of the minnow school, the green heron then runs quickly into the water and tries to pick off a fleeing minnow. This sequence may repeat itself a dozen times as the heron shadows the nonchalantly feeding minnow school.

Menhaden, jumping mullet, spot-tailed bass and even bottlenosed dolphins, sharks and loggerhead turtles all ride the tide miles into the salt marsh. Yet, ironically, the single axiom that covers the spectrum of all marine life is this: The smaller the organism, the more important it is to the food chain; the larger the organism, the less important it is to the food chain. Conversely, the smaller the organism, the less important the individual. The larger the organism, the more important the individual.

The estuarine and tidal-zone waters of the Carolinas are some of the most nutrient-rich in the world. One might think that the crystal-clear waters of the coral reefs of the Caribbean or the tropics would be more fertile than the sometimes greenish, sometimes brownish waters along the coastline. Nothing could be further from the truth. The reason for the crystal clarity of the Caribbean is an almost complete absence of life-sustaining nutrients and organic material suspended in the ocean. By comparison, the ocean off the coast of the Carolinas is a "nutrient soup" swarming with life. Photographs made by the Landsat 5 satellite show that the oceans off North Carolina, South Carolina and Georgia are among the "brightest" or most organically enriched in the world.

The salt marsh ecosystem is vastly different from any other in the region. Spartina or cordgrass prairies extend from horizon to horizon in locations such as Cedar Island, north of Morehead City, North Carolina, as well as the estuaries of the Edisto, Combahee and Ashepoo Rivers in South Carolina and in Cape Romain NWR. The tidal rivers host exotic species such as jet-propelled squid, manta rays, stingrays, sharks and skates. Small islands called "hammocks" support live oak, red cedar, bayberry, palmetto, slash pine, yaupon holly and other tree and shrub species. Paddle your canoe or kayak through these cordgrass prairies, which creak and rattle in the breeze. You may wish to pull your craft out of the water at low tide and walk across the mudflats in a pair of long pants and old tennis shoes. You will push an army of fiddler crabs in front of you. No matter how many times you come here with a cast net, a clam rake or to observe birds, there will always be universes of secrets waiting to be discovered. Two books that help unlock the mysteries of this ecosystem are *Tideland Treasure* by Todd Ballantine and *Nature Guide to the Carolina Coast* by Peter Meyer.

Hot Spots

The larger, more open salt marshes and estuarine areas should be experienced initially under the tutelage of an experienced guide, such as those offered by Coastal Expeditions, located near **Charleston.** For information call (803) 884-7684. Until you are experienced in this environment, you should think small. **Huntington Beach State Park,** South Carolina (chapter 20), offers a protected but diverse salt marsh with extensive spartina grass expanses, mudflats, a dynamic inlet and even a small hammock island called **Drunken Jack Island.** To reach this location, drive 1 mile north of the entrance to the state park. Look for an unmarked turnoff to the right, where a small sign reads "open 6:00 A.M. closed dark." Drive 0.1 mile to the salt marsh. Be careful to park well above

Exploring the salt marsh by canoe.

the high tide line because parking space is limited by trees and foliage.

Another excellent location for exploring the salt marsh is **Bear Island,** located between Wilmington and Morehead City, North Carolina. The Bear Island trip offers a well-marked canoe trail ending at a barrier island whose north end is covered with mixed slash pine–live oak maritime forest, as well as dynamic Bogue Inlet. A strong word of caution: Do not venture out Bogue Inlet, or any ocean inlet, even a short distance on the outgoing tide. You may not be able to paddle against it, and you could be pulled out into the breakers of the ocean. Stop at the Bear Island ranger station and pick up the canoe trail map. Launch your canoe next to the terminal of the Bear Island ferry, which takes pedestrians (no cars) out to the island. For more information, call **Hammocks Beach State Park** at (910) 326-4881. Hammocks Beach–Bear Island is located in Swansboro, North Carolina, north of Wilmington on NC 24.

The nearby mouth of the White Oak River is another good choice for a day trip to explore a salt marsh. The island in the mouth of this river, **Huggins Island,** is privately owned, so exploration of the island is not allowed. But you need not leave your canoe or kayak to appreciate the small live oak forest on this island.

Try to plan your trip to either of these locations so you depart as soon as the incoming tide gives sufficient water depth to paddle your canoe or kayak. In this way you will have the maximum time before the tide reverses itself and begins to rush out. Paddling against a racing ebb tide can be tiring, leaving little energy to enjoy wildlife. It is prudent to stop at Waterway Marina and Store; Tim Simpson, the proprietor, is the most knowledgeable individual on this salt marsh area and is very helpful to salt marsh ecotourists. For information call (919) 393-8008. Waterway Marina is on the north side of the bridge over the White Oak River, a half mile east of Dudley's Marina on NC 24.

A side trip to the pristine **White Oak River** gives an opportunity to experience a sister river to the Black River, near Wilmington. This blackwater river system has the added advantage of being buffered by the largest national forest of North Carolina's coastal plain: Croatan National Forest. This may help explain why the White Oak River has the highest water-quality rating of any blackwater river on North Carolina's coastal plain. On a windy day when paddling the unprotected salt marsh around Huggins Island or Bear Island is not possible, the White Oak River offers an alternative. Take NC 58 north toward Mayville for 8 miles. Turn left and proceed to Haywood's Landing. Here you can paddle upstream, for the current is manageable, and drift back to the landing.

Another splendid side trip, perhaps best taken before the Bear Island or Huggins Island trip, is the nearby **North Carolina Aquarium at Pine Knoll Shores** at Atlantic Beach, just across Bogue Sound from Morehead City. This facility offers numerous exhibits on salt marshes and the ocean environment as well as all manner of field trips. A few of the more popular ones are a canoe trip to Rachel Carson Preserve, exploring the summer beach, a Bear Island trip, a salt marsh walk, a Bogue Sound canoe trip, as well as feedings of the fish in the aquarium. North Carolina Aquarium at Pine Knoll Shores also has an easily walked salt marsh trail. For information call (919) 247-4003.

Kayaks are more seaworthy than canoes, but one-person models offer no space for a companion and little for gear. Two-seater kayaks can be very expensive. For this reason many canoeists have turned to "cross-link," Old Town Canoe's version of Royalex. This quiet, indestructible canoe comes in 16-foot 9-inch and 17-foot 4-inch models. Consider getting the brightest red color available; because powerboaters may be moving at well over 50 mph with poor visibility over the bow of the boat, being seen becomes an important consideration. Pro Canoe of Greensboro, North Carolina, often has reasonably priced "blemished" Discovery cross-link canoes for sale.

Built-in canoe seats place the center of gravity too high, making the canoe tipsy. Beautiful and functional canoe chairs of wood and rawhide can be purchased from Tubbs Snoeshoe Co. in Stowe, Vermont, (802) 253-7398.

The canoe cannot go as safely across the big water as a large kayak. Yet a 17-footer, which tracks better than a shorter canoe, can handle most salt marshes, as well as hold a dog, a companion and a cooler of food. L. L. Bean sells a small outboard motor stern bracket that will accommodate a three-horsepower Johnson outboard, which weighs 33 pounds. McCallum's of Fayetteville, North Carolina [(910) 483-6804], offers the best price for this quiet little motor in the region. If the wind suddenly picks up, the three-horse can quickly become a necessity. It can be used to reach wildlife viewing areas that are quite distant, then be turned off and put in the tilt position as you paddle. This affordable, versatile package is hard to beat for exploring most salt marshes.

57

The Outer Banks: Landbird Traps

Finding a more striking example of a landbird "trap" than North Carolina's Outer Banks would be difficult. As birds move down this ribbon of barrier islands, in some places only several hundred yards wide, they "pile up" in strategic locations, especially after certain weather conditions. In late September and early October, several factors combine to produce fabulous temporary concentrations of landbirds as they migrate southward. Most of these birds are primarily nocturnal migrants who use the night sky as a navigational aid. They ride the northwest winds associated with cold fronts southward. The morning after a night of brisk northwest winds brought by a cold front may see thousands of sparrows, warblers, vireos, thrushes and other small landbirds flitting about in the limited vegetation of the sparse Outer Banks ecosystem. Winds out of the west or north can also produce landbird pileups. A tropical storm or hurricane tends to have the same effect.

The window of opportunity for witnessing this phenomenon is fairly brief. After the middle of October, the frequency of cold fronts with flight-aiding northwest winds increases, but by that time the diversity of landbird species has begun to diminish, for the peak of the migration is over. In late September through early October, watch the weather closely and try to witness one of the most exciting birding events of the three-state region.

Other interesting birds are present at this time, moving down the Outer Banks in their southerly migrations. Pea Island is the best shorebird location in North Carolina, and early October is the tail end of the peak of migration for species such as golden plover, Hudsonian godwit, red knot, whimbrel, willet, yellowlegs and many species of sandpipers. With luck, most of the shorebirds that frequent North Carolina can be seen at this time. For information on where to see shorebirds (see chapter 39).

In addition to landbirds and shorebirds, the Outer Banks has a through-migration of hawks, which opportunistically feed on small landbirds. Raptor species such as sharp-shinned hawks, Cooper's hawks, peregrine falcons and merlins can all be seen in a single day.

Hot Spots

The two wooden observation towers at either end of **North Pond**, behind the **Pea Island** visitor's center, are the best places to see migrating hawks and falcons (chapter 50). The bushes and shrubs on the dikes of North Pond may be alive with passerines after favorable weather conditions. Because the sparse overwash barrier islands offer few brushy thickets, migrating songbirds heavily use the ones here. The dike along the south end of North Pond and the dike following the west shore of North Pond are excellent places to search for migrating landbirds. Of course, identification will be more difficult than during the spring migration, when all these species are in courtship plumage. For directions to the Pea Island visitor's center (see chapter 39).

A second, nearby location for migrating passerines is the brushy area just behind the old Coast Guard station at the north end of Pea Island. Immediately after coming off Oregon Inlet Bridge headed south, turn sharply back to the left and drive as close as you can to the white buildings. Park and walk around behind the buildings. Walk north toward the inlet, watching the bushes for songbirds.

A third location where landbirds concentrate during migration is several hundred miles south of Pea Island. The **Ft. Fisher** area is reached most aesthetically by taking the Southport Ferry. In Southport, located south of Wilmington, turn left (north) on Moore Street, drive 2 miles and take the Southport–Ft. Fisher ferry. Upon reaching the ferry terminal, turn left and drive approximately 1.5 miles to **Ft. Fisher State Historic Site**. Observe the shrubs as well as the live oak forest adjacent to the Ft. Fisher Museum parking lot for migrants. The nearby **North Carolina Aquarium** also offers migrating landbirds refuge in the live oaks and thickets adjacent to the hiking trail that departs from the south side of the aquarium parking lot. This trail is roughly a mile long.

58

Fall Colors by Car and Canoe

Fall colors are much like the constellations of the night sky. One need understand absolutely nothing of either entity to become expert at enjoying them. In the naturalist's world, a technical understanding of behavior, habitat requirements, distinguishing field marks and so on, is the basis for understanding the bewilderingly complex interactions of the creatures that form the chain of life. It is wise to sometimes discipline yourself to turn off the empirical left hemisphere of the brain and "feel" with the right brain. The ability to use the different halves of the brain is what balance is all about. Einstein knew the importance of empiricism better than anyone. He once stated, "Whatever your problems are in mathematics, I can assure you that mine are greater." Yet he also stated that imagination is more important than knowledge. He provides us with an ideal model. The birder with a life list who drives 400 miles to a specific location, identifies a species, places it on his or her list and drives home may be technically expert, but this individual has not achieved balance by "knowing" and appreciating this new species and its environment.

A rudimentary understanding of the miracle of fall color is all that is needed to enjoy it. Certain species of trees turn earlier than others, and different species turn different colors. Each is beautiful. The forest begins to change color earlier at higher elevations.

Try to enjoy the early autumn color, when the mountains "frost" in gold at the higher elevations weeks before the valleys do. Notice how a windy day can produce a blizzard of falling, spinning color. Late in the fall, when many trees are bare, a sugar maple may stubbornly hold its leaves, a bonfire of red, burning in the gray landscape.

Try to make the appreciation of fall colors an exercise in enjoyment as a child would enjoy them. In fact let fall colors be only the first aspect of nature you learn to enjoy as a child would. At the end of his career, after he had mastered nearly every form of

246

Fall colors along the Blue Ridge Parkway.

painting then known, Picasso was asked if there was anything he regretted about his artistic achievements. "I regret," he replied, "that I can no longer paint as I did as a child."

Hot Spots

Fall colors come in according to elevation. Around **Boone, North Carolina**, colors peak about two weeks into October. Colors also peak at this time along higher elevations of the **Blue Ridge Parkway** and **Great Smoky Mountains National Park**. Around the third week of October is the peak of fall color in most of the cove hardwood forest of the southern Appalachians, including **Cade's Cove, Hickory Nut Gorge** and **Lake Lure, Doughton Park, Roan Mountain** and the **TVA lakes** in eastern Tennessee. The **Uwharrie Mountains** of North Carolina's piedmont section may peak several weeks after the mountains of western North Carolina and eastern Tennessee. Refer to chapter 19 for directions to each of these locations, as well as canoe destinations for foliage colors. The canoe destinations outlined are also the best ones for fall foliage color.

59

October Shorttakes

Sugarloaf on the Cape Fear

In **Carolina Beach State Park** stands a 50-foot high sand dune called Sugarloaf. During the Age of Sail, when Wilmington was one of the busiest ports in the colonies, this large dune served as a valuable navigational landmark. During the Civil War, 5,000 Confederate troops camped on Sugarloaf during the siege of Ft. Fisher. Today this sandy promontory, covered in pines and oaks, offers a splended viewing platform for the ecotourist who wants to survey the sprawling, biodiversity-rich Cape Fear estuary. To reach **Sugarloaf Trail,** drive to the marina–boat ramp of Carolina Beach State Park, 15 miles south of Wilmington on US 421. You may wish to pick up a map at the park headquarters. Follow the yellow dot markers along the Cape Fear River and through the dune system. Upon reaching the obvious high point of the dune system, stop and enjoy Sugarloaf. Then retrace your steps back to the marina–boat ramp parking lot. The trail system becomes very confusing if you continue past Sugarloaf. The walk to Sugarloaf should take less than an hour.

On Collision Course

An irresistible force will soon meet an immovable object. The Shell Island Resort Hotel presently stands 155 feet south of **Mason Inlet,** at the north end of Wrightsville Beach near Wilmington. This dynamic ocean inlet has a history of a southward migration. From 1945 to 1963 the inlet·moved 3,000 feet south. Ten years ago the inlet was 1.5 miles north of its present location but in 1986 the resort was built 2,500 feet south of the inlet. Mason inlet moved 150 feet south in 1993 and 200 feet south in 1995. The resort presently stands 155 feet south of Mason Inlet, which separates Figure 8 Island from Wrightsville Beach. Dr. Bill Cleary

Sugarloaf—Carolina Beach State Park

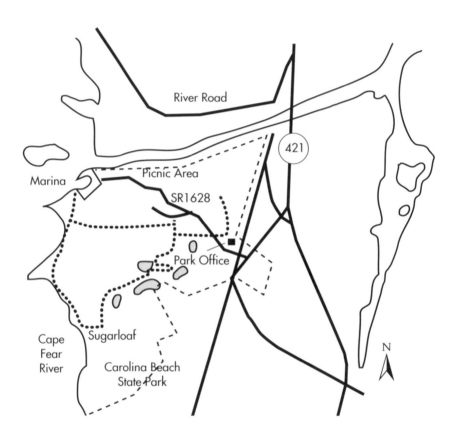

of UNCW predicts that the inlet will stabilize 1,000 feet south of its present location, at which point vegetation will offer some stability against erosion.

The Shell Island Resort Hotel is a study of what happens when humans invite a confrontation with the dynamism of nature. It is worth a trip to see Shell Island Resort, to stand before the folly of this conundrum, which says more than a thousand words.

60

A Closer Look:
Cade's Cove Bucks in Rut

In the Rocky Mountain West, a large, level-floored valley surrounded by mountains was called a "hole" by pioneers. Wyoming's Jackson Hole and Montana's Big Hole are some of the more illustrious examples. In the southern Appalachians, such a geographical feature was called a "cove." In both the American West and the southern Appalachians, these large valleys spawned some of the most stable, self-contained communities ever produced by the American democratic experiment. Cade's Cove was a model of the pioneer-era independent community. Here one man was a blacksmith, one milled grain, one made chestnut shingles, another was a cobbler. Work was traded out. A woman might have great knowledge of mountain herbs or birthing children or spinning wool. Each person had worth, and status could not be bought. Perhaps most important, religion was tied to the land and to nature.

Cade's Cove today is preserved in time in the northwest corner of Great Smoky Mountains National Park. The neat cabins and churches stand in the forest. The pioneers are gone, but the simple order of their lives remains to be seen. There is no more striking time of the year to visit this valley in Great Smoky Mountains National Park than in mid to late October. This is also the time to see the courtship behavior of the bucks of the large white-tailed deer herd that resides in Cade's Cove.

The same bucks that ran here in bachelor groups in August have now rubbed their horns free of velvet and regard each other as enemies. Like a scene from the American West, where bull elk bugle at each other across a meadow, approach regally and fight, Cade's Cove witnesses a southern Appalachian version of the same event. Large, dominant bucks with swollen necks and polished antlers throw caution to the wind. While in rut, they make scrapes in the leaf litter to show the limits of their territory and leave rub marks on saplings, where antlers are polished and cleaned of velvet. A large, dominant buck visits every doe in his territory and breeds with each one as she becomes fertile. He is constantly on the move, checking his does and running off all male challengers. Two bucks who regard each other as equals may meet in the meadow, snort, paw and walk stiff-legged, and then lock horns and fight for the right to breed with the does. The buck with greater strength and tenacity wins out, thereby gaining the privilege to pass on his genes.

This story is acted out by a million players among the species that compose the web of life on earth. No better stage exists than Cade's Cove to watch this ongoing dialectic played out. Walk the woods of Cade's Cove and look carefully in the leaves for scrapes and for small saplings with the bark rubbed off or broken down altogether. In the early morning, or as the sun sinks behind the mountains, if you are lucky you may see the white-tailed bucks gracefully play out the oldest story on earth.

There is one organic difference between a Rocky Mountain hole and a southern Appalachian cove. The coniferous evergreen forest of the shale-sloped Rocky Mountain West has roughly a dozen species of trees that make up most of the biomass of the forest, compared to the southern Appalachian ecosystem with its 159 species of trees. And a western hole never had a backdrop of forested, soil-covered mountains, which change from green to orange, tan, red, yellow, mustard and rust in October. Only the most beautiful, most verdant and most seductive mountains on earth can do that.

To check on the progress of the color at Cade's Cove, call (423) 448-2472. The third week of October is traditionally the peak for fall color.

November

Notes

61

Tundra Swans, Ducks and Geese on Pea Island

Pea Island is the premier location on North Carolina's coastline for shorebirds, "pileups" of southerly migrating songbirds, tundra swans and migrating raptors. Nearby Cape Point at Cape Hatteras is the best place on the East Coast for gull species diversity, as well as the scene of frantic gannet and loon activity from November through February. Throw in the migrating jaeger, scoter, eider and oldsquaw, which all regard Cape Hatteras as important staging grounds, and you have an excellent late fall birding destination.

The five major staging grounds for spring migrating North American shorebirds and waterfowl are the Delaware Estuary; the Bay of Fundy, between New Brunswick and Nova Scotia; Cheyenne Bottoms, Nebraska; Gray's Harbor, Washington, and the Copper River Delta, Alaska. For fall migrating North American shorebirds and waterfowl, North Carolina's Pea Island would have to rank somewhere near the top.

One event that always draws enthusiastic crowds is the arrival of the whistling swans or tundra swans. These are the big boys of the Pea Island crowd, and they begin to arrive, along with Canada and snow geese, during the October full moon. In November the big airships, the geese and swans, as well as hundreds of puddle ducks such as gadwall, mallards, pintails, American widgeon, shovellers, teal and others peak in numbers on Pea Island.

What makes November so special to the empathetic birder is that during late October and into November, the swans are still talking about their trip down from Alaska and the Canadian arctic. On still mornings, not long after light, and at dusk, when the day's work is done, North Pond can be noisy with chatter as the

Pea Island

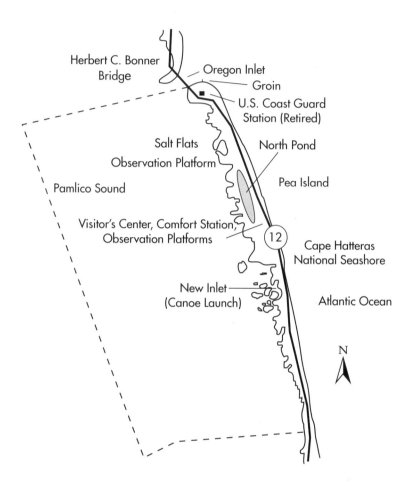

swans and snow geese enthusiastically say whatever needs saying after a flight across one of the remotest regions on the globe. The tundra swans feed like puddle ducks, with their enormous, lovely bottoms up in the air, as they probe the submerged shallows of the ponds. Everywhere is sound, from the yelps and barks of flying snow geese, to the highball call of the hen mallard, to the soft "wows" of the tundra swans. Their sense of sanctuary here is palpable. After a month or so, the excitement in the swan and goose community cools somewhat, as the Outer Banks begin to feel like home for the season. Try to be there early in the winter when these regal birds, so filled with dignity, purpose and resolve, allow a glimpse into a society where no decision is trivial, no joy is not hard-won.

Hot Spots

The tundra swans of **Pea Island** are best seen on North Pond, behind the Pea Island visitor's center. Call the Pea Island Preserve at (919) 987-2394 to check on arriving waterfowl. To see the other large gathering of tundra swans on the North Carolina coast, cross **Pamlico Sound,** either by driving to Manteo and then south on NC 264, or by taking the Swanquarter Ferry from Ocracoke, and then drive to **Lake Mattamuskeet.** By taking the ferry across Pamlico Sound, you may see scoters, oldsquaws and large rafts of black brant that winter here. Pamlico Sound is the most southerly distribution of large numbers of oldsquaw. A drive across Mattamuskeet's causeway may reveal many tundra swans, Canada geese and both puddle ducks and diving ducks. Tundra swans flying low over the causeway appear as big as bombers. An added incentive for a visit to Mattamuskeet is the overwintering bald eagle population. From early November through February, look on the small islands out in Lake Mattamuskeet on the east side of the causeway. The numbers of waterfowl here, as on Pea Island, begin to decline after early December. Check the agricultural fields at the east end of Lake Mattamuskeet for flocks of swans, Canada geese and snow geese, as well as birds of prey. Finally, **Huntington Beach State Park** (chapter 20) has a small population of overwintering tundra swans.

62

Bison and Fall Color in
Land Between the Lakes

It is fitting to combine a trip to see the Land Between the Lakes bison herd with a drive down The Trace Parkway, for it is thought that this splendid scenic drive follows the course of an ancient bison trail. In fact many of the original wagon trails and traces, and even Native American footpaths, followed bison trails. The most famous of these was The Great Wagon Road, which originated in Philadelphia, insinuated its way through the Shenandoah Valley of Virginia, passed through Salisbury, North Carolina, and terminated in Georgia. The Great Wagon Road followed The Warrior's Path, an important trading and warring route between the eastern seaboard tribes. The Indians had, in turn, followed the ancient game trails laid down in large part by the small herds of migrating bison.

In addition to the vast herds of bison that sustained the Plains Indians in the American West, smaller herds also existed in pockets from Georgia to Canada's Hudson Bay. Once the federal government mandated that the Great Plains bison herds be extirpated in order to weaken the Plains Indian tribes, the slaughter was completed in less than a decade. The only reason the plains bison—once the most prolific large mammal the earth has ever known—is not extinct today, is a number of privately owned herds scattered across the country at the turn of the century. The most famous of these were the Goodnight Herd of Texas, the Pablo-Allard Herd of Montana and the Blue Mountain Forest Association Herd of New Hampshire. The 120,000 bison alive today came from crossbreeding these captive animals. The eastern herds of the American bison were shot into oblivion by the colonists before the American Revolution.

Land Between the Lakes has a bison herd of approximately 100 animals. Elk, another species that historically was present in

Bison cooling themselves in pond on Land Between the Lakes.

this corner of Tennessee, were released on the Land Between the Lakes elk range in June of 1996. The elk herd is kept within a fenced-in 750-acre area of L.B.L., the only preserve with separate elk and bison herds in the East. The grazing activity of these two native species, along with naturally occurring burns, once kept tracts of L.B.L. open. A community of prairie grasses and wildflowers was present in these forest openings. L.B.L. is working to restore the prairie component of this oak-hickory ecosystem.

L.B.L. offers the ecotourist unlimited opportunities. The 165 miles of horse trails and hiking trails are only lightly used. The 300 miles of undeveloped shoreline of Kentucky Lake and Lake Barkley offers many canoeing opportunities. These two lakes have a large population of overwintering bald eagles, although they are not as concentrated as Reelfoot Lake's bald eagles. L.B.L. is one of the few places frequented by golden eagles in the region. Twenty-one lake accesses in both Tennessee's and Kentucky's portions of L.B.L. allow a canoeist to find whatever level of solitude he or she might desire. L.B.L. has four developed campgrounds and dozens of undeveloped ones.

The Woodlands Nature Station, located in Kentucky's part of L.B.L., offers programs on raptors, red wolves, ruby-throated hummingbirds, nighttime canoe excursions, heron rookery canoe trips, owl programs and eagle feedings. The Golden Pond Planetarium offers stargazing as well as slide programs.

Hot Spots

Land Between the Lakes is nearly unknown by nature enthusiasts in the three-state region. Nearly all those who use it are from the Upper Midwest. The sheer size of this nature preserve, and the remarkable fact that it forms one of the longest inland peninsulas in the United States, surrounded on both sides by Kentucky Lake and Lake Barkley, make it unique.

The 65-mile North-South Trail, the 14-mile Canal Loop Trail and the 26-mile Fort Henry Trail, plus 30 miles of horse trails and another 40 miles of trails associated with the Woodlands Nature Center, see very little use compared to Great Smoky Mountains National Park and other parks.

Yet the gem in the crown of this 170,000-acre preserve shared by Tennessee and Kentucky is **The Trace Parkway.** This 40-mile parkway winds through uncluttered, uninhabited oak-hickory forest and has much the same feel as the Blue Ridge Parkway. The absence of the southern Appalachians is balanced by the presence of Kentucky Lake and Lake Barkley. Drive this parkway in early November, when the foliage is at its peak. The primary color here is the yellow of nut-tree fall foliage. Sugar maples are absent, so the red color is not as prevalent as in the southern Appalachian ecosystem.

Stop and watch the L.B.L. bison herd on the Tennessee side of the preserve. This creature is the largest land mammal of North America; some of the bulls in this herd weigh nearly 2,000 pounds. These animals are manipulated as little as possible, and their social interaction is unchanged from that of their wild ancestors.

To enjoy the leaf color from the water, launch your canoe on either of these two TVA impoundments. If you wish to remain close to amenities, launch at one of the more developed boating accesses. If solitude is what you seek, drive to one of the undeveloped boating accesses, and have an entire arm of Barkley or Kentucky Lake to yourself. If you are an angler, consider taking a rod and reel and putting out a line. Catching supper out of one of these productive fisheries is one more way to immerse yourself in nature. Both lakes are

Land Between the Lakes

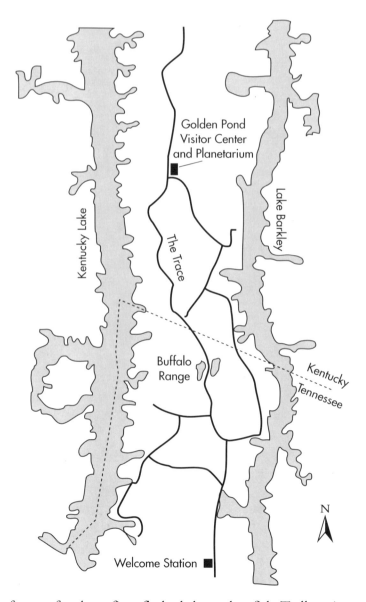

Golden Pond
Visitor Center
and Planetarium

Kentucky Lake

Lake Barkley

The Trace

Buffalo
Range

Kentucky
Tennessee

N

Welcome Station

famous for clean, firm-fleshed channel catfish. Troll a minnow under a cork approximately 6 feet deep, 100 feet behind your canoe, as you enjoy the fall foliage. For questions about L.B.L., call (502) 924-2000 and ask for the wildlife department.

63

Beaver Ponds

The white-tailed deer, the wild turkey and the beaver demonstrate spectacularly the resiliency of nature in rebounding from human abuse. From colonial times until well into the twentieth century, those subsisting off the land harvested whatever wild game they needed whenever they needed it, much as the Native Americans did. Yet unlike the Native Americans, the numbers of immigrants increased to the point that, by the time of the American Revolution, species such as the eastern American bison, the elk and the beaver were extirpated from the three-state region. The passenger pigeon, the red wolf, the cougar, the Carolina parakeet, and the ivory-billed woodpecker soon followed. Concepts such as habitat preservation, protection during breeding seasons and limiting the harvest of wild game would not be understood or implemented for more than a century.

Remarkably, at the brink of the twenty-first century, the white-tailed deer, the turkey and the beaver have returned to the landscape in a big way. If the American chestnut were present in the forest, the numbers of deer, turkey, black bear and other species would probably be at precolonial levels, for the eastern forest has regenerated to a remarkable degree (see chapters 37 and 70). The beaver, too, has made a remarkable comeback. This tree bark–eating rodent, which may weigh 80 pounds, has been reintroduced by Department of Fish and Game stocking programs so successfully that they are now considered a nuisance in some areas.

The beaver only does as it always has done: It builds ingenious dams on all manner of moving water, from small creeks you can step across to arms of large rivers and lakes. Once again beaver-felled trees are a common sight along the waterways of the region.

An element of conflict still exists between humans and beavers, though not nearly as intense as when beaver hats were the height of fashion during the middle of the nineteenth century. Although reintroduction of the beaver is universally acclaimed as a good thing, some landowners resent the flooded pastures and loss of trees. Live trapping of beavers and removal to other locations is a last resort.

Yet, for the naturalist, the reintroduction of the beaver has created numerous oases where wildlife flourishes. Beaver meadows create important vernal breeding pools for salamanders, toads and frogs. Wood ducks nest here, particularly around beaver ponds where nesting boxes have been put out. Otters, another very successfully reintroduced species, depend on the small impoundments created by beaver dams as habitat for rough fish species such as carp, catfish and suckers, the principal prey of otters. Otter pairs and family groups take over abandoned beaver lodges and make residence there. The surest sign of the presence of otters in a beaver meadow is piles of dung, made up chiefly of fish scales and fish backbone vertebrae.

To locate beaver sign, look for "slides" into the water—mud piles at the water's edge that have the smell of the pungent beaver castor the male beaver uses to mark his territory—as well as felled trees and "skinned" sticks scattered about in the shallow water. The marks left by the beaver's incisors are clearly visible on these sticks, which may range from pencil-sized to 5 inches in diameter.

In order to best observe beaver, muskrat and possibly otter and mink, as well as deer that come to beaver ponds to drink, arrive at first light or early evening, and sit quietly with your binoculars. Watch for beavers swimming across the pond. They are fairly observant and will slap their large flat tails on the water as an alarm signal when startled. However, with a little stealth and patience, you may be able to watch a beaver leave the water and peel a stick as it sits, much like a groundhog, surveying the pond created by its engineering skills.

Beavers are active primarily at night, so very early morning and dusk are the best times to look for them. These thickly furred animals are active through even the coldest months of the year, when they offer the ecotourist one of the most interesting ongoing natural spectacles. Once a colony of beavers has taken down most of the easily accessible trees of the preferred species, they move on, dam up a new creek and form another beaver meadow, benefitting the wildlife and perhaps irritating a new landowner.

Hot Spots

Beavers are widespread in the three-state region. Their conical lodges can be seen from the boardwalk of **Reelfoot Lake,** behind the visitor's center. The wildlife viewing area near the **Ft. Pillow State Park** interpretive center beyond the Mississippi River overlook has an active beaver colony. **Merchant's Mill Pond State Park** in northeastern North Carolina's coastal plain has a large beaver population with numerous conical lodges. For information on Merchant's Mill Pond State Park, call (919) 357-1191.

One medium-sized impoundment in North Carolina's Piedmont, which has been heavily utilized by beavers over the years is **Reidsville's City Lake.** Located just north of Greensboro, North Carolina, this lake has at least three active colonies. To reach Reidsville, take US 29 north out of Greensboro. Take the first exit into Reidsville, which is Business Route 29. At the Budget Inn, turn left on Waterworks Road and go 0.5 mile to the entrance of Reidsville's City Lake. Put your canoe in at the boat ramp and turn right at the main body of the lake. Paddle 0.5 mile and pass the brick pump house. Continue past the pump house and through a small inlet into an arm of the lake. During years when the beaver colony is large, this entire arm of the lake may be dammed. If the beaver colony has dropped in size, you may have to paddle up the small creek at the head of this arm of the lake to find beaver scent mounds and feeding stations. For information, call (910) 349-4738.

64

The Roan in Winter

Roan Mountain is described in the 1995 Smoky Mountains Field School brochure as "perhaps the most interesting and beautiful mountain in the eastern United States." It is considered a premier destination for wildflowers, hardwood forests, spruce-fir forest, ravens and songbirds. Yet the Roan is truly a mountain for all seasons. It is the most dependable place for snow in the region and a unique blessing for cross-country skiers and snowshoers. No other location in the three-state region offers such a choice of trails, open balds and closed-off roadways for snow enthusiasts.

In early spring, before any greenery has appeared on the heath balds, you can go there to see nothing in particular, but simply for the "power" that resides there. When the Roan Mountain balds are still mottled yellow, brown, gray and tan in February and March, and the Catawba rhododendron flowers are buds the size of a pencil eraser, the wildflower and songbird fanciers are still waiting in the valleys far below. But even during this sparse season, there are people on the Roan drawn to its unique ambiance. Roan Mountain simply feels different from other places in the region. On a gray, bleak day in March, the heath balds of Roan Mountain look like Katmai National Monument on the wild Alaskan Peninsula. The same gray, ropy storm clouds are often present, with lenticular clouds, or "stacks of plates," sometimes accompanying them. The feel of wildness is there, as are the ravens. Try to experience the power of a large winter storm as the leading edge first reaches the Roan. If the storm is one of great dynamism, the energy of the place will astound you. At such times it sounds as if many great jet turbine engines are running at maximum force, just above the clouds of the pinwheeling storm gyre.

In the winter, the dark green rhododendron leaves are rolled up as tight as soda straws to protect themselves from the cold.

The Roan in winter.

The Roan's heath balds are covered in snow for much of the winter, as are most of the world's great rhododendron areas. Roan Mountain is one of the most transformed places, by the winter season, of any location in the region. After a winter storm, as you drive the last half mile from the Roan Mountain visitor's center to the Carver's Gap parking lot near the summit, the rock outcroppings along the highway, which drip with springwater during the summer months, are sheathed in ice. The spruce-fir forest is nearly black in contrast to the snow.

In the winter the road out of the Carver's Gap parking lot to the Roan Mountain rhododendron gardens and the information stand near the summit is often closed, providing a perfect place for cross-country skiers or snowshoers. Fresh powder is best for this purpose, but more often the snow is hard and crusted, making hiking boots adequate. The hike across the heath bald immediately in front of the Carver's Gap parking lot to Round Bald is easily done in less than an hour. The trail is rather steep. The hike to the Cornelius Rex Parke plaque, a mile beyond Round Bald, takes a bolder individual, especially on a dark and threatening day, for new flakes can appear as if by magic and the evening dark comes early. Approximately one half mile from the marker plaque, the Appalachian Trail, the world's longest continuous footpath, splits off to the left from the path. By taking the Appalachian Trail for about a half mile, you will come to an excellent spring that runs strong during all but the driest weather. Memorize its location for visits during the hot summer months when a drink of cold water is welcome. A second spring on Roan Mountain is much easier to reach than the one just described: Immediately to the left of the public restrooms behind the Carver's Gap parking lot, cold springwater gushes from a pipe placed in the ground.

Often the last several miles to Carver's Gap are snowpacked and icy, even if the roads at the Roan Mountain State Park visitor's center on Doe River are dry. If you are not used to driving on snow, chains are advisable, even if the road has been plowed out. As you drive down the mountain, you'll be glad you have the chains on. The number for the Roan Mountain State Park visitor's center is (615) 772-3303. They sometimes know the road conditions at Carver's Gap (their territory stops at the Forest Service boundary).

Annual wildflower tours and birdwalks are offered around May 6–7 each year and are coordinated at Roan Mountain State Park. Call Jennifer Wilson for information at (423) 772-3303. Naturalist-guided hikes occur all day Saturday and Sunday.

The annual Roan Mountain Naturalist's Rally takes place the weekend after Labor Day and features naturalist-led field trips on such subjects as butterflies, fall wildflowers, the geology of Roan Mountain and stream ecology. For information, call Gary Barrigar at (423) 543-7576.

Cross-country skier on road to Roan Mountain's rhododendron gardens.

Hot Spots

Generally, spring wildflowers are present from mid-April through June. Trout lilies are profuse on parts of Round Bald in late April and early May. Fall wildflowers begin in early September and last well into the autumn. Look along the roadway and along the rivers and creeks as well as on the grass balds and in the forest. Fall colors generally begin between the first and third weeks of October. It is worthwhile to visit the **Roan Mountain State Park** restaurant (O'Delly's) during the summer just to see the ruby-throated hummingbirds that come to the feeders there, buzzing to and fro as hikers rest in rocking chairs on the shaded front porch.

65

November Shorttakes

Footprint on the Landscape

What has been called "the greatest sequence of earthquakes in a continental interior in the world" occurred in the three-state region during an eight week period beginning on December 16, 1811. In the northwest corner of Tennessee, the 20-mile long **New Madrid Fault,** or **Reelfoot Fault,** spawned the largest series of earthquake shocks in the recorded history of North America. Locations as far away as New York and New Orleans experienced shock waves. Seismologists estimate that the three principal shocks each measured 8.0 on the Richter scale. As if this were not pyrotechnical enough, the fault opened up underneath the Kentucky Bend of the Mississippi River, causing the mightiest river in North America to run backward and to pour over waterfalls, according to descriptions from boatmen who survived the event. The bed of **Reelfoot Lake** was created when land along the fault line fell several yards, relative to the adjacent landscape. Reelfoot is not far from Land Between the Lakes (see chapter 62), which offers, as does the loess bluffs of the Mississippi River (chapter 2), the ecotourist opportunities to see world-renown geological "footprints" on the landscape, which time has converted into interesting naturalist destinations. The Reelfoot Lake visitor's center (chapter 1) has a detailed explanation of the great quake and its effect on the surrounding landscape.

66

A Closer Look: South Carolina's Incomparable Lowcountry

No other state on the East Coast has a tidewater region like South Carolina's in terms of productivity and water quality. Fully one-fourth of South Carolina is tidal wetlands. South Carolina, together with its contiguous states, North Carolina and Georgia, forms the largest tidal wetlands region in the lower 48 states. But what is most unusual about South Carolina's estuary and tidal zone is its water quality. Its 350,000-acre A.C.E. Basin and 62,000-acre Cape Romaine NWR are considered the two most pristine tidal zone ecosystems on the East Coast. Contiguous with Cape Romaine NWR are 17,500-acre Hobcaw Barony, 24,000-acre Santee Coastal WMA and 20,000-acre Tom Yawkey Wildlife Center. In 1996, 9,100 acres of Sandy Island in the Waccamaw River was purchased and protected. All combined, these preserves total nearly 800 square miles of some of the cleanest, most productive and most unaltered semitropical tidal wetlands in America. The condition of South Carolina's estuary and tidal marsh is greatly envied by its neighboring states to the north. Given population densities and past and present environmental abuses, it is impossible that either Chesapeake Bay or the Albemarle–Pamlico Sound ecosystems will be restored anytime soon to the pristine condition of South Carolina's tidal zone and estuary.

Waterbirds have voted with their wings that South Carolina's tidewater is unique in the Southeast. The range of the wood stork, the only true stork in the United States, was once limited entirely to Florida. In the 1930s, 60,000 storks bred in the southern Florida wetlands. Then drought, pollution of the Everglades by agricultural runoff and habitat destruction all brought this 3.5-foot-tall

Live oaks and Spanish moss over a sandy lane.

wading bird with a 5.5-foot wingspread to the brink of extinction. Nests were abandoned, and the storks could not find enough food to feed their chicks. By the early 1980s only 6,040 pairs of storks existed, and they began migrating north in search of greener pastures.

South Carolina has now become an important summer residence for these huge wading birds. From 11 pairs of storks in 1981, the number in summer residence in South Carolina has grown to nearly 3,000. These versatile birds have learned that Florida's dwindling wetlands are no longer as productive as those of Georgia and South Carolina. Other species have also voted that South Carolina's coastline is unique among southeastern states. A 1989 count indicated that although North Carolina and Georgia each had approximately 10,000 pairs of wading birds, South Carolina had nearly 60,000 pairs.

The oystercatcher is a large waterbird with a blood-red bill shaped like an oyster knife. This bird has perfected the strategy of quickly inserting its powerful bill inside an oyster or clam and snipping the adductor muscle that opens and closes the oyster's shell. More than half the oystercatchers that winter in North America do so on the South Carolina coast. Because oysters and other plankton-straining bivalves are the most dependable indicator species of the overall health of a tidal zone, the large oystercatcher overwintering population makes a strong statement about South Carolina's incomparable Lowcountry.

Where South Carolina's coastal rivers meet the sea exists a semitropical zone where habitat niche and species diversity are remarkable. Within the A.C.E. Basin alone, more than 50 distinct natural ecosystems have been identified within the forested wetlands, upland hardwood and pine forest, live oak forest, salt marsh, old rice fields and other natural communities. Seventeen endangered or threatened species, including the southern bald eagle, wood stork, loggerhead turtle, alligator and short-nosed sturgeon, all depend on this unspoiled region. Forty percent of South Carolina's nesting bald eagles use the A.C.E. Basin, helping to give South Carolina the largest southern bald eagle population of any state except Florida.

Pristine inlets and estuaries such as Saint Helena Sound at the mouth of the A.C.E. Basin, the North Inlet and Winyah Bay near Georgetown and Bull's Bay in Cape Romaine NWR are all studied as models of clean, dynamic, functioning mixing areas for ocean and salt marsh.

The term "A.C.E. Basin" is derived by taking the first letters of the three rivers that form the huge basin. The Ashepoo, Combahee and Edisto, along with tributaries such as the Chehaw, Coosaw and Salkehatchie, meander through a region spanning 200 miles. These three quintessential Lowcountry rivers all converge at Saint Helena Sound. The rivers were named by the Sewee, Escamacu, Wimbee, Kussah and Stono Indian tribes, who practiced good stewardship of this region before they were displaced by the Europeans. Yet ironically, it was the class society of Europe that actually preserved the region in its pristine state since the arrival of the Europeans.

In the northeastern United States, the shrewd Yankee trader ethos embraced Calvinism and Puritanism to produce the industrialist. In contrast, in Virginia and South Carolina and to a lesser extent North Carolina, the British class society was the principal social model. Such industry was never aspired to in these regions. The South Carolina gentleman who was "to the manor born" placed a great value on sport hunting. Although some clearing of the land was necessary in the creation and management of a plantation, huge blocks of wildlife habitat were left undisturbed so that great quantities of wild game could be produced. The writings of South Carolina's poet laureate, Archibald Rutledge, are an eloquent reflection of this age. In many ways this culture produced the first practicing preservationists of the American democracy. This value system dominated the South Carolina Lowcountry from the late 1600s until the turn of this century, when a new player arrived.

Fabulously wealthy industrialists from the Northeast, drawn to the beauty and bountiful hunting offered by the South Carolina Lowcountry, as well as North Carolina's Currituck Sound region, began to buy up many of the old plantations. Hunt clubs were formed. The value systems of the wealthy industrialists were curiously compatible with those of the remaining Lowcountry gentry. No matter how one views these people, the upshot is that these landholdings were protected jealously, and the ecotourist and the wildlife of the late twentieth century are the ultimate beneficiaries.

Hot Spots

One of the easiest, least expensive ways to see **Cape Romaine NWR** is to take the Bull Island Ferry, which departs from Moore's Landing from March 1 through November 30 on Tuesdays, Fridays and Saturdays at 9:00 A.M. and 12:30 P.M., returning at noon and 4:00 P.M. Moore's Landing is located 20 miles south of McClellanville, South Carolina, just off US 17. Look for signs for Moore's Landing approximately 8 miles south of Awendaw on US 17.

To gain access to the **A.C.E. Basin** (chapter 8), take SC 26 south, just beyond the crossroads called Ashepoo on US 17, approximately 30 miles south of Charleston.

Another interesting side trip is the **Bellefield Nature Center** at Hobcaw Barony. This splendid nature studies center, located just north of the bridge into Georgetown, South Carolina, monitors nekton (shrimp and fish), benthos (worms and small animals that live in salt marsh mud), salt marsh productivity, zooplankton abundance, mobile epibenthos (juvenile shrimp, small crabs and juvenile fish) as well as the overall health of the North Inlet–Winyah Bay ecosystem. This 17,500-acre wildlife preserve is studied as a pristine model for other estuarine systems on the East Coast. The Belle W. Baruch Foundation at the Bellefield Nature Center is one of 11 sites around the continental United States where major North American ecosystems are studied. Other ecosystems covered under the Long Range Ecological Research Program are rivers, lakes, prairie, mountains and various types of forest. The North Inlet–Winyah Bay estuarine research facility is considered an important estuarine research center in America.

Guided van tours of the landholdings of the refuge take place all year on most Tuesdays and Thursdays from 10:00 A.M. to 1:00 P.M. From September 1 to May, the time changes to 1:30–4:30 P.M. There is a $5 charge per seat. This tour covers upland forest, cypress swamp, salt marsh and an old slave village. Call (803) 546-4623 for reservations. Stop at the Bellefield Nature Center to look at the exhibits.

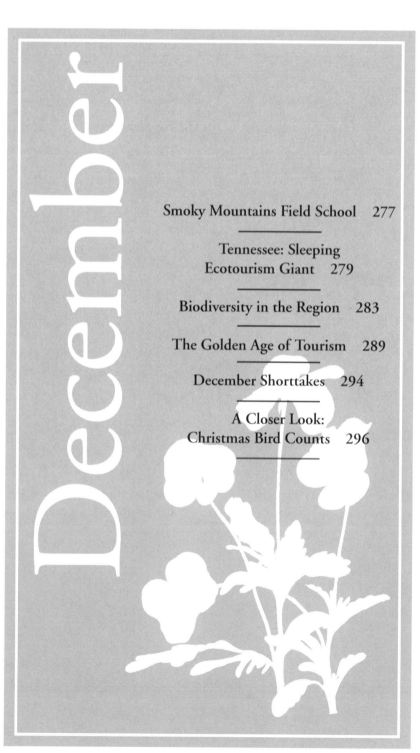

December

Notes

67

Smoky Mountains Field School

For 18 years, the University of Tennessee at Knoxville's Smoky Mountains Field School has been using 800-square-mile Great Smoky Mountains National Park (see chapters 25 and 60) as the ultimate classroom. This nonprofit school studies every aspect of life in the cove hardwood forest and associated ecosystems. The Annual Wildflower Pilgrimage, now in its forty-sixth year, is the most popular event, for it draws hundreds each year (see chapter 26).

The Wildflower Pilgrimage is organized jointly by the Field School as well as the Gatlinburg Garden Club, the University of Tennessee Botany Department, the Southern Appalachian Botanical Association and the Great Smoky Mountains National History Association. This event always occurs on the last full weekend of April.

Yet the Wildflower Pilgrimage is only one of the "classes" offered through the Field School. Some of the programs offered in the 1995 brochure included such diverse topics as Winter High Country Camping, Introduction to Orienteering, Geological Evolution of the Smokies, Incredible Edibles, Traditional Medicines, Nature Sketching, Fly Fishing in the Smokies, Waterfalls of the Smokies, Butterflies and Other Insects of the Smokies, Native Plant Propagation and Appalachian Trail Experience.

Other courses are more traditional and deal specifically with flora and fauna: Wildflowers of Roan Mountain, Birds of the Smokies, Spring Wildflower Photography, Wild Mammals of the Southern Appalachians and Black Bears of the Smokies. The 1995 program schedule offered 49 different classes. No classes are offered in January and December.

None of these classes offers credits toward degrees; they are considered "continuing education" for those who seek knowledge simply for its own value. Many of the instructors are regarded as luminaries in their area of expertise. Many classes are completed in a single day, but others can span an entire weekend. Some of the excursions involve overnight camping, such as the day hike into 6,593-foot Le Conte Lodge. For information on the Great Smoky Mountains Field School courses, call (800) 284-8885 or (423) 974-0150. For information on the Annual Wildflower Pilgrimage, call Don DeFoe at (423) 436-1262.

68

Tennessee:
Sleeping Ecotourism Giant

Tennessee was once called "America's first frontier," and to a remarkable degree, the state has never lost the vigor and vitality for which it was known. The southern Appalachians served as a physical and mental barrier to the immigrants who came south on the Great Wagon Road in search of land. The region to the west of the mountains was the domain of the French as well as hostile Indians.

Two centuries later, many people living in the Carolinas still have little idea of what lies over the mountains in Tennessee. Few North or South Carolinians ever think of going there to enjoy its superlative flora and fauna (see chapter 30). This is their loss, for Tennessee has experienced far less modification by humans than either of the Carolinas.

That Tennessee had an extraordinary flora and fauna was known early in its history. The Paleoindians left perhaps the richest archeological occupational record in the Western Hemisphere in what is now Tennessee, particularly along the course of the Tennessee River. The Paleoindians were mastodon hunters drawn to Tennessee by abundant large mammals at the end of the last ice age. The mastodons in turn were drawn by the rich floral life web west of the Appalachian Mountains. In many ways these characteristics are still present across the Tennessee landscape.

Few states can match Tennessee's eight distinct geographical regions, which attract geologists from all over the world. Tennessee's list of natural superlatives is very long. Within its half of Great Smoky Mountains National Park are the lion's share of the 100,000 acres of virgin hardwood forest, the largest stands of never-logged hardwood forest in the nation (see chapter 25). Savage Gulf State

Botanist among endangered Tennessee coneflowers.

Natural Area (see chapter 72), in Tennessee's limestone heartland, contains one of the few remaining stands of never-logged hardwood forest outside the southern Appalachians. Roan Mountain's highland grass balds (see chapter 31), shared by Tennessee and North Carolina, are regarded as the finest example of this cloud-level natural community type in the nation. Upper eastern Tennessee's South Holston and the Clinch River below Norris Dam are arguably the finest mayfly–brown trout–rainbow trout rivers in the East. The lakes on the upper end of the TVA chain, Holston Lake and Watauga Lake (see chapter 19), are the equals of any mountain lakes in the East in terms of overall water quality and sheer beauty.

The vast Cumberland Plateau, which contains limestone strata just beneath a thin layer of topsoil, has regenerated its forests to a remarkable degree. While one drives between Knoxville and Nashville on I-40, the forested, northeast-southwest trending mountains form an essentially unaltered landscape from horizon to horizon. The underlying reason—limestone—is clearly visible in roadcuts, some dynamited through up to 50 feet of horizontally layered white limestone. This limestone substratum saved the region from "clean farming" techniques which have altered much of the Carolinas. This essentially reforested area, roughly 200 miles wide and stretching north from the Alabama state line to the Kentucky state line, is largely undisturbed.

Nashville's 1,025-acre Radnor Lake and 2,665-acre Warner Parks are the city parks every metropolitan area in America wishes it could have. The cedar glades of middle Tennessee have the normal wildflower communities found in the southeastern United States, but the glades also have a large disjunct prairie wildflower community (see chapter 38). In Tennessee's Highland Rim limestone region is one of the finest examples of karst topography in the country. The area has more than 500 caves, the largest number of any karst region in the United States. On the Kentucky-Tennessee border is a vast sandstone region with some of the most striking water-eroded "rock houses" and stone pillars anywhere.

The 300 miles of undeveloped lakeshore of Tennessee and Kentucky's Land Between the Lakes forms an inland peninsula bordered on either side by Lake Barkley and Kentucky Lake. Land Between the Lakes is the only park in the East with both bison and elk herds (see chapter 62).

On Tennessee's western border flows one of the world's great rivers (chapter 51). This section of the Mississippi River contains the best-preserved large blocks of lower Mississippi River floodplain hardwood forest, remnants of the greatest riverine deciduous hardwood forest the world has ever known (see chapter 6). Tennessee's share of this mighty river, with its associated hardwood forest, oxbow lakes and sloughs, preserves one of the best remaining examples of a large riverine ecosystem in the country. Reelfoot Lake, on the north end of Tennessee's section of the Mississippi River, has one of the largest easily accessible, overwintering bald eagle populations in the United States.

Within the banks of the Mississippi River, a large-scale biodiversity center waits to be discovered. The sandy islands of the river offer wonderful camping opportunities for those respectful of the river's power (chapters 40 and 51). Mosquitos can be fierce here, so plan your trip accordingly. The Mississippi Flyway is one of the great flyways of North America, and has flights of waterfowl, neotropical migrants and even migrating eagles.

These are only a few of Tennessee's statewide biodiversity and geological treasures. Many others wait for ecotourists on the other side of the mountains.

69

Biodiversity in the Region

If one took a giant cookie-cutter and attempted to cut out a region of North America the same size as North Carolina, South Carolina and Tennessee, with as much biodiversity present, he or she would essentially have one choice: California, long recognized as one of the great areas of botanical diversity in the world. In fact these two regions would have to rank as biodiversity heavyweights, by anyone's yardstick, in the temperate (nonequatorial) zone of the world. This becomes particularly evident when one discusses the issue of biodiversity on the levels of natural community types and landscape.

Great biodiversity is generated by factors such as mixing of species where northern and southern ranges overlap and also by numerous natural communities within a landscape, each one containing many individual species. The Cape Hatteras–Outer Banks onshore, offshore ecosystems are a textbook example of both components. The Wilderness Society's Bolle Center for Forest Ecosystem Management states, "It [biodiversity] includes the entire range of life forms—from the smallest virus to the living monuments we call giant sequoia.—From the top carnivore that depends on prey, to the prey that depends on plants, to the plants that depend on other organisms to produce carbon dioxide and to cycle nutrients." Viewed on this level, North Carolina's marine mixing grounds off Cape Hatteras reveal a remarkable degree of species richness.

North Carolina has five mixing components at work in its territorial waters. Here one finds both continental shelf and deep ocean floor. These two vast ecosystems, one based on sunlight reaching the ocean floor and the other existing in the water column and the deep ocean floor, mix freely. Many soundings off Cape Hatteras are as shallow as 14 fathoms. One fathom equals 6 feet. Near the mouth of the Cape Fear River, soundings may be only a few fathoms deep, giving rise to a rich ecosystem based on sunlight interacting with ocean floor.

Yet, 50 miles off Cape Hatteras, offshore depths of more than 2,000 fathoms are common. Here, truly remarkable species diversity exists. On the deep ocean floor, one 21-square-meter area, the size of a small living room in a house, was recently found to possess 898 species, most new to science. Extrapolation from these new data strongly suggests that millions of species are still undiscovered by science. The deep ocean floor, it is now thought, possesses a small marine animal species diversity that may equal the species diversity of the rain forest. Their value and relevance to land-based creatures like us are yet undetermined.

Just off Cape Hatteras are two important global currents, the tropical Gulf Stream and the cold Labrador Current, mixing just offshore and giving rise to great diversity of northern and southern marine species. Other species are flushed into this ecosystem by dynamic upwelling from great ocean depths. Still other species are involved because of the sargasso component. Floating rafts of sargassum seaweed, as well as clouds of fish larvae, zooplankton, small crustaceans and squid boiled up from great depths by dynamic upwelling, are carried along North Carolina's coastline off Cape Hatteras by the Gulf Stream. These fertile waters attract a host of fish, marine mammals and pelagic bird species. It is no accident that the Gulf Stream region off Cape Hatteras is the best location in the western Atlantic for observing pelagic (open-ocean–dwelling) birds. Jaegers, skuas, petrels, northern fulmars, Cory's shearwaters, masked boobies, black-legged kittiwakes and Atlantic puffins are some of the dozens of species that use these waters.

The northern-southern plant and animal ecotone on North Carolina's Outer Banks at Cape Hatteras also creates overlapping webs of life that produce great species diversity. Cape Hatteras Point is one of the premier gull-watching locations in North America, once again reflecting the mixing of northern and southern species. Even the harbor seal has extended its range southward and now terminates its winter range in the cold waters just north of Cape Hatteras. Apparently all of this is well known to whales and other marine mammals. North Carolina has documented sightings of more species of marine mammals in its waters than any other location in the hemisphere.

Also on the coastline of the region, the mouth of the Cape Fear River is another important biodiversity hotspot. This river mouth has a unique Florida-Caribbean connection: Water manatees once terminated their northern range here. Occasionally even now, a manatee enters the mouth of Cape Fear. It is hoped that someday they can be reintroduced here.

In nearby Green Swamp, 1 square meter of longleaf pine–wire grass savanna may have greater small-scale diversity of plant species than any other place in the world, including the Amazon Basin. On The Nature Conservancy's Lanier Quarry site, as many as 104 species may exist in 1 square meter of the forest floor. Here, as well, are more species of insectivorous plant species than anywhere else in the world except New Zealand.

The longleaf pine–wire grass savannas in Green Swamp, the Sand Hills of the Carolinas and Ft. Bragg–Camp MacKall are fire ecosystems. It is significant that the four areas of greatest diversity of floral species in the temperate zone of the world all occur in longleaf pine–grass savannas. The 65,000 acres of longleaf pine forest on Ft. Bragg–Camp MacKall, as well as the other longleaf pine preserves mentioned in chapter 29, are regarded as some of the best remaining examples of this natural community type in America. The most recent fieldwork indicates that 975 endemic species are found in the Southeastern Coastal Plain longleaf pine ecosystem. Many of these species occur in the splendid longleaf pine stands of the Carolinas. By way of comparison, according to the "Rare and Endangered Plant Survey and Natural Area Inventory for Ft. Bragg and Camp MacKall Military Reservations, North Carolina" by Raven and Axelrod, the entire state of California has a total of 1,517 endemics.

Much of South Carolina's coastline contains incomparable semitropical tidal marsh and estuary, the most pristine on the East Coast (see chapter 66). South Carolina's A.C.E. Basin, Cape Romaine, Santee Coastal, Hobcaw Barony and Tom Yawkey preserves total approximately 800 square miles of protected pristine salt marsh, maritime forest, barrier island and estuarine ecosystems. Clouds of insect larvae; fish larvae; tiny floating plants called phytoplankton, which make up 80 percent of all plant life on earth; zooplankton; diatoms; dinoflagellates; coccolithophores and algae make South Carolina's estuarine ecosystem a "green pea soup" of organic material, which in turn supports great species diversity.

In the A.C.E. Basin, 50 distinct ecosystems have been identified within the forested uplands, swamp forest, barrier islands, salt marsh and ocean inlets. Each tidal exchange sees an invasion of marine predators from the high end of the food chain. Some of these species are bottlenosed porpoises, loggerhead sea turtles, skates, manta rays, sharks and squid. This area produces alligators in densities greater than any region of Florida or Louisiana.

Some barrier islands, such as Deveaux Bank in A.C.E. Basin, support as many as 13,000 pairs of royal and sandwich terns, as well as hundreds of pairs of brown pelicans and wading birds. Tropical species such as Mississippi and American swallowtail kites terminate their northern range in the three-state region.

How many states possess both the Fraser fir, a northern species, and the palmetto palm, a southern species, as North Carolina does? The Fraser fir forest and the Fraser fir–red spruce forest ecosystems exist at the highest elevations of the southern Appalachian ecosystem. As one descends in altitude, one encounters northern hardwood forest, mixed mesophytic hardwood and finally cove hardwood forest. This vast forested landscape is regarded as one of the two most important areas of forest biodiversity in the United States, according to the Bolle Center for Forest Ecosystem Management.

The 520,408-acre Great Smoky Mountains National Park, as well as the adjacent 3.2 million acres of National Forest, creates a biosphere of more than 6,000 square miles of protected public land that supports 690 vertebrate species and 3,000 species of vascular plants, including an astonishing 159 species of trees. With 54 species, the southern Appalachian ecosystem has the world's largest salamander fauna, and with 500 endemic species, it has 20 percent of all floral species found in North America (see chapters 25 and 26).

The many mountain bogs and the spray cliff plant communities created by waterfalls add still more pieces to the mosaic of great natural community–level biodiversity (see chapter 38). The Asheville, North Carolina, area is an important "break point" for northern and southern trillium species. The trillium genus finds one of its worldwide centers here in the southern Appalachians. Orchid species flourish here too.

Within Great Smoky Mountains National Park alone are 130 species of trees, more than in all of northern Europe, an area 1,000 times larger than the park. Fifteen hundred flowering plants, 50 species of fern and fern allies, 330 mosses and liverworts, 230 lichens and 1800 fungi also enrich this remarkable International Biosphere Reserve. Great Smoky Mountains National Park is a world center for mushroom species. Of 36 species of eastern warblers, 24 nest here. The other 12 species migrate through on their way to the spruce-fir-larch forest of Canada. This park is one of the most splendid examples of temperate-zone hardwood forest in the world. Great Smoky Mountains National Park contains more than 100,000 acres of virgin hardwood forest, more than any other location in America.

A day hike from 1,500 feet elevation to 6,643-foot Clingman's Dome, the highest point in the park, carries the hiker through nearly every deciduous and evergreen forest configuration that exists between Georgia and Newfoundland in a stunning statement of natural community–type biodiversity.

Eastern and middle Tennessee possesses the world's greatest species diversity of freshwater darters (see chapter 30). These little-known 3-inch fish are as colorful as tropical fish, and their names reflect it. Some of the 91 darter species of eastern and middle Tennessee are: greenside darter, tangerine darter, copperhead darter, emerald darter, splendid darter, orangefin darter, rainbow darter, fantail darter, bronze darter, harlequin darter, greenbreast darter, firebelly darter, orangethroat darter, jewel darter and gilt darter. The best place to see them is the darter exhibit in the Chattanooga Freshwater Aquarium in Chattanooga. In fact this is about the only place one can see them, for they tend to live in slower-moving, mud-bottomed rivers and creeks, although some live in clear-water, gravel-bottomed streams. Darters do not give themselves up to observation easily.

This section of Tennessee can make other superlative claims in terms of freshwater fauna. Upper eastern Tennessee takes in the southern edge of the Ohio River freshwater mussel fauna, the world's greatest. A few of the species found here are the shiny pigtoe mussel, pimpleback mussel birdwing pearly mussel and fine-rayed pigtoe mussel. Freshwater mussels are the most endangered faunal group in the United States. Middle Tennessee's Duck River, which flows through Henry Horton State Park, supports the largest single river freshwater mussel fauna in the world.

Tennessee's freshwater fish species diversity is the equal of any state in the nation. On a small-scale level, the diversity of freshwater fish species of the Central Basin of middle Tennessee's limestone country is considered remarkable in the world.

Finally, at the western edge of the three-state region is one of the world's great rivers. Although the Mississippi River Riparian zone forest does not have numbers of species on the level of the southern Appalachian cove hardwood forest, a river that disgorges four million gallons of precious freshwater per second at its mouth is, by its very character, a world-class component on the landscape biodiversity level. The Mississippi offers an interesting riverine fauna including shortnosed gar, alligator snapping turtles, soft-shelled turtles, freshwater drum buffalo and others (see chapter 51).

The southern Appalachian ecosystem, the Outer Banks–Cape Hatteras offshore-onshore ecosystem, the estuarine-tidal marsh of South Carolina's Lowcountry, middle Tennessee's limestone-enriched Cumberland Plateau, and western Tennessee's section of the Mississippi River illustrate major components of landscape-level biodiversity on a plane that few relatively small regions can transcend.

70

The Golden Age of Tourism

The opening lines of Dickens's 1859 novel, *A Tale of Two Cities,* are so contemporary that they give one pause: "It was the best of times, it was the worst of times ... it was the age of wisdom, it was the age of foolishness ... it was the epoch of belief, it was the epoch of incredulity, it was the season of Light, it was the season of Darkness, it was the spring of hope, it was the winter of despair— we had everything before us, we had nothing before us, we were all going direct to Heaven, we were all going direct the other way."

The same could be said today of the prospects for human-kind, as well as for wild things, wild places and the diversity of life-forms on earth. With the human population increasing by nearly a billion each decade, educational excellence eroding away and value systems moving ever further from the old axiom "Live simply so that others may simply live," these could be construed as the worst of times. However, there are glimmers of hope. The human being is seldom placed at the apex and considered to be, with all others, a beast of earthly origin. Humans are increasingly viewed, both genetically and in terms of ultimate survival, as shar-ing the same fate as their fellow earthly creatures. Global commu-nications have made the rain forest and the spotted owl causes célèbres.

During the administration of Abraham Lincoln, the Potomac River was little more than an open sewer. Now it is a popular location for bass tournaments. With DDT out of the environ-ment, the number of bald eagles has soared. The toxicity levels of the Great Lakes drop significantly each decade. Much of the night landscape along North Carolina's Blue Ridge Parkway is unblem-ished by the lights of a single dwelling. Similarly, the 800-square-mile biosphere of Great Smoky Mountains National Park has been emptied of families and has returned to a nearly pristine state. Yet it has not been without bitterness and sacrifice on the part of those families who owned and loved the land. Looking at a map of Alaska, one sees that half the state is classified as Bureau of Land Management, military, Forest Service, National Park System or National Wildlife Refuge land. In many western states, huge blocks are claimed by the Forest Service or the BLM. The ecotourist has never enjoyed such freedom to venture across North America on land that belongs, as John Muir said, to those who have the time to go there.

Scattered across the three-state region are vast, forested tracts where human populations are lighter now than at any time in the last two centuries. Scotch-Irish and English immigrants traveled the Great Wagon Road headed for the southern colonies, and after the American Revolution, the southern states, in search of available land. No matter how remote the location, log cabins sprouted in virtually every hollow, valley and cove. Often, bitter disputes arouse over hunting rights. The most graphic example in the region may be the "Night Riders," who fought over the fishing and hunting rights to northwestern Tennessee's Reelfoot Lake. Lynching and murder took place as local hunters and fishermen bitterly opposed the efforts of the J. C. Harris Land Company to ruthlessly exploit the resources of Reelfoot Lake. Today Reelfoot Lake is a state park. Over the last 80 years a remarkable change has come over the landscape.

The great environmental story of the United States during this century, states Bill McKibben in his landmark article "An Explosion of Green," is not the American West, but rather the return to forest of the eastern seaboard states. McKibben observes that when the colonists arrived in North America in the 1600s and 1700s, three quarters of the forests of what is now the United States were in the eastern third of the nation. Remarkably, the eastern hardwood forest has regenerated to the point that once again three fourths of the country's forests are in the East. Deep core samples of swamps and bogs on Cape Cod reveal that oak pollen is now approaching pre-Columbian levels, indicating that the hardwood forest of the East is much as it was before colonization by the Europeans.

In addition, many of the huge, privately owned estates of western North Carolina, where the fabulously wealthy turned loose Russian boar to be hunted, are now national forests. Much of the vast hinterlands of western North Carolina and eastern Tennessee contained in national forests is virtually uninhabited, in sharp contrast to two centuries ago, when families occupied and farmed every flat piece of ground in the southern Appalachians.

The age group most active in ecotourism, those 40 years or older, have destination choices that did not exist a few decades ago. Some of the public lands now treasured by birders, wildflower enthusiasts and anglers were privately owned through much of this century, and were off-limits to the public.

One of the earliest large acquisitions within the region created most of what is now North Carolina's Pisgah National Forest. Acting on the authority of the Weeks Act passed by Congress, the U.S. government bought 80,000 acres of land from Edith Vanderbilt, widow of New Yorker George Vanderbilt, the builder of Biltmore House in 1911. This land, purchased for $5 an acre, formed the nucleus of Pisgah National Forest.

Cape Romaine NWR in South Carolina, now recognized as possessing the highest water purity on the eastern seaboard, came under federal protection in 1932 (see chapter 66). The land for the Blue Ridge Parkway was purchased between 1933 and 1935 (see chapter 19). In a totally new concept at the time, the roadbed for this scenic drive was cut along the ridges of mountains, looking down on valleys. Taking this world-renowned scenic drive today, whether enjoying fall foliage, spring songbirds or night skies, it is difficult to appreciate how bold the concepts of Cornell graduate Stanley Abbott of Yonkers, New York, were at the time.

Great Smoky Mountains National Park once supported small communities where now there is only forest. In the 1850s, Cade's Cove could count 685 residents, and Cataloochee, 1,200. In 1934 the 800-square-mile region became an uninhabited area and is now the nation's most visited park. Cape Hatteras National Seashore, with its miles of sparse, elegant barrier island, followed in 1937 (see chapter 8). Pea Island, the single most productive birding location in North Carolina, became a National Wildlife Refuge in 1938. Hunting Island, South Carolina, with 4 miles of beach and the most splendid example of a semitropical, palmetto palm–slash pine maritime forest in the region, was created in 1938. In 1964 Hammock's Beach State Park was donated to the state of North Carolina by a African-American teachers' group, the North Carolina Teacher's Association (see chapter 56).

Yet there is a uniquely personal element to the story of the golden age of tourism in the region, relating to the most pristine tidewater region on the East Coast: the South Carolina Lowcountry. During the first four decades of this century, wealthy northern industrialists bought many plantations along the South Carolina coastline in order to hunt waterfowl and deer and enjoy the mild winters there. In almost every case, however, these people were seduced by the Lowcountry. Belle Baruch gave up her residence in New York and spent her last years in the Lowcountry. Upon her death in 1964, 17,500-acre Hobcaw Barony was stipulated in her will to become a self-funding nature preserve. The Baruch Institute for Marine Biology is now one of the 11 most important environmental study sites in the United States (see chapter 55).

Tom Yawkey of New York City, owner of the Boston Red Sox for 43 years, willed his beloved South Island Plantation to the South Carolina State Wildlife and Marine Resources Department. Upon his death, the 20,000 acres of South Island Plantation became an important "anchor" in the pristine blocks of South Carolina coastal habitat that stretches for 60 miles between Georgetown and Charleston. South Island Plantation was named a South Carolina Heritage Preserve in 1976, when Yawkey died at the age of 76.

In 1974 the Santee Gun Club, composed primarily of wealthy Northeasterners, donated 24,000 acres of critical waterfowl, alligator and wood stork habitat to The Nature Conservancy. Now called Santee Coastal WMA, this preserve includes the Washo Reserve, mentioned by Audubon in his journals, a place of great importance to wading birds and other wildlife.

In 1930, New Yorker Archer Huntington and his wife, American sculptress Anna Hyatt, bought Brookgreen Plantation and three adjoining plantations north of Georgetown, South Carolina. In 1960, Huntington Beach State Park, one of South Carolina's premier birding locations, was created out of these landholdings.

Other preserves are still in the process of being assimilated. The protection of 350,000-acre A.C.E. Basin, called "one of this country's natural jewels" by John C. Sawhill, president and chief executive officer of The Nature Conservancy, was accomplished in large part by the efforts of area landowners. About 25 large, privately owned plantations account for most of the land in A.C.E. Basin (chapter 9). It has been said that nowhere else in the United States has so much private money been invested in managing land in such a way that its natural character would be preserved, as in South Carolina's A.C.E. Basin. In fact, if not for the leadership role of Ashepoo Plantation owners Gaylord and Dorothy Donnelley and others in placing conservation easements on many of the plantations of the A.C.E. Basin, this flagship project in nature preservation could have never happened. In A.C.E. Basin private landowners who place conservation easements on their property that prohibit any future commercial development, as well as the efforts of The Nature Conservancy, Ducks Unlimited, South Carolina Wildlife and Marine Resources and the U.S. Fish and Wildlife Service, have set an example emulated as far away as western Tennessee's section of the Mississippi River. Here efforts are under way to create another A.C.E. Basin–type preservation program along the Mississippi River (see chapter 5). Anyone not familiar with the A.C.E. Basin should look at the coffee-table book *South Carolina's Wetland Wilderness—The ACE Basin* by Tom Blagden, Jr.

And so it is that the birder, the angler and anyone who would study a pristine salt marsh or a cove hardwood forest in the southern Appalachians owe a great deal to a few who have given us the opportunity to make the next century the best of times for wild places and the people and creatures who depend upon them.

71

December Shorttakes

Savage Gulf

One of Tennessee's superlative claims in terms of flora and fauna is the approximately 3,000 acres of old-growth timber growing in the Cumberland Plateau's gorges. This is one of the few stands of virgin hardwood forest in the East outside the southern Appalachian biosphere. Located in Tennessee's limestone heartland, Savage Gulf was so rugged and inaccessible that no attempt was made to cut the ancient trees. Even now only parts of this forest are open to hiking due to the inaccessibility of the gorge. The timber of Savage Gulf is scattered throughout three gorges that converge to form one large gorge. To obtain a map with public hiking trails write to Savage State Natural Area, Route 1, Box 253, Palmer, Tennessee, 37365. Wayne Morrison of the Savage Gulf ranger station can be reached at (615) 779-3532 any day except Wednesday and Thursday. One may obtain the same map at South Cumberland State Park visitor's center in Monteagle. Monteagle is located approximately 100 miles south of Nashville on I-24. To reach the South Cumberland visitor's center take Exit 134 off I-24. Follow US 41 south for 3 miles to the visitor's center.

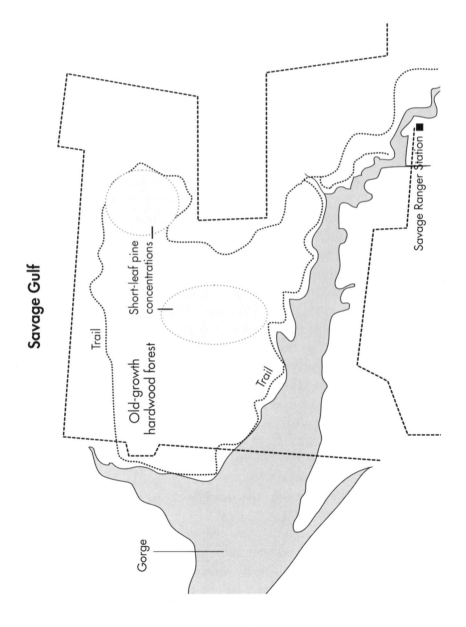

Savage Gulf

Trail

Old-growth
hardwood forest

Short-leaf pine
concentrations

Gorge

Trail

Savage Ranger Station

N

72

A Closer Look: Christmas Bird Counts

By regularly placing food in a location safe for wild birds, one can enjoy nature without leaving the house. Both parties benefit, for the birds can use a little help during the bleak winter months. During weather calamities such as ice storms a feeder can become very important to them. Yet certain ground rules should be observed. It is best to let wild birds fend for themselves until the leaves are off the trees and the grass and weeds are dead. Pick a place that is easily observed from inside the house, but do not put the feeding station in a location that forces the birds to leave protective cover by more than 50 feet or so.

The birds that respond best to feeding are primarily those of the thicket, such as towhees, white-throated sparrows, tufted titmice, Carolina chickadees and cardinals. Place the feeding station fairly close to protective thickets, hedges or shrubs so that "your" birds will not be overly exposed to predators. If you use a hanging feeder or one mounted on a pole, clear out a space underneath so the birdseed knocked from the feeder by titmice and Carolina chickadees and finches will be found by those species that prefer to feed on the ground: the towhees, cardinals and mourning doves. Be careful not to put out too much bird feed. By attracting too many birds, predators such as feral cats and sharp-shinned or Cooper's hawks will appear as well. A dozen or so regulars is a nice-sized family of songbirds to help out through the winter months. You may wish to enrich the wild bird mix you buy with sunflower seeds and millet. A suet feeder will attract woodpeckers and nuthatches. There is no better way to introduce young people to the pleasures of observing wildlife than by attracting songbirds.

In times of extremely harsh weather, be more generous than usual.

The Christmas Bird Count is another way to enjoy songbirds during the winter months. This event spans the period from one week before Christmas to one week after Christmas, and combines business with pleasure. The tallies compiled by Christmas Bird Count volunteers are useful in tracking upward and downward trends or range expansions among species. "Explosions" of species invading a region will also be noted. Such an event might take place during a year when lemmings or vole populations in the Far North crash, forcing hundreds of snowy owls into states such as Pennsylvania, New Jersey and New York. Christmas counts are an ideal way to meet other birders, in particular if you are new to an area. Connections made during this event may come in handy in April and May, when the neotropical migrants are passing through.

Typically each Christmas Bird Count covers the same 15-mile-diameter circle on the map year after year. In this way the ups and downs within the same bird populations can be easily noticed. These counts usually span the individual states thoroughly. North Carolina alone has 30 counts, which encompass the state from the Outer Banks to the Tennessee border.

North Carolina has Christmas Counts in Cape Hatteras, Buncombe County, Charlotte, Brevard, Chapel Hill, Greensboro, Morehead City, New River, Stone Mountain, Tyron, Lake Lure and other locations.

South Carolina has counts in Charleston, Clemson, Greenville, Hilton Head, Pawley's Island, Spartenburg, Rock Hill and other locations.

Tennessee has counts in Chattanooga, Clarksville, Cookeville, Dresden, Elizabethton, Great Smoky Mountains National Park, Hiawassee, Jackson, Knoxville, Nickjack Lake, Reelfoot Lake, Roan Mountain and other locations.

For information on contacts for each of these counts, call local bird clubs, nature or environmental centers or science museums. In addition, you can get phone numbers of contact people by writing: Christmas Bird Count editor, American Birds, National Audubon Society, 950 Third Avenue, New York, NY 10022.

The National Audubon Society will assist in starting new Christmas Counts. The Christmas count has become quite popular, with as many as 40,000 participants across the nation and around the world.

Appendix

The following agencies, organizations and centers may be useful in locating additional sites for enjoying the biodiversity found in the three-state region.

NATIONAL PARKS, MONUMENTS, AND SEASHORES

Cape Hatteras National Seashore
Route 1, Box 675
Manteo, NC 27954
(919) 473-2111

Cape Lookout National Seashore
131 Charles Street
Harker's Island, NC 28531
(919) 728-2250

Congaree Swamp National Monument
200 Caroline Sims Road
Hopkins, SC 29061
(803) 776-4396

Great Smoky Mountains National Park
National Park Service
Gatlinburg, TN 37738

NATIONAL FORESTS AND RANGER DISTRICTS
REGIONAL OFFICES

USDA Forest Service—Southern Region
Information Center, Room 154
1720 Peachtree Road Northwest
Atlanta, GA 30367-9102

National Forests in North Carolina
100 Otis Street
Asheville, NC 28801
(704) 257-4200

Witherbee Ranger District (South Carolina)
P.O. Box 1532
Monck's Corner, SC 29461
(803) 336-3248

Cherokee National Forest
2800 North Ocoee Street
Cleveland, TN 37312
(615) 476-9700

NATIONAL WILDLIFE REFUGES

North Carolina

Alligator River NWR (National Wildlife Refuge)
708 North Hwy. 64
P.O. Box 1969
Manteo, NC 27954-1969

Cedar Island NWR
Route 1, Box N-2
Swanquarter, NC 27885

Currituck NWR
State Route 615
P.O. Box 39
Knotts Island, NC 27950-0039

Great Dismal Swamp NWR
3100 Desert Road
P.O. Box 349
Suffolk, VA 23434-0349

Mackay Island NWR
State Route 615
P.O. Box 39
Knotts Island, NC 27950-0039

Mattamuskeet NWR
New Holland, NC 27885

Pea Island NWR
P.O. Box 1969
Manteo, NC 27954-1969

Pee Dee NWR
Route 1, Box 92
Wadesboro, NC 28170

Pocosin Lakes NWR
Route 1, Box 195-B
Creswell, NC 27928

Roanoke River NWR
102 Dundee Street, Box 430
Windsor, NC 27983-0430

Swanquarter NWR
Route 1, Box N-2
Swanquarter, NC 27885

South Carolina

A.C.E. Basin NWR
P.O. Box 848
Hollywood, SC 29449-0848

Cape Romain NWR
5801 Hwy. 17 North
Awendaw, SC 29429

Carolina Sandhills NWR
Route 2, Box 330
McBee, SC 29101-2975

Pinckney Island NWR
1000 Business Center Drive
Savannah, GA 31405 (SC)

Santee NWR
Route 2, Box 370
Summerton, SC 29148

Tennessee

Chickasaw NWR
4343 Hwy. 157
Union City, TN 38261

Cross Creeks NWR
643 Wildlife Road
Dover, TN 37058

Hatchie NWR
4172 Hwy. 76 South
Brownsville, TN 38012-0187

Lake Isom NWR
4343 Hwy. 157
Union City, TN 38261

Reelfoot NWR
4343 Hwy. 157
Union City, TN 38261

Tennessee NWR
810 East Wood Street
P.O. Box 849
Paris, TN 38242-0849

U.S. FISH AND WILDLIFE SERVICE

U.S. Fish and Wildlife Service
P.O. Box 33096
Raleigh, NC 27636
(919) 856-4786

U.S. Fish and Wildlife Service
1835 Assembly Street, Suite 971-B
Columbia, SC 29201
(803) 765-5626

U.S. Fish and Wildlife Service
220 Great Circle Road, Suite 150
Nashville, TN 37228
(615) 736-5532

U.S. Fish and Wildlife Service
Ecological Service—Endangered Species
446 Neal Street
Cookeville, TN 38501

STATE AGENCIES

North Carolina Wildlife Resources Commission
512 North Salisbury Street
Raleigh, NC 27604-1188
non-game and endangered wildlife: (919) 733-7291
enforcement division: (800) 662-7137

North Carolina Department of Environment,
Health, and Natural Resources
P.O. Box 27687
Raleigh, NC 27611-7687
(919) 733-4984

South Carolina Department of Natural Resources
Attention: Dot Walker
P.O. Box 167
Columbia, SC 29202
(803) 734-3886

Wildlife Management—Wildlife Diversity—
Freshwater Fisheries
163 Hopewell Road
Clemson, SC 29633
(864) 654-1671

Wildlife Management—Wildlife Diversity—
Freshwater Fisheries
420 Dilerton Road
Georgetown, SC 29440
(803) 546-8119

TWRA (Tennessee Wildlife Resources Agency)
Central Office
P.O. Box 40747
Nashville, TN 37204
(615) 781-6500

Tennessee Department of Natural Resources
675 U.S. Courthouse
801 Broadway
Nashville, TN 37203
(615) 736-5471

TWRA West Tennessee
225 Martin Luther King Blvd.
State Office Building, Box 55
Jackson, TN 38301
(901) 423-5725

TWRA Middle Tennessee
Ellington Agricultural Center
P.O. Box 40747
Nashville, TN 37204
(615) 781-6622

TWRA Cumberland Plateau
216 East Penfield
Crossville, TN 38555
(615) 484-9571

TWRA East Tennessee
6032 West Andrew Johnson Hwy.
Talbott, TN 37877
(423) 587-7037

Selected State Parks

North Carolina

Carolina Beach State Park
P.O. Box 475
Carolina Beach, NC 28428
(910) 458-8206

Eno River State Park
6101 Cole Mill Road
Durham, NC 27705
(919) 383-1686

Hammocks Beach State Park
1572 Hammocks Beach Road
Swansboro, NC 28584
(910) 326-4881

Hanging Rock State Park
P.O. Box 278
Danbury, NC 27016
(910) 593-8480

Lake Waccamaw State Park
1866 State Park Drive
Lake Waccamaw, NC 28450

Lumber River State Park
P.O. Box 10
Orrum, NC 28369
(910) 628-9844
(910) 646-4748

Merchants Millpond State Park
Route 1, Box 141-A
Gatesville, NC 27938
(919) 357-1191

Morrow Mountain State Park
49104 Morrow Mountain Road
Albemarle, NC 28001
(704) 982-4402

Mount Jefferson—New River State Park
P.O. Box 48
Jefferson, NC 28640
(910) 246-9653

Mount Mitchell State Park
Route 5, Box 700
Burnsville, NC 28714
(704) 675-4611

Pettigrew State Park
2252 Lake Shore Road
Creswell, NC 27928
(919) 797-4475

Stone Mountain State Park
Route 1, Box 17
Roaring Gap, NC 28668
(910) 957-8185

South Carolina

Caesars Head State Park
8155 Greer Highway
Cleveland, SC 29635
(864) 836-6115

Kings Mountain State Park
1277 Park Road
Blacksburg, SC 29702
(803) 222-3209

Rose Hill Plantation State Park
Sardis Road, Route 2
Union, SC 29379
(803) 427-5966

Lake Wateree State Park
Route 4, Box 282 E-5
Winnsboro, SC 29180
(803) 482-6126

Redcliffe Plantation State Park
181 Redcliffe Road
Beech Island, SC 29841
(803) 827-1473

Santee State Park
251 State Park Road
Santee, SC 29142
(803) 854-2408

Edisto Beach State Park
8377 State Cabin Road
Edisto Island, SC 29483
(803) 869-2156

Hampton Plantation State Park
1950 Rutledge Road
McClellanville, SC 29458
(803) 546-9361

Hunting Island State Park
1775 Sea Island Parkway
St. Helena Island, SC 29920
(803) 838-2011

Huntington Beach State Park
Murrells Inlet, SC 29576
(803) 237-4440

Old Santee Canal State Park
900 Stoney Landing Road
Moncks Corner, SC 29461
(803) 899-5200

Tennessee

Fort Pillow State Historic Park
Route 2, Box 109-A
Henning, TN 38041
(901) 738-5581

Hiwassee State Scenic River State Park
P.O. Box 255
Delano, TN 37325
(423) 338-4133

Long Hunter State Park
2910 Hobson Pike
Hermitage, TN 37076
(615) 885-2422

Meeman—Shelby Forest State Park
Route 3
Millington, TN 38053
(901) 876-5215

Mousetail Landing State Park
Route 3, Box 280-B
Linden, TN 37096
(901) 847-0841

Norris Dam State Park
1261 Norris Freeway
Lake City, TN 37769
(615) 426-7461

Paris Landing State Park
Route 1
Buchanan, TN 38222
(901) 642-4311

Reelfoot Lake State Park
Route 1
Tiptonville, TN 38079
(901) 253-7756

Roan Mountain State Park
Route 1, Box 236
Roan Mountain, TN 37687
(423) 772-3303

South Cumberland Recreation Area
Route 1, Box 2196
Monteagle, TN 37356
(615) 924-2980

T.O. Fuller State Park
1500 Mitchell Road West
Memphis, TN 38109
(901) 543-7581

Tims Ford State Park
570 Tims Ford Drive
Winchester, TN 37398
(615) 967-4457

Warrior's Path State Park
P.O. Box 5026
Kingsport, TN 37663
(423) 239-8531

PRIVATE, NONPROFIT CONSERVATION ORGANIZATIONS

National Audubon Society
(212) 979-3000

North Carolina

The Nature Conservancy
Southeast Regional Office
P.O. Box 2267
Chapel Hill, NC 27515-2267
(919) 967-5493

The Nature Conservancy
North Carolina Field Office
Michael Andrews, Regional Director
4011 University Drive, Suite 201
Durham, NC 27007
(919) 403-8558

North Carolina Wildlife Federation
Katherine Skinner, Vice President
Box 10626
Raleigh, NC 27605
(919) 833-1923

American Fisheries Society—NC Chapter
3205 Bedford Avenue
Raleigh, NC 27607

Conservation Council of North Carolina
Box 37564
Raleigh, NC 27627

NC Herpetological Society
Ann Berry Somers
Department of Biology UNC-G
Greensboro, NC 27412-5001

Carolina Bird Club
The Ornithological Society of the Carolinas
P.O. Box 29555
Raleigh, NC 27626-0555

Wildlife Society—NC Chapter
1394 Utah Mountain Drive
Waynesville, NC 28786

New Hope Audubon Chapter
Phil Manning
315 East Rosemary Street
Chapel Hill, NC 27514

Sierra Club
Chuck McGrady
104 Sunningdale Drive
Flat Rock, NC 28731
(704) 696-0672

South Carolina

The Nature Conservancy
South Carolina Field Office
P.O. Box 5475
Columbia, SC 29250
(803) 254-9049

SC Wildlife Federation
Patrick Morgan, Director
715 Woodrow
Columbia, SC 29205

SC Association for Conservation District
James MacLeod
P.O. Box 612
Camden, SC 29010

Wildlife Society—SC Chapter
Robert Perry
State Route 1, Box 226
Georgetown, SC 29440

Columbia Chapter—Sierra Club
P.O. Box 2388
Columbia, SC 29202
(803) 256-8487

Columbia Audubon Society
2505 Hardscrabble Road
Columbia, SC 29223

Francis Beidler Forest
336 Sanctuary Road
Harleyville, SC 29448
(803) 462-2150

Tennessee

The Nature Conservancy
Tennessee Field Office
50 Vantage Way Suite 250
Nashville, TN 37228
(615) 255-0303

Tennessee Conservation League
300 Orlando Avenue
Nashville, TN 37209-3200

Tennessee Citizens for Wilderness Planning
130 Tabor Road
Oak Ridge, TN 37830

Tennessee Environmental Council
1700 Hayes Street, Suite 101
Nashville, TN 37203

Wildlife Society—Tennessee Chapter
William Wathen
Tennessee Wildlife Resources Agency
P.O. Box 40747
Nashville, TN 37204

Tennessee Forestry Association
Box 290693
Nashville, TN 37229

Chattanooga Audubon Society
Linda Harris
1000 North Sanctuary Road
Chattanooga, TN 37421
(423) 892-1499

Cumberland—Harpeth Audubon Society
Shelia Shay
2408 Belmont Boulevard, Apt. A-3
Nashville, TN 37212
(615) 298-5154

Sierra Club
Shelia Shay
2408 Belmont Boulevard, Apt. A-3
Nashville, TN 37212
(615) 298-5154

Nature Centers

North Carolina

Western North Carolina Nature Center
75 Gashes Creek Road
Asheville, NC 28805
(704) 298-5600

NC Arboretum
P.O. Box 6617
Asheville, NC 28816
(704) 665-2492

Cape Fear Botanical Gardens
P.O. Box 53485
Fayetteville, NC 28305
(910) 486-0221

Piedmont Environmental Center
1220 Penny Road
High Point, NC 27265
(910) 883-8531

Discovery Place
301 North Tryon Street
Charlotte, NC 28202
(704) 372-6261

Cradle of Forestry
U.S. Forest Service
10001 Pisgah Highway
Pisgah Forest, NC 28768
(704) 877-3130

Cape Fear Museum
814 Market Street
Wilmington, NC 28401
(910) 341-4350

Carolina Raptor Center
P.O. Box 16443
Charlotte, NC 28297
(704) 875-6521

Forest Discovery Center
Cradle of Forestry in America
1001 Pisgah Highway
Pisgah Forest, NC 28768
(704) 877-3130

North Carolina Aquarium at Fort Fisher
P.O. Box 130
Kure Beach, NC 28449-0130
(910) 458-8257

North Carolina Aquarium at Pine Knoll Shores
P.O. Box 580
Atlantic Beach, NC 28512
(919) 247-4004

North Carolina Aquarium at Roanoke Island
P.O. Box 967, Airport Road
Manteo, NC 27954
(919) 473-3494

North Carolina Botanical Garden
Totten Center—UNC-CH
Chapel Hill, NC 27599-3375
(919) 962-0522

Duke Marine Laboratory
135 Duke Marine Lab Road
Beaufort, NC 28516
(919) 504-7503

South Carolina

Silver Bluff Sanctuary
Wildlife Rehabilitation Center
4542 Silver Bluff
Jackson, SC 29831
(803) 827-0781

Charleston Museum
Dr. Albert Sanders, Curator of Natural History
360 Meeting Street
Charleston, SC 29403

SC State Museum
301 Gervais Street
Columbia, SC 29202
(803) 737-4921

Savannah River Ecological Lab
P.O. Drawer East
Aitken, SC 29802
(803) 725-2472

Bellefield Nature Center
Route 5, Box 1003
Georgetown, SC 29440
(803) 546-4623

Belle W. Baruch Institute for Marine Biology
and Coastal Research
University of South Carolina
Columbia, SC 29208

Tennessee

Center for Global Sustainability
1817 White Avenue
Knoxville, TN 37916
(423) 524-4771

Clinch River Environmental Studies Organization
Oak Ridge Schools
P.O. Box 6588
Oak Ridge, TN 37831-6588
(423) 482-6324

East Tennesse Discovery Center
Chilhowee Park
516 Beaman Street
P.O. Box 6204
Knoxville, TN 37914
(423) 637-1121

Great Smoky Mountains Institute at Tremont
Great Smoky Mountains National Park
Route 1, Box 81
Townsend, TN 37882
(423) 448-6709

Ijams Nature Center
2915 Island Home Avenue
Knoxville, TN 37914
(423) 637-5331

Owl's Hill Nature Center
545 Beech Creek Road
Brentwood, TN 37027
(615) 370-4672

Radnor Lake State Natural Area
1160 Otter Creek Road
Nashville, TN 37220
(615) 373-3467

Save Our Streams
Izaak Walton League of America
4021 Sunnybrook Drive
Nashville, TN 372053834
(615) 665-2324

Steele Creek Park and Nature Center
City of Bristol Leisure Service Maintenance
P.O. Box 1189
Bristol, TN 37620
(423) 989-5616

Tennessee Environmental Council
1725 Church Street
Nashville, TN 37203
(615) 321-5075

University of Tennessee
Forestry Experiment Station and Arboretum
901 Kerr Hollow Road
Oak Ridge, TN 37830
(423) 483-3571

Warner Park Nature Center
7311 Hwy. 100
Nashville, TN 37221
(615) 352-6299

Wesley Woods Environmental Education Camp
329 Wesley Woods Road
Townsend, TN 37882
(423) 448-2246

FERRY SYSTEM

North Carolina Ferry System
(800) BY-FERRY: (800) 293-3779

BIRDER'S HOTLINES

North and South Carolina Birder's Hotline
(704) 332-2473

Tennessee Birder's Hotline
(615) 356-7636

Selected Bibliography

Alexander, John, and James Lazell. *Ribbon of Sand—The Amazing Convergence of the Ocean and the Outer Banks.* Chapel Hill, North Carolina: Algonquin Books, 1992.

Alsop, Fred J., III. *Birds of the Smokies.* Galtinburg, Tennessee: Great Smoky Mountains National Park Natural History Association, 1991.

Baker, Mary L. *Whales, Dolphins and Porpoises of the World.* New York: Doubleday and Company, 1987.

Ballantine, Todd. *Tideland Treasure.* Columbia, South Carolina: University of South Carolina Press, 1991.

Bell, C. Ritchie, and Anne H. Lindsey. *Fall Color and Woodland Harvests.* Chapel Hill, North Carolina: Laurel Hill Press, 1990.

Bierly, Michael Lee. *Bird Finding in Tennessee.* Nashville, Tennessee: Michael Lee Bierly, 1980.

Boone, D. Daniel, and Gregory H. Aplet. *The Living Landscape—Sustaining Biodiversity in the Southern Appalachians.* Atlanta, Georgia: Wilderness Society, 1994.

Campbell, Carlos C., William F. Hutson and Aaron J. Sharp. *Great Smoky Mountains Wildflowers.* Knoxville, Tennessee: University of Tennessee Press, 1992.

Carlton, Mike. *Tennessee's Wonders.* Nashville, Tennessee: Rutledge Hill Press, 1994.

Carter, Robin. *Finding Birds in South Carolina.* Columbia, South Carolina: University of South Carolina Press, 1991.

Clapham, W. B., Jr. *Natural Ecosystems.* New York: MacMillan Publishing Company, 1983.

Clark, William S., and Brian K. Wheeler. *Peterson Field Guide Series—A Field Guide to the Hawks of North America.* Boston: Houghton Mifflin Company, 1987.

Coffey, Timothy. *The History and Folklore of North American Wildflowers.* Boston: Houghton Mifflin Company, 1993.

Constantz, George. *Hollows, Peepers and Highlanders—An Appalachian Mountain Ecology.* Missoula, Montana: Mountain Press Publishing Company, 1994.

Cox, Barry, Peter D. Moore and Philip Whitfield. *The Atlas of the Living World.* Boston: Houghton Mifflin Company, 1989.

DeBlieu, Jan. *Hatteras Journal.* Golden, Colorado: Fulcrum Publishing, 1987.

Ehrlich, Paul R., David S. Dobkin and Darryl Whege. *The Birder's Handbook—A Field Guide to the Natural History of Birds.* New York: Simon and Schuster, 1988.

Elphick, Jonathan. *The Atlas of Bird Migration.* New York: Random House, 1995.

Etnier, David A., and Wayne C. Starnes. *The Fishes of Tennessee.* Knoxville, Tennessee: University of Tennessee Press, 1993.

Fussell, John O, III. *A Birder's Guide to Coastal North Carolina.* Chapel Hill, North Carolina: University of North Carolina Press, 1994.

Grimm, William Carey. *The Illustrated Book of Trees.* Harrisburg, Pennsylvania: Stackpole Books, 1983.

Gupton, Oscar W., and Fred C. Swope. *Fall Wildflowers of the Blue Ridge and the Great Smoky Mountains.* Charlottesville, Virginia: University Press of Virginia, 1987.

Hamel, Paul. *Tennessee Wildlife Viewing Guide.* Helena, Montana: Falcon Press, 1993.

Harrar, Ellwood S., and J. George Harrar. *Guide to Southern Trees.* New York: Dover Publications, 1962.

Harrison, George H. *Roger Tory Peterson's Dozen Birding Hot Spots.* New York: Simon and Schuster, 1976.

Hemmerly, Thomas E. *Wildflowers of the Central South.* Nashville, Tennessee: Vanderbilt University Press, 1990.

Houk, Rose. *A Natural History Guide to Great Smoky Mountains National Park.* Boston: Houghton Mifflin Company, 1993.

Hutchins, Ross E. *Hidden Valley of the Smokies—With a Naturalist in Great Smoky Mountains National Park.* New York: Dodd, Mead and Company, 1971.

Kirby, Peter. *Georgia's Mountain Treasures—The Unprotected Wildlands of the Chattahoochee National Forest.* Atlanta, Georgia: The Wilderness Society, 1995.

Kraus, E. Jean Wilson. *A Guide to Ocean Dune Plants Common to North Carolina.* Chapel Hill, North Carolina: University of North Carolina Press, 1990.

Kricher, John C., and Gordon Morrison. *A Field Guide to Eastern Forests of North America.* Boston: Houghton Mifflin Company, 1988.

Luther, Edward T. *Our Restless Earth—The Geologic Regions of Tennessee.* Knoxville, Tennessee: University of Tennessee Press, 1977.

McClane, A. J. *McClane's New Standard Fishing Encyclopedia.* New York: Holt, Rhinehart and Winston, 1965.

Meinkoth, Norman A. *The Audubon Society Field Guide to the North American Seashore Creatures.* New York: Alfred A. Knopf, 1981.

Milne, Lorus, and Margery Milne. *The Audubon Society Field Guide to North American Insects and Spiders.* New York: Alfred A. Knopf, 1990.

Newcomb, Lawrence. *Newcomb's Wildflower Guide.* Boston: Little, Brown and Company, 1977.

Niering, William A., and Nancy C. Olmstead. *Audubon Society Field Guide to North American Flowers (Eastern Region).* New York: Alfred A. Knopf, 1979.

Parker, Steve. *Pond and River.* New York: Alfred A. Knopf, 1988.

Peterson, Roger Tory. *Peterson Field Guide to Eastern Birds.* Boston: Houghton Mifflin Company, 1980.

Rotter, Charles. *Wetlands.* Mankato, Minnesota: Creative Education Publishers, 1991.

Schafale, Michael P. *Inventory of Longleaf Pine Natural Communities in North Carolina.* North Carolina Natural Heritage Program, 1994.

Schafale, Michael P., and Alan S. Weakley. *Classification of the Natural Communities of North Carolina.* Raleigh, North Carolina: North Carolina Natural Heritage Program, 1990.

Schoenbaum, Thomas J. *Islands, Capes and Sounds of the North Carolina Coast.* Winston-Salem, North Carolina: John F. Blair Publishers, 1982.

Simpson, Marcus B., Jr. *Birds of the Blue Ridge Mountains.* Chapel Hill, North Carolina: University of North Carolina Press, 1992.

Sutton, Ann, and Myron Sutton. *Audubon Nature Series—Eastern Forests.* New York: Alfred A. Knopf, 1985.

Thorne-Miller, Boyce, and John Catena. *The Living Ocean.* Washington, D.C.: Island Press, 1991.

Weidensaul, Scott. *Mountains of the Heart—A Natural History of the Appalachians.* Golden, Colorado: Fulcrum Publishing, 1994.

Whitman, Ann H. *National Audubon Society Pocket Guide to Familiar Trees of North America (East).* New York: Alfred A. Knopf, 1986.

Wilson, Edward O. *The Diversity of Life.* Cambridge, Massachusetts: Belknap Press of Harvard University Press, 1992.

Zim, Herbert S., and Alexander C. Martin. *Trees—A Guide to Familiar Species.* Racine, Wisconsin: Western Publishing Company, 1991.

Index

About the Author

John Rucker is an avid photographer and naturalist who has lived in many areas across the United States. After graduating from the University of North Carolina at Chapel Hill, he moved to Montana to work as a ranch hand. He taught high school English in Montana for two years, then moved to Alaska to continue teaching and buy a commercial fishing boat. After nine seasons of commercial fishing, John returned to his roots. A published author of books, including *Melancholy Bay, North Carolina: Portrait of the Land and Its People* and *The Barney Years*, and articles appearing in *Gray's Sporting Journal* and *Wildlife in North Carolina*, he is a promoter of ecotourism and biodiversity, especially in the Southeast. John now concentrates on his writing while living in the southern Appalachians with his boiken spaniel, Jeb Stuart.